Reconstructing
FORT UNION

Reconstructing
FORT UNION

John Matzko

University of
Nebraska Press
Lincoln & London

Portions of chapters 4 and 5 have been previously published as "Ralph Budd and Early Attempts to Reconstruct Fort Union, 1925–1941," *North Dakota History* 64 (summer 1997): 2–19.

© 2001 by the University of Nebraska Press
All rights reserved
Manufactured in the United States of America

Library of Congress Cataloging-in-Publication Data
Matzko, John Austin.
　Reconstructing Fort Union / John Matzko.
　　p. cm.
　Includes bibliographical references and index.
　ISBN 0-8032-3216-0 (cl. : alk. paper)
　　1. Fort Union Trading Post National Historic Site (N.D. and Mont.)—History.
2. Historic sites—Conservation and restoration—North Dakota—Fort Union Region. 3. United States. National Park Service—History—20th century. 4. Fort Union Region (N.D.)—History.
I. Title.

F739.F5 M38 2001
978.4'73—dc21   2001018120

Publication of this volume was assisted by The Virginia Faulkner Fund, established in memory of Virginia Faulkner, editor in chief of the University of Nebraska Press.

To Mother
and to the memory of my father,
John F. Matzko (1912–91)

CONTENTS

List of Illustrations ix *List of Maps* x
Acknowledgments xi *Introduction* xiii

1 Historical Reconstructions and the National Park Service 1
2 Historic Fort Union 10
3 The Neighboring Ruin 22
4 Ralph Budd and the Upper Missouri Historical Expedition 33
5 Depression Years 46
6 State Ownership 55
7 A New National Historic Site 65
8 Winning Congressional Authorization 73
9 Reenergizing the Project 82
10 Winning the Appropriation 95
11 Groundwork for the Reconstruction 105
12 Reconstructing Fort Union 118
13 The Business of a Park 128
  Conclusion 145

APPENDIX A *The "Old Tunnel"* 151
APPENDIX B *The Snowden Bridge* 153
List of Abbreviations 155
Notes 157 *Selected Bibliography* 213 *Index* 219

ILLUSTRATIONS

1. Fort Union, 1833, by Karl Bodmer   17
2. Bourgeois House, 1866   20
3. Mondak   28
4. Invitation to the Upper Missouri Historical Expedition, 1925   40
5. Columbia River Historical Expedition at Fort Union   44
6. Ralph Budd, Gen. Hugh Scott, and Yakima chief Minninick during the Columbia River Historical Expedition, 1926   44
7. Fort Union site, 1924   49
8. Fort Union site, 1937   50
9. Ben Innis   74
10. The Snowden Bridge   89
11. Rick Collin, Gov. Allen Olson, Sen. Mark Andrews, and Secretary of Transportation Elizabeth Dole   93
12. Friends of Fort Union lobbying in Bismarck   101
13. Archaeologist Bill Hunt and Lord Astor   110
14. Waldorf Astoria reception   111
15. Superintendent Paul Hedren and NPS director William Penn Mott   116
16. Interior, Fort Union Trading Post NHS   124
17. Relaying trade house hearth stones   126
18. Members of the reconstruction team, 1989   126
19. Greg Hennessy and members of the Gold Star Caviar management committee   140
20. Aerial view of Fort Union NHS   147

MAPS

MAP 1. The Confluence Region xv
MAP 2. Fort Union Trading Post National Historic Site xvi

ACKNOWLEDGMENTS

THIS HISTORY has been immeasurably improved by those who read various drafts in whole or part and who made comments and suggestions. I am grateful for the contributions of Mark Andrews, Priscilla Baker, Andrew Banta, Bart Barbour, Audrey Barnhart, John Bennison, Dennis Borud, Ethan Carr, Mike Casler, Ralph Chase, Rick Cronenberger, Janet Daley, Scott Eckberg, Bill Hunt, Marv Kaiser, Randy Kane, Carla Kelly, John Lancaster, Orville Loomer, Neva Hydle MacMaster, Jackson W. Moore, Dwight F. Rettie, Ed Richards, Doug Scott, James Sperry, Richard Stenberg, Tom Thiessen, Robert Utley, Bill Wellman, and Rodd Wheaton. Some also provided interviews, as did Greg Hennessy, Wilfred Husted, Jane Innis, Mike Jones, Earle Kittleman, Sylvester Putnam, and Tom Rolfstad.

Librarians, of course, aided me everywhere. Jim Davis of the State Historical Society of North Dakota and Pat LeMaster, the Bob Jones University interlibrary loan librarian, made particularly thorough attempts to accommodate my requests. Jim Hargis, cartographer for the Bob Jones University Press, graciously provided preliminary sketches for the maps.

National Park Service personnel, past and present, contributed answers to many questions about the Service and its previous reconstructions: Paul Ghiotto, David Hansen, Don Hill, F. Ross Holland, Larry Ludwig, David Nathanson, Vivien Rose, Don Spencer, Arthur Sullivan, Erwin "T" Thompson, and Gary Warshefski. With a remarkable knowledge of his agency, Barry Mackintosh, NPS Bureau Historian, supplied information and encouragement throughout the project.

Like Mackintosh and Carla Kelly, Rick and Andrea Winkjer Collin read the entire manuscript in draft—some of it twice—and were gracious in offering suggestions although they had once considered writing a history of the reconstruction themselves. Kim Vivier proved an exemplary copyeditor whose careful reading detected numerous inconsistencies and syntactical lapses. My wife, Rachel Smith Matzko, a teacher of English composition and grammar, noted other errors and was usually able to restrain my rhetorical flights of fancy. I would not have written this book without the encouragement of Paul Hedren, who gave several candid interviews, read the entire manuscript critically, and provided numerous suggestions for improvement. Most important, he believed—on limited evidence—that I could effectively tell a story he might have recounted from his own perspective.

The maps and illustrations in this book have been generously funded by the Fort Union Association.

INTRODUCTION

UNLIKE MOST North American fur trading posts, Fort Union was built to protect and impress for the indefinite future. In the event, it survived nearly forty years, dominating the upper Missouri Valley from 1828 until its dismantling in 1867—the longest-lived fur trading post in the history of the United States.

Today the historic fort is commemorated at Fort Union Trading Post National Historic Site, a unit of the National Park System. Located on the border of North Dakota and Montana, some seventy miles south of Saskatchewan, and on the Missouri River, a few miles above its confluence with the Yellowstone, the park boasts a partially reconstructed fort, even more solidly built than its predecessor and set in countryside largely unchanged from the mid–nineteenth century.

More than three times forty years have passed since the destruction of the historic fort. Until 1895 Fort Buford, a nearby military post, presided over the confluence. After its abandonment northwestern North Dakota receded even further from the national consciousness. Today the area has fewer residents than it did in 1920, and when mentioned in the media, it is usually because of its weather.

Yet for reasons of geography and simple good fortune, the archaeological ruins at Fort Union survived. A transitory Indian village and a hard-drinking frontier town disappeared with minimal impact on the site. Farmers plowed to the outside of its stone foundations. The river, which once seemed to threaten the ruins, eventually cut into the opposite bank instead. Relic seekers were partially deterred by the fort's isolation, New Deal agencies came too late to destroy with good intentions, and the final threat from gravel mining aroused men and women of goodwill to the site's protection.

Local supporters experienced years of frustration in their attempts to contrive Fort Union's incorporation into the National Park System and years more trying to have the park developed. Proponents of the fort's reconstruction and their political allies clashed with preservationists on a scale that attracted national attention. Eventually, Fort Union became the site of one of the largest archaeological excavations ever mounted by the National Park Service, and its partial reconstruction was the consequence of both the political power and the fortuitous timing necessary to overmaster preservationist scruples and a deliberate bureaucracy.

The new Fort Union was the last reconstruction of a major historic structure attempted by the National Park Service in the twentieth century. How a small group of enthusiasts in a remote section of the country managed to recreate a mid-nineteenth-century trading post is a story worthy of contemplation by both those who support and those who oppose the technique of historic reconstruction.

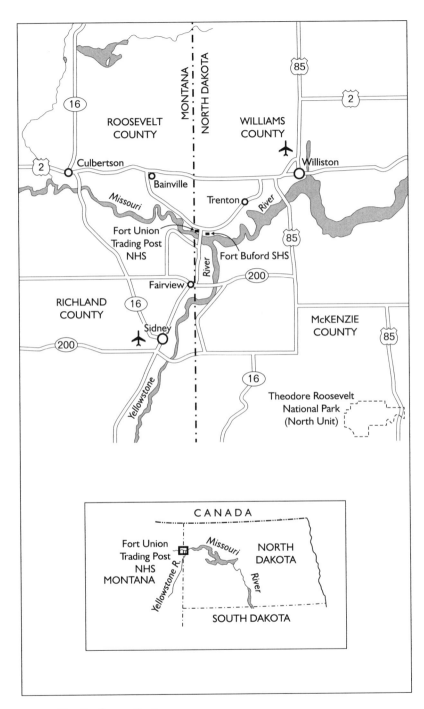

Map 1. The Confluence Region

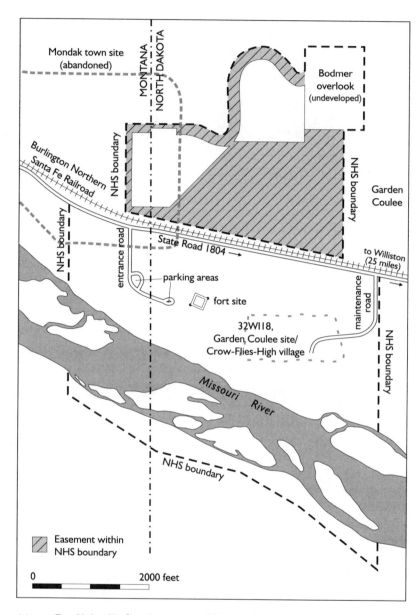

Map 2. Fort Union Trading Post National Historic Site

1 | Historical Reconstructions and the National Park Service

PRESENTING HISTORY to the public by reconstructing historical structures that no longer exist is a comparatively recent phenomenon. Attempts to save existing buildings fully occupied nineteenth-century American preservationists. They had neither the money nor the expertise to reconstruct buildings that had been destroyed. Nevertheless, the urge to reconstruct non-extant buildings sprang from the same commemorative instinct and the same economic prosperity that had begotten the preservation movement.

The reconstruction of historic buildings—usually called *restoration* during the first half of the twentieth century—was not at first distinguished from historic preservation. As late as 1965 Charles B. Hosmer Jr. treated the reconstruction of vanished buildings as simply "a new phase in historic preservation." But some early restorations of historic structures, notably at Sutter's Fort in Sacramento, California (1891–93), and at Fort Ticonderoga, New York (which began in 1908), were so extensive that they verged on reconstruction.[1]

The first historic building suggested for reconstruction in the United States was probably that early loss to the preservation movement, the John Hancock house of Boston, demolished in 1863. The Hancock house was rebuilt in 1926, albeit in Ticonderoga, New York.[2] The first historic building to be reconstructed on its original site was Theodore Roosevelt's birthplace at 28 East 20th Street, New York City. Completed by the Women's Roosevelt Memorial Association in 1923—four years after the sudden death of President Roosevelt and only seven years after the original building had been demolished—the project followed in the commemorative tradition of the Mount Vernon Ladies' Association. Hermann Hagedorn, the director of the Roosevelt Memorial Association, declared the reconstructed Roosevelt House "only incidentally a building." It was, he said, "a rallying place, a spiritual headquarters for those Americans who look on their country as Roosevelt looked on it."[3] Yet the *New York Times* considered a restoration that contained none of its "original material" so novel (and perhaps so dubious) that Hagedorn had to make it clear that the ladies responsible had never pretended to be rebuilding the structure from original fabric.[4]

It took the invention of Colonial Williamsburg in the late 1920s and early 1930s to tempt Americans into believing that, given enough time, money, and expertise, a reasonable facsimile of the past could be recreated almost anywhere. Colonial Williamsburg inspired historical replicas throughout North America. (Even a Canadian opponent of historical reconstructions admitted to having "swelled with pride" after overhearing fellow vacationers pronounce Louisbourg "better . . . than Williamsburg.") At the same time, however, John D. Rockefeller Jr.'s transformation of Virginia's colonial capital served as the first American training ground for preservation professionals—who were shortly to become some of the sturdiest opponents of historical reconstruction.[5]

The Historic Sites and Buildings Act of 1935 explicitly authorized the National Park Service (NPS) to reconstruct historic structures. Even the National Historic Preservation Act of 1966 (as amended in 1980) defined preservation to include reconstruction. Nevertheless, reconstruction of non-extant buildings as a means of interpreting historic sites swiftly fell from favor within the National Park System.[6]

Early NPS reconstructions hardly raised confidence in the technique. First among embarrassments was the reconstruction of George Washington's birthplace in Westmoreland County, Virginia. Inaugurated by a private association in a haze of patriotic good intentions, the "memorial mansion," completed by the Park Service in 1932, was the wrong size, had the wrong shape, and faced the wrong direction on the wrong site.[7]

By 1937 the Park Service had formally adopted policy guidelines for historic preservation that included the preservationist shibboleth: "Better preserve than repair, better repair than restore, better restore than construct." The guidelines also declared, however, that appropriate treatment for any historic site ultimately depended on balancing disparate objectives. The highest aesthetic, archaeological, and educational good might each be reached with a different interpretive solution, and the deadlock could be broken only by "the tact and judgment of the men in charge."[8]

Not surprisingly, the men in charge differed in tact and judgment. For example, both NPS director Newton Drury and chief historian Ronald Lee opposed the reconstruction of the McLean House at Appomattox, although clear photographs and architectural drawings of the building existed and more than five thousand original bricks lay stacked beside the foundation. After World War II the Park Service bowed to political reality (in this case, Virginia senators Glass and Byrd) and fulfilled a promise to reconstruct the building. At its dedication Drury frankly admitted his earlier misgivings but expressed pride in a "model Service project" that seemed, in the end, to have satisfied everyone.[9]

The same could not be said of the major reconstructions conducted by the Service in the fifteen years between 1963 and 1978. With one exception, all were forts, and all were imposed on the Park Service hierarchy by political forces beyond its control.[10] For instance, Fort Stanwix, an eighteenth-century fort, was rebuilt in the 1970s as part of an urban renewal project. The fort had convincing documentation, significantly augmented by archaeology, but downtown Rome, New York, hardly resembled its historic scene.[11]

Fort Vancouver, a fur trading post across the river from what is now Portland, Oregon, had less documentation but a much more insistent member of Congress, Julia Butler Hansen. A writer of children's literature, Hansen had won a statewide reputation for *Singing Paddles* (1935), a fictional story of Kentucky emigrants befriended and resupplied by John McLoughlin, Vancouver's chief factor. Elected to the House of Representatives in 1960—partly on her reputation as a writer—Hansen became the first woman to serve as a member of the Appropriations Committee and, in 1967, the first chairwoman of the House subcommittee responsible for National Park Service appropriations. From 1961 until even after her retirement in 1974 Hansen channeled money into the rebuilding and interpretation of her favored historic site. The reconstructed Fort Vancouver was an interpretive success. Nevertheless, even a site handbook noted the incongruity of a mid-nineteenth-century stockade wedged between an airport and interstate traffic on the Columbia River bridge.[12]

A historic site with less significance but an even more persistent champion was Fort Scott, a mid-nineteenth-century army post in eastern Kansas. The district's congressman, Joe Skubitz, was an amateur historian obsessed by the place. Congressional powerhouse Phillip Burton recalled that

Skubitz's "one interest in life was Fort Scott." After Park Service personnel repeatedly denigrated its importance, Skubitz visited the Service's historical office, scrutinized its files, and made clear his goal of national historic site status for the post. Since Skubitz sat on the parks subcommittee of the House and eventually became the ranking Republican on the Interior Committee, he was not easily denied. Nine original buildings had survived to some extent, but the inclusion of Fort Scott in the Park System (1978) actually followed an NPS reconstruction of much of the fort. Shortly before Skubitz retired in 1978, the last of his four appropriation bills for Fort Scott obliged the Service to fund reconstruction of the fort's dragoon stables, "notwithstanding an almost total lack of information on their appearance."[13]

Perhaps the least successful attempt at Park Service reconstruction was the rebuilding of Fort Caroline (near modern Jacksonville, Florida) to commemorate a brief French Huguenot settlement in 1564. The original site could not be located and had probably disappeared into the St. Johns River. Congressman Charles E. Bennett, prime mover of the reconstruction, was not a member of an Interior or an appropriations committee, but he was a serious amateur historian who had written a history of the fort.[14] The Park Service based its reconstructed Fort Caroline (1963–65) on a contemporary drawing but did not attempt an exact reproduction. The new fort was approximately three-fourths the size of the original, lacked interior buildings, and had a parapet composed of cinder blocks occasionally visible "despite efforts to cultivate a grassy veneer." Recent interpretive staffs referred to the structure as an "exhibit."[15]

Nevertheless, the reconstruction of most consequence for the Fort Union project was that achieved at Bent's Old Fort (1974–76) in rural eastern Colorado. Bent's had been a fur trading post on the Santa Fe Trail and a shorter-lived contemporary of Fort Union. Like the North Dakota site, Bent's had been saved through local interest and was later transferred to state ownership. Its remains, like those of Fort Union, were "identifiable only as a rough spot on a rather undistinguished landscape." With a nudge from Colorado's congressional delegation, Bent's Old Fort became a national historic site in 1960, six years before Fort Union. Archaeologist Jackson W. Moore conducted the major excavation at Bent's Old Fort before being sent to excavate the North Dakota site. When Park Service officials proved recalcitrant about providing the promised reconstruction, further political pressure was applied by Senator Gordon Allott, a member of the Senate Appropriations Committee. Reconstruction began in 1974.[16]

In view of its parallels with Fort Union, the Colorado reconstruction might have been expected to aid the rebuilding of its northern counterpart. Instead, it proved a detriment. One ironic problem with the reconstruction at Bent's Old Fort was that it sought a higher degree of authenticity than had earlier been attempted. By combining historic and modern building techniques, its historical architect turned the reconstructed fort into a maintenance nightmare. Adobe walls, designed to weather, weathered with a vengeance. Bent's Old Fort had no sooner been completed than the Park Service had to reconstruct the reconstruction. (Experience eventually provided some maintenance solutions, but tens of thousands of dollars are still allocated annually to restucco adobe surfaces.) Although Bent's Old Fort was better documented than most earlier NPS reconstructions and its historic scene better preserved than most others, opponents of historic reconstruction seized on the site's maintenance problems to disparage the technique.[17]

While these five forts were being rebuilt by the National Park Service during the 1960s and 1970s, anti-reconstructionist sentiment continued to grow at its Washington headquarters. After the retirement of older officials such as Roy Appleman, whose priority had been interpretation, policy making shifted to Ernest Connally, director of the Office of Archeology and Historic Preservation (OAHP), and his titular subordinate, Robert M. Utley. Utley, both a gifted scholar and an effective administrator, developed into a strong preservationist and became a most influential critic of historic reconstructions from his successive positions as chief historian (1964–72), director of the OAHP (1972–73), and assistant director for park historic preservation (1973–77).[18]

By 1975 NPS *Management Policies* sanctioned reconstructions only if (1) no "significant preservable remains" would be destroyed, (2) sufficient information allowed "an accurate reproduction with a minimum of conjecture," (3) the structure could be built on its original site, (4) all "prudent and feasible alternatives to reconstruction" had been considered, and (5) the reconstruction was *"essential* to public understanding" of the park. Fulfilling the criteria was intended to be virtually impossible. As Utley later admitted, the requirements "could never be professionally met, only declared met by management when deemed politically expedient."[19] The "essential-to-public-understanding" criterion was itself a nearly insurmountable barrier if taken literally. The phrase seemed to imply that no model, film, display, or interpretive talk could adequately convey a park's story to the public—a preposterous idea.[20]

The *Management Policies* also foreclosed the possibility of off-site reconstruction, a middle-of-the-road solution that might have allowed replicas to be built near historic sites without being built on top of them. Although credible off-site reconstructions were achieved by Parks Canada at L'Anse aux Meadows, the private Plimoth Plantation in Massachusetts, and the state-owned Jamestown Settlement in Virginia, the technique was prohibited by the National Park Service. The on-site requirement was primarily motivated by a concern for accuracy, but it also served as an additional impediment to reconstruction for structures whose original sites had been lost to erosion or subsequent development.[21]

Opponents of historical reconstruction more often articulated their arguments than did proponents of the technique. When the noted landscape architect Frederick Law Olmstead Jr. was asked to design gardens for the "replica" of Washington's birthplace, he refused, urging the promoters instead to preserve and mark the foundations "as all that is left of the 'real thing.'" Opponents of historical reconstruction continue to argue that historic fabric destroyed in the reconstruction process can never thereafter be investigated by future researchers asking different questions or using more advanced technologies.[22]

Moreover, anti-reconstructionists claimed that resources spent on reconstructions might better be devoted to preserving authentic structures and artifacts, or at least to studying those about to be destroyed by development. Added to the cost of planning, researching, and executing reconstructions were the increased expenditures for maintaining and interpreting them. Critics claimed that as long as the Park Service had authentic resources in need of conservation, spending money on reconstructions was wasteful and perhaps even in violation of the Organic Act of 1916, which mandated Park Service preservation of cultural resources.[23]

Anti-reconstructionists also contended that historical reconstructions, no matter how accurate, could not be faithful in every detail. All required some guesswork. Even when considerable accuracy had been achieved, critics objected that a reconstruction could be accurate only for a moment in the structure's history. In an attempt to recreate the past, reconstruction frequently obliterated both the previous and subsequent history of the site.[24]

Finally, anti-reconstructionists criticized the interpretive weaknesses of reconstruction. As early as 1938 NPS architect Albert H. Good reflected that every man ought to have a right to reconstruct vanished structures in his own imagination. To Good, "the faint shadow of the genuine often [made] more intelligent appeal to the imagination than the crass and visionary replica." Even more trenchant was Walter Muir Whitehill, art historian and director of the Boston Athenæum, who asserted that reconstructions were "expensive life-size toys, manufactured for children of all ages who have forgotten how to read." Some opponents complained that reconstructions trivialized genuine structures and weakened the interest of the public in saving originals. Others warned that only a slippery slope separated Williamsburg from Disneyland.[25]

Proponents of historical reconstruction have less frequently defended their position with logical argument. Albert Good to the contrary, the wider public enjoyed reconstructions; and what the public would visit, the local chamber of commerce would usually endorse.[26] Theoretical argument frequently took a back seat to political maneuver in the struggle to re-erect historic structures. Nevertheless, the reconstructionist position was as logically defensible as that of its opponents.

Although it was true that historic fabric was nearly always lost when a reconstruction was built on site, the loss was often reduced to insignificance by prior archaeological investigation. Archaeological remains rarely provide more than minimal information before being excavated—and sometimes not even then. Burying sites in an attempt to preserve them for future investigators may actually hasten their destruction. And occasionally, even comparatively well-publicized features have been lost to development before they could be investigated.[27]

Furthermore, like reconstruction, preservation could be both expensive and unsuccessful. At the "other" Fort Union—Fort Union National Monument in New Mexico—misguided attempts to preserve the structure's adobe walls resulted in the loss of nearly one-third of the remaining square footage.[28] Similar treatment of the Fort Bowie ruins in eastern Arizona proved even more damaging. A 1979 NPS Historic Structures Report conceded that most of the "change" in the historic structures at Bowie had resulted from "National Park Service stabilization and maintenance work."[29] Preserving the shell of the chapel at Women's Rights National Historic Park in Seneca Falls, New York, required stripping away later additions and, in the end, resulted in a structure both unattractive and as much a maintenance burden as Bent's Old Fort.[30]

Alternatives to reconstruction posed other difficulties. The "ghost reconstruction" of Benjamin Franklin's house in Philadelphia—a steel framework within a sterile courtyard—was widely admired by cultural resource professionals, but what visitors learned from it was a mystery. Elaborate visitor centers too near a site, as at Gettysburg and Fort Union National Monument, endangered remaining fabric, whereas those too far away discouraged visits to the cultural resource itself. Furthermore, the Park Service proved more willing to construct visitor centers of a contemporary design on historic landscapes than to build structures that blended with the interpreted period.³¹

Authentic structures in the Park System undoubtedly deteriorated for lack of money to preserve them, but historical reconstructions played little demonstrable role in that decline. That Congress might have redirected toward preservation appropriations intended for reconstructions was as probable as Congress eliminating billion-dollar bombers to aid the school lunch program. More likely, reconstructions benefited historic preservation by increasing public awareness of American history.

Historical reconstructions also provided an excellent interpretation of the historic scene for children and for the many adults who were only functionally literate. Instead of serving as toys for those who had forgotten how to read, reconstructions often served as tools for those who had never learned how. Daniel J. Boorstin argued that Colonial Williamsburg was an appropriate medium for Americans of the "middling sort," a "place where people often go 'because of the children,'" a place "intelligible and interesting to nearly everybody." In any case, the union of education and entertainment long preceded Disney, extending at least as far back as the lyceum movement and chautauqua.³²

Park Service professionals sometimes tended toward an elitism in which concern for the "public good" slipped easily into assertions of professional expertise. Unlike the directors of Colonial Williamsburg and Plimoth Plantation, NPS policy makers worked largely outside the market economy. They could more easily take the position of a Canadian museum official who declared that his institution was not in the business of adapting its product to public taste but of educating public taste to appreciate the museum's offerings.³³

Finally, preservationists accorded undue weight to the importance of surviving artifacts. Reflecting a contemporary materialism, in which reality was viewed as the accumulation of things, preservationists behaved as if the essence of the past was embodied in its material survivals. Hollywood took the same tack when it created minutely accurate reproductions of historic clothing and landscapes and then suffused accompanying scripts with presentist dogmas.³⁴

In any case, artifacts do not look to us as they looked to contemporaries. Most have been altered by age and use. Further, the modern viewer does not see even a well-preserved artifact, such as a pit saw, as it was seen by its original owner: to him it was a tool, to us a *former* tool, an antique in a glass case. Worse yet was the preservationist implication that the authentic past lay in rusty nails, broken glass, and other accidental survivals of which their former owners would have been ashamed.[35]

Such was the history and theory that served as shadowy backdrop to the Fort Union reconstruction controversy. Ideas had consequences. Even so, the partial reconstruction of Fort Union might just as easily be credited to factors of geography, chance, and the singularities of human personality, to which it is now appropriate to turn.

2 | Historic Fort Union

THE FUR TRADE, which had already transformed Siberia and Canada, came with a rush to the upper Missouri. Even as Lewis and Clark descended the river in 1806 on their return from the Pacific, they encountered fur trading parties laboring upstream. By the mid-1820s "mountain men" were operating throughout the Rockies from the Missouri and Yellowstone drainage, in season trapping beaver and out of season enriching the steely entrepreneurs who supplied their cravings at annual rendezvous.

Independent, buckskin-clad "free trappers" are part of the American romantic tradition, but like the Pony Express, their ascendancy was short lived. Profits of the western fur trade shortly aroused the acquisitive instincts of eastern capital. John Jacob Astor, soon to be the richest man in the United States, dreamed of a fur empire extending from the Missouri to the Pacific under the aegis of his American Fur Company. Astor's money made many friends in Washington, including Secretary of War Lewis Cass and Missouri senator Thomas Hart Benton. Cass and Benton helped Astor eliminate the "factory system," the federal trading posts that had operated from 1796 to 1822 in competition with private traders.[1]

Astor did not have it all his way. In 1827 he was forced to come to terms with the St. Louis firm of Bernard Pratte and Company, an enterprise conducted by interrelated merchants of French descent and dominated by Pierre Chouteau Jr., a man as brilliant and as ruthless as Astor himself. Similarly, an understanding had to be reached with the Columbia Fur Company, managed by Kenneth McKenzie, a Scotsman with prior Canadian experience, whose energy, ambition, and executive ability—though not capital—rivaled those of both Astor and Chouteau.[2] McKenzie's organization, renamed the Upper Missouri Outfit (UMO), became, in theory, a subsidiary of the American Fur Company's Western Department. In fact, McKenzie and his partners remained as independent as before but with the advantage of Astor's capital as wind to their sails. When Astor retired in 1834 and sold the Western Department to Chouteau, the change was so imperceptible that the operation continued to be known as the American Fur Company.[3]

In the fall of 1828—or perhaps 1829 (the dated is controverted)—McKenzie dispatched a keelboat up the Missouri to construct a new trading post at the mouth of the Yellowstone.[4] Palisades and living quarters were hastily thrown up—probably between October and December—on the north bank of the Missouri about five miles upstream from the confluence. Why the fort was called *Union* is unclear, although perhaps McKenzie intended to suggest UMO control of the fur trade from both the rivers and the mountains.[5]

The site could hardly have been better chosen. Other military and commercial structures were built near the mouth of the Yellowstone both before and after the construction of Fort Union, and only the merest trace of any of them has yet been uncovered. Unlike its predecessors and competitors, Fort Union was grounded on a high gravel bank—an extremely unusual formation on the Missouri—at least twenty feet above the river. At that height the fort was safe from the annual spring floods. Yet during the historic period the Missouri held to its north bank, almost immediately below the fort, so that cargoes could be easily unloaded. The area also boasted above-average timber resources and a plain to the north and east that could accommodate large Indian encampments.[6]

The Fort Union palisade of 1828 was built as a parallelogram rather than a square—about 198 feet north to south and 178 feet wide—in order to avoid construction and drainage problems in the northwest and southeast corners.[7] After a serious fire in February 1832 that destroyed employee dwellings and the west wall, the fort was enlarged to a quadrangle 240 by 220 feet nearly oriented to the compass. Palisade walls of cottonwood timbers were set on stone foundations, and two-story stone bastions were constructed to guard the northeast and southwest corners. By 1834 Fort Union was the most solidly built trading post on the Missouri and perhaps in the entire West. Kenneth McKenzie, its bourgeois, presided over a territory "greater than that of many a notable empire."[8]

In many ways Fort Union was only a more sophisticated version of the typical fur trade establishment. The post included a long dwelling range for employees on the west interior with an ice house at its north end. On the opposite side was a storage range of similar dimensions, and to the north a vaulted limestone powder magazine. Near the north wall stood an impressive bourgeois house, the administrative heart of the fort, which was rebuilt in the early 1830s and then extensively remodeled before 1851.[9] A north gate opened to the prairie, but the main gate faced south toward the river. Immediately to its west stood the trade house and Indian reception room. Eventually, the main gate was fitted with two sets of doors. Small groups of Indians could trade in the "strong room" between them without being admitted to the fort itself, and at night or in times of uncertainty, trade could be conducted through a wicket in the palisade.

Although McKenzie was prepared to supply any white trappers who appeared at Fort Union, his intent was to attract the trade of Indian tribes along the Missouri and Yellowstone. The fort itself was located in the territory of the Assiniboines, who had trapped furs for Europeans even before the tribe had moved onto the prairie.[10] The UMO also pursued trade with the Crows on the upper Yellowstone and the Blackfeet (long enemies of the Americans) on the western Missouri. In time subsidiary posts were built to accommodate both.

Transporting trade goods more than eighteen hundred miles upriver from St. Louis to Fort Union was a difficult and expensive process. During the earliest years keelboats were dragged up the river by human muscle power at the rate of twelve to fifteen miles a day. McKenzie was soon arguing that despite the dangers from obstructions and shallow water, steamboating the upper Missouri River was possible. Chouteau eventually backed him with a strong endorsement to the New York office in 1830.[11]

In 1832 the American Fur Company's new sidewheeler *Yellow Stone* successfully navigated the upper Missouri and arrived at Fort Union bearing Chouteau himself as well as the artist George Catlin. The achievement convinced the American Fur Company that steamboats could crush competitors who were unable to afford them. The *Yellow Stone* also proved a public relations triumph among UMO customers. Indians were in awe of the boat. According to Catlin, some called it "the big medicine canoe with eyes" and shot their horses and dogs to propitiate the Great Spirit.[12]

Tribes along the Yellowstone and the Missouri found themselves unwittingly drawn into the stream of international commerce. Traders were extremely sensitive to the tastes of the Indians, and in meeting their demand the American Fur Company supplied Fort Union with goods from all over the world. Bells and mirrors were imported from the German states, beads from Venice and Bohemia, calico from France, woolen blankets and guns from Britain, and vermilion pigment from the Far East. Dentalium shells were obtained from the Pacific coast of North America, and marine shell hair pipes were conveyed from the Caribbean via New Jersey, where they had been fabricated into barrel shapes.[13]

In return, the traders wanted furs. During Fort Union's first decade beaver "plew" were the most highly prized, largely for use in the manufacture of beaver hats for men. A large beaver plew brought four to eight dollars in a period in which a farm laborer might make fifty cents a day plus meals. But toward the end of the 1830s nutria fur became cheaper, the French introduced a more fashionable silk hat, and improvements in the textile industry allowed the British to manufacture comfortable and attractive woolen hats and caps. At Fort Union trade in beaver declined dramatically following the panic of 1837 and the smallpox epidemic of the same year.[14]

Fort Union had never restricted itself to the beaver trade. In 1851 artist and Fort Union clerk Rudolph Kurz noted that the skins of twenty species were represented in the press room, from grizzly bear to mouse. After the mid-1830s bison "robes" became the mainstay of Fort Union trade—a robe being the tanned skin of a winter-killed buffalo cow or young bull dressed with the fur on. Although an Indian woman could process only eighteen to twenty robes a year, Chouteau's headquarters in St. Louis received roughly seventy thousand of them annually between 1834 and 1844. From St. Louis the robes were shipped east for use as floor coverings, carriage and sleigh robes, and overcoats for men.[15] Hundreds of skins, butchering waste, livestock within the palisades, and scores of unwashed human beings gave Fort Union at the height of summer an odor that must have been potent even by nineteenth-century standards.

A common interpretative theme at Fort Union Trading Post National Historic Site is the cooperative relationship that existed between traders and their clients at the historic fort. Although that relationship was usually cautious and occasionally strained—there were one or two serious attempts to seize the fort, and some depredation of the fort's livestock and gardens was taken for granted—neither side wished to disturb the ongoing trading relationship from which both profited.[16] Usually, Indians were content to do violence to other Indians, and fort personnel likewise assaulted one another. The keen-eyed company man Charles Larpenteur noted that when Fort Union employees decided to massacre the troublesome Deschamps family in 1835, they first forced them to turn out their Assiniboine women, whom they did not want to kill for fear of retaliation by the tribe.[17]

That there were no interracial atrocities committed at Fort Union was due in part to good fortune, in part to the strong leadership provided by the successive bourgeois who commanded the post. McKenzie and Alexander Culbertson were physically vigorous as well as mentally keen; James Kipp, a seasoned veteran of the trade, "was a favorite of the Indians"; and Edwin Thompson Denig, another old-timer on the upper Missouri, proved to be a considerable intellect, if a less dynamic personality than his predecessors.[18]

Exacting work from the fort employees was no easy task for the bourgeois. Rudolph Kurz wrote in 1851 that since the bourgeois had "no recourse to police control or to any outside assistance," he had to manage his men "with ability, courage, and tact . . . for every one of them is armed and, though not courageous in general, are nevertheless touchy and revengeful."[19] To complicate matters, Fort Union employees came from all over the United States and Europe—including Britain, Germany, French Canada, Russia, Spain, Mexico, and Italy. Even to describe the employees as "white" (or its euphemism, "Euro-American") is misleading because their number included African Americans and many hunters and interpreters of mixed European and Indian blood.[20] Nevertheless, given the crowded isolation of men heavily armed and recreating in drink, there was probably less violence at Fort Union than might have been expected.[21]

If the inhabitants of Fort Union were rarely exemplars of Western civilization, neither were the Indians who traded there gentle children of nature. Recent attempts to romanticize them reflect more the anomie and lost spirituality of contemporary society than nineteenth-century reality. The life of Indians along the upper Missouri was often nasty, brutish, and short. Before the coming of Europeans their condition rarely rose much above subsistence. The Indians were bound by fear of their enemies, fear of their leaders, and fear of a capricious spirit world. Edwin Denig, a sympathetic but objective observer, noted the Crow custom of mutilating hands to mourn the dead, the garbage-strewn villages and venereal diseases of the Arickaras, and the practice among the Crees of making their old chiefs "the butt and ridicule of the camp." Denig praised the Crees for allowing a husband to beat his wife three times with "a small stick" before receiving a refund on his bride price. He commended the Crows for taking women and children prisoners "instead of dashing their brains out as the rest of the tribes do." In an account of the infamous Assiniboine chief The Gauche, Denig described how the chief's band massacred nearly an entire village, with children being "roasted alive by a pointed stick being run through the body and planting it in the ground before a hot fire." Shortly afterward smallpox nearly annihilated The Gauche's band.[22]

Smallpox came to the upper Missouri aboard a company steamboat that arrived at Fort Clark about 15 June 1837 and at Fort Union nine days later. In a desperate attempt to prevent an epidemic at Fort Union, "Dr. Thomas's medical book" was consulted, and the resident Indian women were inoculated with live virus. The gamble proved a disaster. Within a few days the "stench in the fort . . . could be smelt at the distance of 300 yards." Attempts were made to warn the Assiniboines, who were coming in to trade, but the Indians, suspecting some sort of trickery, could not be dissuaded. Once abroad in a population isolated from Old World diseases for millennia, the smallpox raced from tribe to tribe, producing an epidemiological catastrophe perhaps as far away as the Pacific. The number of dead has been variously estimated, from fifteen thousand for the upper Missouri to more than two hundred thousand for the entire epidemic.[23]

Both company and Fort Union personnel have been censured for their failure to prevent the calamity, but those in authority probably did the best they could considering the limited medical knowledge of their day and the realities of the upper Missouri trade. Even if the smallpox epidemic could have been contained, other Old World diseases were waiting their turn: measles, chicken pox, typhoid fever, cholera, scarlet fever. Modern field studies suggest that even today, "when isolation ceases, decimation begins."[24]

More reprehensible was the company's distribution of alcohol. For more than two hundred years Europeans had understood what exposure to alcohol did to Indian people and their cultures. In 1802 Congress authorized the president to restrict the sale of alcohol to the Indians, and in 1834 it absolutely prohibited the introduction of "spirituous liquor or wine into the Indian country." Nevertheless, the laws were nearly impossible to enforce, especially on the upper Missouri, where the American Fur Company competed head to head with the Hudson's Bay Company and the latter's unlimited liquor supplies. Alcohol was easily smuggled upriver to Fort Union, perhaps with the connivance of officialdom in the interest of Manifest Destiny.[25]

In 1833 Kenneth McKenzie brought a still to Fort Union and began producing corn whiskey. Taking leave of his usual common sense, McKenzie boasted of his coup to all comers, including his business rivals. Inevitably, the information reached the Indian commissioner, and serious consideration was given to suspending the company's trading license. The situation was not improved by Chouteau's (perhaps sardonic) excuse that the still was intended "to promote the course of Botany." Friends of the company, including Secretary of War Cass, weighed in on its behalf, but McKenzie was never after quite as comfortable at Fort Union, and eventually he retired to St. Louis to enter the wholesale liquor business.[26]

The liquor trade was fantastically profitable. Larpenteur once traded five gallons of alcohol to a band of Crees for about two hundred buffalo robes, worth perhaps eight hundred dollars at the time. There is also little doubt about the effect alcohol had on the tribes of the upper Missouri. Before contact with Europeans they had had no previous experience with intoxication. Furthermore, their religions contained few ethical or moral values and put a premium on "vision quests" of altered consciousness. Right from the start the history of the confluence became, in the words of Ian Frazier, "the history of a binge."[27]

We owe our knowledge of both good and evil at Fort Union to the many careful observers who recorded descriptions of the post, its inhabitants, and its neighbors. Among the most significant visitors were the famous painters George Catlin (1832) and John James Audubon (1843), who ironically left better word pictures of their experience than paintings. The best drawings were produced by the lesser-knowns Karl Bodmer (1833) and Rudolph Friederich Kurz (1851–52). Bodmer and his employer, scientist-prince Maximilian of Wied, are especially important because they arrived in 1833, before the tribal cultures along the upper Missouri were swept away by smallpox. Nor should the important contribution of Edwin Thompson Denig be overlooked. Denig, who arrived at Fort Union as a bookkeeper in 1837 and left as bourgeois in 1855, matured into a creditable naturalist and ethnologist and wrote a detailed description of Fort Union at its height.[28]

Pierre Chouteau was one of the first American businessmen to aid government-sponsored, as well as private, scientific expeditions. Like many modern corporate executives, Chouteau was motivated by both the public relations value of his contributions and a genuine interest in natural history. Chouteau's "favorite scientist" was Ferdinand Vandeveer Hayden, a talented and ambitious geologist.[29] Hayden was a distasteful personality, "self-centered," "a notorious womanizer, an abject flatterer [and] an unashamed self-promoter" who hated Indians and repaid Denig's kindness by plagiarizing his ethnological manuscript, mutilating and mangling it in the process. Hayden was too consumed by professional politics and his extracurricular activities to contribute much of consequence to our knowledge of Fort Union, but he did name the bedrock formation on which it rested the "Fort Union Formation."[30]

Hayden's controversies with his academic peers about the scientific meaning of the Fort Union Formation are beyond the scope of this work, but one practical implication of the formation may be noted: when water percolates

Fig. 1. The first Fort Union, drawn in 1833 by Swiss artist Karl Bodmer. At this date the Bourgeois House was less than two stories high, and a blockhouse straddled the main gate facing the river. Bodmer used artistic license to portray the fort much closer to the viewer than it would have seemed from the spot where he made the sketch. Courtesy, Joslyn Art Museum, Omaha NE, gift of Enron Art Foundation.

through it, the water becomes very hard. A recent geologist noted discreetly that the water might cause "physical distress" in those unaccustomed to it. Edwin Denig, less discreetly, said that the water had "a mineral taste and possess[ed] active cathartic properties."[31]

Other geographic and climatic realities of the confluence are more significant. In the spring, when the frozen Missouri and surrounding landscape thaw, the resultant ice jams and flush of water inundate the floodplain. Another flooding occurs when snowmelt from mountains five hundred miles away reaches the area. Before the building of the Fort Peck dam the flooding was even greater. Once the bourgeois at Fort Union smugly watched an opposition post slide into the river.[32] The flooding also provided a suitable environment for timber growth on the south bank, as well as a window of opportunity for the annual steamboat traffic. Less pleasantly, thousands of bison would annually drown while attempting to cross the half-frozen Missouri in the spring. When their carcasses washed ashore, the air reeked with decay.[33]

The bison, of course, are gone, but mosquitoes remain an annoyance in spring and summer. In 1806 William Clark left the confluence before Lewis's arrival, in part because the "musquetors [were] excessively troublesome." During the wet summer of 1835 the acting bourgeois reported that the insects came in clouds, and the men cried "out terribly and not without cause." During the summer of 1843 Audubon preferred to sleep on the boards of the Bourgeois House "piazza" to avoid the mosquitoes inside.[34] Presumably, a breeze kept them at bay.

At regular intervals, however, the breeze at Fort Union turns to a gale. Rudolph Kurz complained that the fort was "exposed to every wind that blows from any point of the compass," and on 14 December 1833 two sides of the fort blew down. The construction of X-shaped interior braces solved this problem and also provided support for a walkway around the palisades—"a favorite place from which to shoot Wolves after nightfall and for standing guard in time of danger."[35]

High winds were especially dangerous when combined with extreme winter temperatures. Kurz heard that Fort Union was colder than any other trading post in North America, even those on Hudson Bay. Low temperatures of minus thirty degrees Fahrenheit are not uncommon. On the expedition that concluded with Larpenteur in possession of two hundred robes and the Crees with bad hangovers, one of the trader's mules froze to death standing up. Denig noted that during every cold winter some Assiniboines died and others were weakened because of wet feet, lack of proper clothing, and the necessity of sleeping on damp ground. Considerably less snow falls at the confluence than might be expected, but an occasional blizzard of fine snow driven by gale-force winds is capable of producing a fatal loss of bearings in those caught outdoors.[36]

In the summer, temperatures of over one hundred degrees have been recorded in every month from May to September, although the climate is semiarid and low humidity prevents the heat from becoming as oppressive as in the East. Denig believed that hardy livestock might survive the heat and aridity but was less sanguine about crops. Fort Union employees grew oats, corn, potatoes, and garden vegetables, but the success rate was only one out of three seasons, the remainder failing "from drought and destruction by grasshoppers, bugs and other insects"—a lesson early settlers would have to relearn. On the positive side most of the rain falls in the spring and summer, and the northern latitude provides long hours of daylight despite a short growing season.[37]

By the 1860s the garden was abandoned for good, not for lack of rain but because raids by the Sioux made it too dangerous to tend. Denig had predicted that the Sioux would become an increasing menace, and shortly after his retirement in 1856 the forays began. At first it was mostly horse stealing, but at dawn on 22 August 1860 two hundred fifty mounted Sioux launched a full-scale assault on the fort. They killed twenty-five head of cattle and burned all the outbuildings, several tons of lumber and hay, and two mackinaw boats. The Indians also attempted to fire the fort but retreated when one of their number was killed. Thereafter Fort Union remained under intermittent siege and experienced another brush with an Indian takeover in 1867.[38]

Meanwhile, events in the larger world helped hasten the end of Fort Union. In 1860 the first steamboat reached Fort Benton, Montana Territory, which then became the head of navigation on the Missouri. Fort Union was reduced to a way station and a depot for the distribution (and theft) of Indian annuities.[39] Henry Boller, a visitor to Fort Union, noted that the "gradual approach of civilization" and "the increasing ease with which steamers navigate the river" had changed the character of the trade: "Fort Union, in 1863, was (and had been for several years past) simply a Post for the Assiniboine Indians, and as they are notoriously poor robe-makers, its trade had fallen away very considerably."[40]

The discovery of gold in western Montana was publicized in 1862, and gold seekers flocked to Fort Benton, from which point they proceeded overland to Virginia City. Although Chouteau's company transported and supplied the miners as a matter of course, the new emigration was a further setback to the fur trade, which could prosper only if Indians were free and mobile. Every miner and settler—and every hostile Indian that they created—threatened the life of the trade.[41]

During the summer of the same year, the Santee Sioux of Minnesota attacked and killed several hundred whites. Two of their own chiefs who had been friendly to the government and had accepted annuities were assassinated. Other tribes, whom Denig had described just a decade before, were pushed out of their homelands by the Sioux.

In the resulting punitive expedition against them General Alfred Sully was sent to the upper Missouri. In 1864 Sully ordered troops garrisoned at

Fig. 2. The only known extant photograph of the Bourgeois House, taken in 1866 shortly before it was destroyed. Despite the frowziness of the structure at this date, this photograph provided important details for the National Park Service reconstruction. Courtesy, Montana Historical Society, Helena.

Fort Union to guard supplies for a new military post to be constructed nearer the confluence. For two years, until Fort Buford was built two and a half land miles away, soldiers and traders shared accommodations at Fort Union.[42]

The outbreak of the Civil War in 1861 struck another blow against Fort Union. The price of robes fell in St. Louis, and commercial traffic on the lower Missouri was disrupted by military operations for the first two years of the war. Furthermore, since the Chouteaus were slaveholders and suspected of Confederate sympathies, the Republican Indian agents sent to the upper Missouri treated them with undisguised antipathy. Competition from opposition companies stiffened when the latter displayed ardent

Northern sentiments. Finally, in 1865, the Chouteaus were denied a trading license by the Lincoln administration, and Charles Chouteau sold the UMO to James Hubbell and Alpheus F. Hawley, major partners in the newly formed North Western Fur Company.[43]

The fraudulent operations of the new company rendered the questionable business practices of its predecessor pale by comparison. The North Western Fur Company had "no long term stake in the country . . . and little interest in the Indian trade." Its game was "flagrant deception and extortion of the government . . . a sleazy take-the-money-and-run mentality." This slipshod attitude was mirrored in the physical decline of the fort. Two photographs from 1866 show a partially collapsed northeast bastion and a Bourgeois House with sagging roof and broken windows. A visitor in 1866 noted that the fort "had a sort of 'played out' look."[44]

On 4 August 1867 Charles Larpenteur, who had been witness to much of Fort Union's history, noted that the fort had been "sold to the government to build up Fort Buford. . . . Indians and old Squaws about the establishment all drunk." On the same day, the steamboat *Miner* arrived at the fort, and its crew demolished the kitchen for fuel. In September laborers and cooks moved to Fort Buford. October and November were spent hauling away remaining materials and supplies. On the last day of November Larpenteur wrote, "Nothing left at Union but adobes."[45] To the old trader, who knew Union in its prime, that was certainly true; but to archaeologists of another century, it would prove a gross exaggeration.

3 | The Neighboring Ruin

THE SIOUX dogged river traffic on the Missouri for more than a decade before the nearly contemporaneous uprising of the Santee Sioux in Minnesota and the western Montana gold rush of 1862 brought a clamor for army protection on the high plains. By June 1866 the army began to build a one-company, palisaded fort at the confluence. Like Fort Union, Fort Buford enjoyed a fine location well above the high-water level during the spring floods. Although Buford had no steamboat landing below its front gate, it did have an unobstructed view of the Missouri and the Yellowstone Rivers, an asset the army considered more valuable.[1]

The Sioux rightfully regarded the construction of a military post as an intrusion into their territory, "a spear thrust deep into the Hunkpapa world." For four years Sitting Bull and his people warred on Buford.[2] They were not able to take the fort, but work details, hunting parties, and outbuildings fell to their raids. In May 1867 the army began construction of a far larger establishment, and it was to this second fort that the salvaged materials from Fort Union were consigned. (The powder magazine, one of the few historic structures that remain at Fort Buford State Historic Site today, was almost certainly built of stone recycled from Fort Union.) Danger from Indian attack was so great that soldiers guarded the route between Buford and Union while wood and stone were moved.[3]

A third, even larger fort was authorized in 1871. By then the Sioux had directed their thrusts away from the upper Missouri, and Fort Buford became a base of supplies for military expeditions farther west. (In November there was time to engage a group of prisoners in the grim business of moving bodies from the Fort Union cemetery to the new one at Buford.) The

Custer debacle of 1876 sealed the fate of the nomadic Sioux, and finally, on 19 July 1881, Sitting Bull returned from Canadian exile to surrender at Fort Buford.[4]

Thereafter mundane police duties were all that remained to Buford's soldiers. On 11 June 1887 the tracks of the St. Paul, Minneapolis, and Manitoba Railway—soon to become the Great Northern—reached the fort. The last details from Buford were ordered out to protect railroad property during the Pullman Strike of 1894. The army abandoned Fort Buford the following year. Its buildings were auctioned, and a military reservation of thirty square miles—more than five hundred thousand acres, including the Fort Union site—was transferred to the Department of the Interior in 1900 for dispersal through the General Land Office.[5]

During the 1870s memories of Fort Union remained fresh among the men who had worked and traded there. In 1872–73 James Stuart, a frontier jack-of-all-trades and post trader at Fort Browning, Montana, collected reminiscences of Fort Union from old trappers and traders. The resulting article, printed in the fledgling journal of the Montana Historical Society, was not entirely accurate, but it had been researched carefully enough to occasion regret that the interviews were not systematically conducted and preserved.[6]

Even during the Sioux years the Fort Union site remained a travelers' landmark, its foundational stonework still intact. On 20 April 1872, after performing a difficult amputation, the post surgeon at Fort Buford rode over to Union to measure its foundations and to prove to his satisfaction that George Catlin had exaggerated the fort's size by eighty feet. A year later Luther S. "Yellowstone" Kelly, an experienced army scout temporarily stationed at Buford, noted the "burned stockade and blackened chimneys" at the old trading post.[7]

In 1875 George Custer's scout "Lonesome Charley" Reynolds and his friend, businessman-explorer Philetus W. Norris, spent "hours of pensive wanderings among the ruins of old Fort Union and the cemetery near Fort Buford" where friends of each were buried. Almost exactly a year later Lt. Edward Settle Godfrey, a Seventh Cavalry survivor, passed the site on his return from the Battle of the Little Big Horn, at which Reynolds had died. Godfrey noted that of Fort Union there was nothing left "but stones out of which the chimneys were built, wells, sinks, etc."[8]

These visitors to Fort Union did not mention the presence of a nearby Indian village, although they hinted at its existence. Norris wrote that when he and Reynolds arrived at Fort Union, they saw "the old target-pole, which is now surmounted by the head, horns and mane of a huge buffalo bull. Thence we made our way through some patches of really good corn, potatoes and vegetables and over the plateau to the cemetery near Fort Buford."[9] Perhaps, too, Yellowstone Kelly's "burned stockade and blackened chimneys" were the product of Indian fires that blazed after salvageable building materials had been removed.

The Assiniboines, in whose territory Fort Union had been established, continued to camp and hunt near the site well into the 1870s. Assiniboine men were occasionally employed as scouts at Fort Buford, and after 1867 tribal annuities were distributed there. In 1868 "thirty or forty lodges" at the point of starvation camped near Fort Buford and subsisted for several weeks on "the offal from the butcher's shop and corn picked out of dung heaps." The Assiniboines came under repeated attack from the Sioux, and on 20 August 1868 several Assiniboine women and children were killed by Sioux near the old trading post.[10]

More important for the history of the Fort Union site was a village occupied periodically between 1869 and 1884 by a band of Hidatsas (Gros Ventres) at Garden Coulee, a few hundred yards east of the fort.[11] Today its scant archaeological remains lie within the boundaries of Fort Union Trading Post National Historic Site. Although the band eventually called itself the Hoshka or Hoska, both contemporaries and historians referred to it as the band of Crow Flies High.[12]

Crow Flies High, the son of a tribal elder, had been orphaned by the 1837 smallpox epidemic. As a young man he became a successful military leader but proved less effective at religio-political intrigue. In 1869 or 1870 he complained to the Indian agent that his faction within the consolidated Hidatsa-Mandan settlement, Like-a-Fishhook Village, on the Fort Berthold Reservation, was being slighted in the distribution of government beef rations. It was no small matter since the Hidatsas were starving. The agent's attempt to provide an equitable solution resulted in jealousy and bitterness among Crow Flies High's rivals. His life was threatened, and the putative chief, his supporters, and their families withdrew from Like-a-Fishhook Village.[13]

Secession was probably in the best interest of the Hidatsas because government subsidies at Fort Berthold were inadequate to provision the entire tribe. Game had declined, and attacks by the Sioux had increased. Fort Buford offered the dissident band at least the illusion of military protection as well as access to the post trader. The confluence was also nearer traditional hunting grounds, and buffalo still ran in the Yellowstone Basin.

At Garden Coulee the band built both log cabins and earthlodges, as if to symbolize its intermediate position between the white and Indian worlds. The subtribe seems to have survived largely by hunting, at least until the game played out; then it relied more on agriculture. Some Hidatsas served as scouts at Fort Buford. Others reportedly sold wood to Missouri River steamboats. Still others engaged in begging, stealing, and prostituting their women to Fort Buford soldiers.[14]

As the bad feelings between Hidatsa factions diminished over time, Garden Coulee became an intermediate destination for Fort Berthold residents engaged in hunting, eagle trapping, and escaping misdeeds on the reservation. Delegations from the confluence also traveled to Fort Berthold. Relatives visited one another; some men took wives in both camps.[15]

By the mid–twentieth century most surface features of the Crow-Flies-High encampment at Garden Coulee had been obliterated by subsequent land-leveling and farming. Only the remains of a few cache pits survived.[16] At Fort Union itself, however, archaeologists discovered six relatively complete skeletons interred during the post-fort period. Although it is possible that these were Assiniboines, most probably they represent members of the Crow-Flies-High band killed by Sioux and buried in depressions of convenience inside the ruins of the old trading post. Of the six, three were killed by massive blows to the head or body, the others by an arrow to the chest, a gunshot wound to the head, and a thrust of a lance or saber. Since the injuries were inflicted from above, it is reasonable to assume that the attackers were mounted.

Beyond the evidence of violent death, the skeletons suggest the harshness of the Hidatsas' existence at Garden Coulee. One female between twenty-five and thirty years old suffered from severe arthritis, and an adult male from serious sinus infections. Another woman, approximately twenty-five to thirty-five years old, was afflicted with tuberculosis or a fungal infection, as well as a type of osteoporosis usually seen only in the elderly. Both maladies were likely the result of malnutrition. Two skeletons revealed tooth wear so severe that the pulp cavity was exposed. Three had grooving in their teeth caused by using a pick to clean them or to relieve the pain of tooth decay.[17]

Nevertheless, even if the band suffered from dismal health, its numbers increased. In 1883 there may have been as many as 240 members of the subtribe. The encampment probably spread westward toward the Fort Union ruins; several contemporaries located the village at the site of the old trading post.[18]

In 1884 the commander at Fort Buford ordered the removal of the Crow-

Flies-High band because its members "were not doing much for themselves and were a great annoyance" at the fort. Crow Flies High left Garden Coulee but did not return to Fort Berthold. Instead, his band built a new village on unsurveyed government land opposite the mouth of the Little Knife River—another confluence—where its members continued to hunt, fish, and garden. Crow Flies High also discovered the marketability of Indian dances, which whites considered picturesque.[19]

Several times government agents attempted to return the dissidents to the reservation, and Crow Flies High appeared to concede, "always managing to sidestep the actual return." Finally, the Indian agent at Berthold refused to issue rations to the band whenever its members appeared, and in 1894 Crow Flies High and his people were returned to Fort Berthold under armed guard. Thus the Crow-Flies-High Hidatsas may have been the last group of Indians forced onto a reservation.[20]

Settlement of the confluence by white homesteaders had been inhibited by the Great Sioux War, but it was well under way before Fort Buford was abandoned and the Crow-Flies-High band was returned to Fort Berthold. The greatest stimulus to homesteading was the inauguration of regular railroad service in July 1887.[21] Railroad baron James J. Hill was a shrewd, efficient, and farsighted manager. Operating without the land grants enjoyed by his competitors, Hill realized the necessity of developing the hinterlands of his Great Northern Railroad. He built feeder lines, laid out model farms, and attracted immigrants from Europe. Thousands of agricultural pioneers were enticed west by the railroad's colonization program.[22] Hill's promotion contributed both to the Great Northern's de facto control of northwestern North Dakota and to the agricultural disaster that was to befall the region during the dry years to come.[23]

In the normal course of events the confluence should have become the site of a regional center. But no city could be built there before 1900 because the land was included in Fort Buford's thirty-square-mile military reservation. Instead, the railroad all but created a town at the junction of the Missouri and the Little Muddy River, twenty-five miles east of Fort Union. Hill ignored the locals' name for their tent-and-log hamlet and arbitrarily christened "Sidetrack No. 25" *Williston* after one of his major stockholders, D. Willis James. Thus, through one of those coincidences that played a significant role in the destiny of the Fort Union site, the confluence remained undeveloped and the surrounding landscape continued to look much as it had during the historic period.[24]

Even after Fort Buford was abandoned, the area might have supported a market town. The post traders had relocated their store to the Great Northern main line, about a mile north of the fort, and the store had become the nucleus of the community of Buford. Clement A. Lounsberry, the editor of the *Bismarck Tribune* and one of North Dakota's first historians, invested heavily in Buford property, believing that the confluence would again play an important commercial role.[25] Unfortunately for Lounsberry, two political factors nullified Buford's natural advantages. First, North Dakota had entered the Union in 1889 as a dry state; and second, the North Dakota–Montana border had been drawn at the 104th meridian, three miles west of Buford and only a few hundred yards west of the Fort Union site.

Apparently, the idea of establishing a town on the state line to sell liquor to North Dakotans first occurred to George Stevens, the manager of a ranch in eastern North Dakota owned by Hamm's Brewing Company. Long on ideas but short on money, Stevens discussed his plan with rancher Luke Sweetman, who lived near the confluence. Sweetman invested in the project himself and enlisted several other North Dakotans, including a lawyer from Minot and Jacob Seel, the owner of the most suitable location for the town. At the time, there were few white homesteaders in the area, and most of them (like Seel) had been previously employed at Fort Buford. Only a few years before the establishment of the new border town the area immediately west of the Fort Union site remained a bivouac for Indians, and scaffold burials could still be seen on the surrounding hills.[26]

In 1903 the investors formed the Mondak Townsite Company, platted the town, and laid out the streets. The first building, a triangular land office, was constructed in 1904. Some structures were hauled from Fort Buford on the frozen Missouri to serve as houses and small businesses. Larger buildings were constructed on site. By the end of its first decade the town included a bank, two hotels, some rooming houses, three general stores, two drugstores, and several grain elevators. A weekly newspaper, the *Yellowstone News*, began publication in January 1905 and continued until the death of its second editor in 1920. Before its decline Mondak could boast of telephone service, a two-story brick school, and a part-time electric generating plant.[27]

In the short run the investors had chosen an excellent location. The Great Northern Railroad, which crossed the townsite, also owned a spur down to the Missouri River. Manufactured goods from the East could be transshipped from Mondak to more isolated settlements. One Montana pioneer even ordered a house from Sears, Roebuck in Chicago and had the building materials ferried across from Mondak.[28]

Fig. 3. Mondak in its heyday. Taken from the ridge to the north of town, this photograph does not show the Fort Union site, which is to the east (left) of the frame.
Courtesy, State Historical Society of North Dakota, Bismarck.

Farm products were also delivered by ferry from the south side of the Missouri, which had the best farming and grazing acreage in the region. A hamlet soon appeared at the landing on the opposite bank. Named Java, after its founder Anton Jevnager, the town served the owners of wagons that were sometimes lined up for half a mile or more on occasions when the river was impassable. Java included a few stores and the inevitable saloons on the Montana side of the state line.[29]

The Great Northern hoped to build a bridge near Mondak and Java, but the bedrock proved to be too deep for the piers. In 1912 the railroad began construction approximately two and a half miles west. Mondak enjoyed a temporary boom from hundreds of free-spending laborers, but once the Snowden Bridge was completed in 1913, rail access to the lower Yellowstone greatly reduced ferry traffic across the Missouri. Java collapsed immediately, and Mondak, with its limited hinterland to the north, entered a period of slow decline, forced to depend almost entirely on its founding purpose—to peddle alcohol.[30]

During its heyday Mondak had at least seven saloons and five warehouses for storing alcohol. The Mondak station became one of the most profitable on the Montana section of the Great Northern line, and crews reportedly worked twelve-hour days unloading the cars. A good portion of the town was engaged in supporting the alcohol traffic. Even children hunted up discarded beer and whiskey bottles, for which they received from three to fifteen cents at the back door of the saloons.[31]

Not surprisingly, the sale of alcohol was accompanied by gambling and prostitution, both technically illegal but winked at by county authorities. Gambling generally occurred on a small scale in the back rooms of saloons. Similarly, the two or three "sporting houses" were discreetly managed southeast of the town, across the tracks and near the ferry landing. (One, surrounded by a white picket fence, was called the "White Dove.")[32]

The human cost of Mondak's trade is difficult to discover. Crime, violence, gambling, and prostitution were not subjects of polite conversation at the turn of the twentieth century, even in places like Mondak. Certainly Mondak had a high crime rate for its size. The Great Northern refused to billet a section crew there.[33] Even the boosterish *Yellowstone News* reported many acts of violence, ranging from armed robbery to shootings—the scene of one incident described circumspectly as "between the track and the river in the house near the state line."[34] Mondak's most notorious murder was the killing of the sheriff and a deputized citizen by a black construction worker on 4 April 1913. Residents lynched the murderer.[35]

Although drunks were not infrequently robbed, their worst enemy was the environment. Alcohol, extreme cold, and railroad trains were not a happy combination. For instance, one Knute Bakke was discovered in a haystack "in a drunken stupor" with both legs frozen from the knees down. A man named Payne, an employee of the bridge construction company, died in December 1912 "from the effects of booze, exposure and an over supply of cocaine, or as it is commonly called 'snow.'" A presumed suicide with two whiskey bottles in his pocket was killed by a train, as was another man "after taking a few drinks." Reportedly, more drunken men were killed by Great Northern trains at Mondak than at any other station on the railway.[36]

Though Mondak subsisted on vice, it simultaneously sought the middle-class respectability that was obligatory for all small towns in early-twentieth-century America. In its quest Mondak displayed enough societal schizophrenia to stir the most jaded sociologist. Mondak's first ferry was the *Sam Lilly*, named for an early homesteader who proved up, sold out, and then drank himself to death on the profits. Children sent to Sunday school absorbed the aftermath of barroom brawls and were shushed when they asked about the brothels. Simon Riddle, a fearsome character who operated a blind pig on the state line and "always wore his cartridge belt and carried a revolver under his arm," urged the town's newsboy not to smoke or drink and grew nostalgic when he reminisced about local history.37

Mondak also maintained a sort of "Potemkin" Methodist church, assiduously tended by the Ladies Aid Society but nearly devoid of a congregation. Townspeople paid special homage when the beloved Methodist superintendent and prohibitionist Rev. William Wesley "Brother Van" Van Orsdel appeared to preach, "and no greater honor came than to entertain him at their homes." The *Yellowstone News* explained that without the church, towns would be "hot beds of vice, drunkenness and crime" and, further, that a "great many people" would shun a potential business location that had no church.38

In 1908 poet-philosopher John Neihardt (1881–1973) descended the Missouri in a small boat from Fort Benton, Montana, to Sioux City, Iowa, a trip that resulted in a book, *The River and I* (1910). Neihardt stopped briefly at Fort Union and thereby became the first to publish a description of the ruins with a photograph of the site. Neihardt's comments were brief and self-consciously literary. But he had read Larpenteur, and the poet affirmed the importance of the trading post's story—"the unwritten Iliad of a stronghold forgotten." "I looked off a half-mile to the modern town of Mondak," Neihardt mused, "and wondered how many in that town cared about this spot where so much had happened, and where the grass grew so very tall now."39

The answer was that not many cared. Mondak residents were too absorbed in the present to concern themselves with preserving the past. Although the memory of Fort Union was not totally lost during the early Mondak years and a few old-timers remembered the fort before its destruction, there seems to have been little interest in discovering the fort's history.40 The *Yellowstone News* never published anything substantive about the site, although extracts from Audubon or Larpenteur might have filled satisfyingly large amounts of newsprint.

When Kate Hammond Fogarty, the author of a school history of Montana, arrived by train from Butte determined to discover if Fort Union had been located in her state, she was first directed to the remains of Fort Buford several miles away. When she finally discovered that the remains of the Fort Union site were only a few blocks from the train station, she predicted that the "small heaps of crumbling stones" would in a short time be "entirely effaced."[41]

Fogarty's prophecy was nearly fulfilled. Grass-covered ridges that for almost four decades had outlined the fort's palisades and outbuildings were destroyed within a few years by the removal of stone for Mondak foundations and by farmers who plowed the land to the fort's substructure.[42] Still, damage to the site could have been worse. Mondak, despite its name, was located almost entirely in Montana, and a 1912 attempt to extend the town into North Dakota proved abortive.[43] Furthermore, the American Fur Company had put so much stone into the palisade foundations that it was uneconomical to level the fort site itself for the plow. But had North Dakota been wet and Montana dry, the ruins almost certainly would have been obliterated.

Mondak residents found the interior depressions of the fort a convenient dumping ground. They piled empty bottles and car bodies into the old ice house—and unknowingly on top of the graves left by the Hidatsas decades before. Outside the palisade foundations residents hunted souvenirs. When the land around the fort was farmed, "people, like blackbirds, would follow the plow."[44] On only one occasion, the discovery of three large ax heads in 1919, were the finds mentioned in the newspaper and the artifacts promised to a museum.[45] Some Mondak residents went a ghoulish step further and dug up Indian graves. The *Yellowstone News* warned its readers that this "nuisance" was a statutory crime that might initiate an epidemic of "black small pox," of which the Indians had supposedly died.[46] In the end, Mondak was repaid for the desecration, not by disease but by souvenir hunters who, within a few decades, began combing through its own remains.

Montana went dry in 1919, a full year before the Eighteenth Amendment and the Volstead Act took effect. Prohibition cramped Mondak's style but never completely ended its trade in alcohol. When saloons were forced out of business, alcohol was cached around town—even in haystacks, since the whiskey wouldn't freeze.[47]

Factors beyond Prohibition played at least as great a role in Mondak's decline. In 1916 another drought cycle began, and this inevitable feature of the northwest prairie forced many homesteaders from their claims. Rural automobile ownership also increased dramatically during the second decade of the century. Area farmers could more easily bypass Mondak to shop in Williston, at least when the roads were passable.[48]

Then there were the fires. Mondak was threatened by two major fires in 1916, the first of which might easily have taken the entire town. There were two less serious fires in 1917 and another in 1918. Undoubtedly, some were the work of arsonists who, as townspeople said, had an "insurance policy rubbing on [their] pocketbook." To fight the blazes, Mondak had only two chemical carts and no city water supply. In March 1917 several warehouses were saved only because a Great Northern crew raced west to the new bridge and brought up a tank of water that could be sprayed on the buildings with a hose from the engine.[49]

Ironically, in 1919, the first year of Prohibition, Mondak experienced a short-lived boom. A county-splitting movement swept the state with "fast talking promoters and political con-men" igniting enthusiasm for "the blessings that a county courthouse and its payroll might bring to any village, no matter how remote." When Roosevelt County was created in February 1919, Mondak became its temporary seat, partly because of the mutual jealousy of the larger towns and partly because Mondak had several vacant buildings suitable for offices.[50]

Government business was "like a blood transfusion to the dying town." A new concrete vault—today one of the few remaining structures on the townsite—was constructed to hold county records. Nevertheless, after two years the county seat was moved to Poplar and then to Wolf Point. Mondak entered an inexorable decline. The railroad station closed in 1920, and one of the last viable businesses, the town bank, moved to Fairview in 1925. By that date, wrote former resident Ralph Chase, "Mondak remained a place to live only for those who had no other place to go." Homes and stores were once again moved on the frozen Missouri.[51]

The final catastrophe occurred on 30 September 1928, when most of the remaining buildings, including the Great Northern depot, a general store, and an elevator filled with grain, were destroyed by fire possibly ignited by sparks from a train carrying John Philip Sousa's band away from a concert in Williston.[52] Ironically, Mondak's destruction occurred during the centennial of Fort Union's construction—perhaps during the very month—an anniversary made more poignant both because it passed virtually unnoticed and because by this time Mondak bore Fort Union's name.

4 | Ralph Budd and the Upper Missouri Historical Expedition

IT WAS Ralph Budd, president of the Great Northern Railroad, who changed Mondak's name to Fort Union in 1925. The new name proved of small benefit to the dying town. And beyond the confluence the change generated confusion when map readers encountered a "Fort Union" in the state of Montana. Nevertheless, Budd's creation of a new Fort Union symbolized a revival of interest in the old fort site. Budd was first to promote the ruins as a tourist attraction, first to seek federal ownership of the site, and first to plan a reconstruction of the fort. In many ways Budd was the father of Fort Union Trading Post National Historic Site. During the three decades that followed his commemoration of the site in 1925, his vision of a historical reconstruction faded, but never entirely disappeared, from the consciousness of local residents.

Like many nineteenth-century railroad men, Ralph Budd (1879–1962) rose from humble circumstances—in his case, an Iowa farm. Inculcated with the conviction "that it was a privilege to go to school," he completed the civil engineering program at a small Des Moines college by age nineteen. Throughout his life Budd remained a serious reader. He gave his most important innovation, a streamlined, diesel-powered engine, the name *Zephyr*, after Chaucer's god of the west wind.[1]

Budd entered railroading almost immediately out of college. On the Rock Island line he met John F. Stevens, who, as chief engineer for the Panama Canal, had him rebuild the Panama Railroad. Budd completed the work ahead of schedule. Stevens then had him survey a right-of-way from the Columbia River south toward California for James J. Hill. Budd's relaxed but judicious demeanor impressed Hill, and he put the young man in line for the presidency of the Great Northern.[2]

Like his older contemporary Theodore Roosevelt, Budd was fascinated by cartography and the nomenclature of plants, but the great love of both men was history. Budd's specialty was the history of the Northwest from St. Paul to the Pacific. His associates liked to say that if the histories of the early Northwest were destroyed, Budd could replace the important ones from memory.[3]

Budd possessed keen intelligence and exceptional energy, but it was his modesty as much as any other virtue that won him friends and enhanced his gift for leadership. Budd refused to allow any part of his railroad empire to be named for him, and in his own office he was once mistaken for a file clerk. When Budd met with Williston businessmen in the spring of 1925, an associate reported their immense satisfaction with his demeanor. Budd, they said, was not "high toned."[4]

James J. Hill, a man of a different temper, once told a group of farmers that they were the railroad's "children." But, he added, "we are in the same boat with you, and we have got to prosper with you or we have got to be poor with you." Hill refused to believe that western North Dakota and eastern Montana were beyond the reach of agricultural productivity. After 1909 he and the Great Northern promoted emigration to the upper plains—the last great land rush of American history—along with its scientific justification, "dry farming."[5]

Even in Hill's lifetime North Dakota farmers were skeptical about the mutuality of interest that was supposed to exist between agriculture and the railroads. When the inevitable dry cycle returned, the relationship deteriorated quickly. In 1916, after North Dakota farmers noted the subsidized grain rates on Canadian lines, they endorsed a platform of home-grown socialism in the belief that government could produce what the ground could not. Simultaneously, federal regulation (to Hill, the product of "college tackhead philosophers") began challenging every railroad manager. In this difficult business climate Ralph Budd worked assiduously and, to a large extent, successfully to enhance the profitability of the Great Northern.[6]

Despite growing automobile traffic on government-subsidized roads, the Northwest in the 1920s remained a domain of rail, especially for the long-distance traveler. Jim Hill had a "low regard for passenger trains and Rocky Mountain scenery," but his son Louis, Budd's titular superior as chairman of the board, endorsed both and threw the assets and influence of the Great Northern behind the development of Glacier National Park in western Montana. The Great Northern lobbied Congress for the creation of the park, built hotels and lodges for wealthy easterners, and even developed park roads for automobiles. The railroad itself named the park "Glacier," and Louis Hill also bestowed romantic names on smaller Montana stations in the interest of tourism.[7]

In hindsight it seems almost inevitable that a man of Ralph Budd's interests would take note of the Fort Union ruins, which were visible from the Great Northern's tracks and roughly half the distance from St. Paul to Glacier National Park. By 1924 Budd had mastered Chittenden's two-volume *History of the American Fur Trade* and other published descriptions of the historic fort, and in October the railroad's architectural office completed a series of blueprints for the "restoration" of the Fort Union palisade and bastions.[8]

Considering what was known of the fort at the time, the drawings are remarkably accurate, but turning plans into reality posed two major problems for Budd. First, Budd considered the cost too high for the railroad to bear— $19,900 by the conservative estimate of the Great Northern's chief engineer.[9] Even the cost of reconstructing the northeast bastion, the one nearest the track, was estimated at $4,400. Perhaps, wrote Budd, the railroad would "simply have to clear off the ground, put a wire fence around it, and erect a cairn of rough stone at about the center of the site."[10]

A second problem was that the Great Northern did not own the land. In theory, acquiring it should not have been difficult. Mondak was headed for extinction, and the price of agricultural property had declined under poor harvests and postwar deflation.[11] Nevertheless, Budd prudently approached the owner through an intermediary, M. L. Wilson, an official of the Department of Agriculture, fearing a sudden rise in price if it were known the Great Northern wished to buy the property. Like Budd, Wilson was a former Iowa farm boy who had an interest in the history of the northern Great Plains. More important, Wilson had known Frank A. Weinrich, the owner of the Fort Union site, for at least fourteen years and had on occasion discussed the old fort with him.[12]

Weinrich, in turn, was one of the most successful farmer-ranchers at the confluence and was currently serving as a Roosevelt County commissioner. To Budd's gratification, Weinrich expressed an interest in preserving the fort site and none in extorting the highest dollar from a purchaser. Weinrich told Wilson he believed the property should be "forever reserved . . . as a park or public place of historic interest." He even used the heartwarming word "donate" in response to Wilson's first query. When Budd and Weinrich met a few months later, the railroad president pronounced the farmer a "high grade man."[13]

Coincidentally, a group of Williston businessmen approached Weinrich about the Fort Union site a few weeks later. Weinrich soon learned that the businessmen were acting as representatives of the North Dakota State Historical Society and its secretary, Orin G. Libby. Libby (1864–1952) was perhaps the most influential historian who has ever made North Dakota his professional home. A man of broad interests, he had written an authoritative analysis of constitutional ratification, investigated Indian history and folkways, and barely avoided being dismissed from the faculty of the University of North Dakota for supporting the state's socialist movement and opposing American involvement in World War I.[14]

Libby effectively created the North Dakota park system. By 1924 he had already acquired six properties for the State Historical Society, including three fort sites. Nevertheless, Libby and Budd did not compete for the Fort Union site. Willard B. Overson, a Williston lawyer who had served as an attorney for the Great Northern and who was a former member of the Historical Society board, discerned that Budd had the greater resources and thus the better chance to develop the site.[15] Despite a report in the *Minneapolis Tribune* that Libby had purchased Fort Union, the Historical Society abandoned the field to the Great Northern.[16]

Still, before the issue was finally decided, M. L. Wilson suggested to Weinrich that he "play a waiting game and protect himself from giving the site to some one who would do nothing with it." Weinrich had earlier considered requiring free public access to the site and a title reversion if the new owner abandoned it.[17] By May 1925 he had drawn up a list of conditions that included demands that the site never be used for any "domestic, business, commercial, or railroad purpose" and that the Great Northern be required to convey the property to the state of North Dakota or the federal government should either decide to reconstruct the fort. Budd, to his credit, had no objection to these conditions. Nevertheless, although on several occasions he and his subordinates believed themselves close to an agreement with Weinrich, the transfer never occurred, and the Great Northern never took possession of the Fort Union site.[18]

Meanwhile, Budd, concerned about the expense of restoring the fort "in the very best way," now tried to interest the federal government in it, an idea simultaneously naive and farsighted. In 1925 the preservation movement in the United States remained largely the domain of eastern society ladies who hoped to save structures associated with patriotic heroes, usually historic houses that could be treated as shrines. It would be another year before John D. Rockefeller Jr. was introduced to Williamsburg; and William Sumner Appleton, a pioneer in the modern preservation movement, remained hostile to government involvement in administering historic sites.[19]

Perhaps federal regulation of the railroad industry made it easier for Budd to envision a federal presence in historic preservation as well. Nevertheless, during the 1920s no single federal agency had charge of historic structures owned by the United States, none had the mandate or a professional staff to interpret them, and no policies governed new acquisitions. Despite National Park Service responsibility for some Pre-Columbian Indian ruins in the Southwest, the War Department controlled most federally owned historic sites, largely Civil War battlefields.[20]

Possibly uncertain about where to apply for federal assistance, Budd first contacted Calvin Coolidge's secretary and gatekeeper, C. Bascom Slemp, and Slemp assured him that the president would approve having "the War Department cooperate with [him] in the work." Nevertheless, when Budd sent his senior vice president to meet with War Department officials, he learned that the department had few funds for, and no interest in, maintaining historic sites. But, War Department officials advised, if the Great Northern could bring political pressure to bear, Budd's plan would "receive necessary consideration."[21]

The counsel was more than polite dodge. A month later Rep. Louis C. Cramton of Michigan pushed through a congressional resolution authorizing the War Department to restore Arlington House (the Custis-Lee Mansion) to its pre–Civil War condition. Although Arlington House was already government property and, in the late-nineteenth-century tradition, was intended as a shrine to the revered Robert E. Lee, Cramton's success could only have encouraged Budd.[22]

The method Budd chose in his effort to raise political support for the Fort Union project was unusual even by contemporary standards—but then Budd, unlike Cramton, had first to bring his historic site into the consciousness of the educated elite. Under Budd's leadership, the Great Northern had already spent considerable sums in creative advertising. Attempting to increase passenger traffic, the railroad had used lectures, radio, motion pictures, window displays, and colorful print materials. Budd had sent out Minnesota's first locomotive, *William Crooks* (under its own steam), to fairs and similar events, and he had paid a writer to produce pamphlets on the history of the Northwest. In 1924 Budd and Louis Hill also entertained twenty eastern writers on a "Publisher's Edition of the *Oriental Limited*," during which the reporters met local residents at farms and factories.[23]

A year later Budd combined these seasoned promotional tools into the "Upper Missouri Historical Expedition," a week-long rail excursion (16–21 July 1925), part high-toned vacation, part study tour, part advertising campaign. Near the end of the trip Budd told his guests that the trip had been planned to "attract travel to the Northwest" in the expectation that most of it would "ride over the Great Northern Railway." Yet there was more to the Historical Expedition than simple promotion. Budd's heavy investment and careful planning reflected his own love of regional history at least as much as any anticipated financial return for the railroad. One correspondent even praised Budd for "turning from the materialistic side of his work" to do something "that wouldn't pay."[24]

Budd easily obtained official sponsorship for the expedition from the fledgling historical societies of Minnesota, North and South Dakota, and Montana. Five thousand elaborately decorated invitations were distributed to writers, professors, public officials, and other opinion makers, inviting them "to attend a series of memorial celebrations" commemorating "the notable explorations and discoveries of several distinguished pathfinders of the Great Northwest." Those invited were expected to purchase tickets, although presumably "distinguished guests" (as one reporter called them, including himself in that number) were suitably recompensed. Most of the latter were second-rate magazine writers, but among them were men of truly national influence, such as Lawrence Abbott, editor of the influential *Outlook*; Pierce Butler, a Supreme Court justice; and Maj. Gen. Hugh Scott, a former army chief of staff, a distinguished veteran of the Indian Wars, and a specialist in the culture of the plains tribes.[25] Representative Cramton also came aboard.

During the early months of 1925 Budd and his assistants ironed out details of the trip. For instance, considerable effort was expended on the logistical problems of transporting and housing the Knickerbocker Boys' Band of Ray, North Dakota, an incidental feature of the Fort Union ceremonies.[26] Budd commissioned a series of booklets on the sites to be commemorated and checked their drafts before publication. He even drew up an eight-page bibliography, carried its books on the expedition train, and arranged for a librarian to make them available to the passengers.[27]

Planning for the expedition also included changing the names of three small towns. Felsen, North Dakota, became "Verendrye" to honor the French explorers of that name. Bombay, Montana, was renamed "Meriwether" for Meriwether Lewis, and Mondak became "Fort Union." Town naming was a virtual prerogative of the railroad, although the residents of Mondak were at least asked for their approval. (The people of Verendrye seem to have been less enthusiastic. One reporter said that the inhabitants, "with a pleasing but not exactly truthful irreverence," called the hamlet "Verydry.")[28]

The approximately seventy-five expedition members assembled at St. Paul on 16 July 1925, enjoyed a luncheon given by the Budds, and then visited local historic sites before departing on a special train of fourteen Pullmans and private cars. The next morning the train stopped at Verendrye for the dedication of a large granite globe, a monument to the notable English geographer David Thompson (1770–1857). Although Thompson's relationship to the site was tenuous, the North Dakota governor graciously accepted Budd's gift of monument and site. After the reading of papers on Thompson and the Verendryes, as well as a picnic and a baseball game, the expedition moved on to Minot for more banqueting and speech making.[29]

Saturday was spent at Fort Union. On the remaining three days of the trip, expedition members visited the battlefield where Chief Joseph had been captured, dedicated two more monuments (one to Meriwether Lewis and another to Budd's mentor, John F. Stevens), and enjoyed a reception at the home of western artist Charley Russell in Glacier National Park.[30]

In this potpourri of history remembered, recovered, and invented, Fort Union was intended as the centerpiece. The design of the invitation was itself a celebration of the fur trade and made no pictorial reference to David Thompson, Meriwether Lewis, or Frank Stevens. The invitation showed a stylized buffalo robe lashed to a framework of birch boughs. Between the robe and the frame were eleven hoops containing pictures of such features of the fur trade as an earthlodge, a dog travois, and mackinaw boats. At the top of the invitation the largest of the hoops contained a drawing of Fort Union loosely based on Bodmer.[31]

Not surprisingly, planning the Fort Union event proved more time-consuming for Budd and his staff than any of the other expedition stops. The railroad president generated enthusiasm for the Fort Union celebration by addressing a group of regional leaders in Williston on 27 May, laying special emphasis on the tourist traffic and even emigration that might be expected to follow the planned "historical pageant." The Great Northern's local attorney, W. B. Overson, whose own interest in the site had predated Budd's, was made general chairman for the celebration. An enthusiastic Weinrich became half the Committee on Grounds, and Libby was enlisted as a judge of Indian contests.[32]

Budd arranged to have a Fort Union sign placed on the railroad right-of-way, and when a subordinate suggested adding the names of two rival forts and Fort Buford, Budd replied that Fort Union was "so much more impor-

Fig. 4. Invitation to the Upper Missouri Historical Expedition "memorial celebrations," with various images suggesting the early-nineteenth-century fur trade on the upper Missouri. The original of this elaborate, full-color document is 13 inches by 21 inches. Courtesy, Fort Union Trading Post NHS.

tant than the others" that the latter could remain unmentioned.[33] Because no memorial was to be dedicated at Fort Union—the reconstructed palisades and bastions were to be the eventual memorial—Budd planned a symbolic flag raising. He personally approved a flagpole of what he deemed an appropriate size and shape,[34] authorized the division of concessions between the Elks and local churches, and even approved a baseball game in the belief that those attending the Fort Union celebration ought to have "all the fun they want."[35]

The most difficult event to arrange was an "Indian congress" with representatives from eleven tribes. As Budd's advertising director had anticipated, it proved "wonderful copy for magazines and newspapers," but assembling and provisioning the Indians entailed considerable expense and logistical complications. Horses had to be rented and fed, tepee poles had to be cut and shipped from Glacier, and five hundred pounds of pipestone had to be carried from a Minnesota quarry to supply the pipe-making contest. Logs for a Mandan earthlodge, built just outside the southern perimeter of the historic fort, were inadvertently taken without permission from a local landowner, who, of course, had to be reimbursed. Assembling the Indians cost more than $3,000 at a time when reconstructing a bastion was estimated at $4,400.[36]

The Great Northern spent perhaps three or four times that amount in building a timber approach ramp to its railroad bridge across the Missouri (known locally as the Snowden Bridge) and in planking the roadbed to accommodate automobile traffic. The unusual combination of a toll and railroad bridge was immediately popular and continued to serve the confluence until 1985. On 18 July, its first day of operation, more than a thousand cars crossed to participate in the ceremonies at Fort Union.[37]

The crowd attending the event was probably the largest ever assembled in western North Dakota to that date. Local newspapers estimated it at ten thousand, a number entirely conceivable given the more than three thousand cars parked in a thirty-five-acre wheatfield cut by Frank Weinrich for the occasion. Most Williston businessmen shuttered their stores for the day. Some people drove more than a hundred miles to attend, and cars from eight states were spotted on Williston streets the following Monday.[38]

When the expedition train arrived, the assembled Indians greeted the guests with a variety of dances and contests. During the formal ceremony that followed, the flags of France and England were raised and lowered. Then the American flag was raised to the shouts of the crowd and the singing of the "Star Spangled Banner." (The Great Northern crew that erected the pole had aimed for the exact spot where the original had stood but fortunately missed by a few yards, thereby saving its archaeological remains for future investigation.) General Scott talked with the assembled chiefs in sign language, at which he was an expert, and the Indians responded. Although the picturesque exchange was thoroughly photographed, it was more than a stunt. Scott actually knew most of the tribal leaders from his days as an Indian fighter. Local people, too, searched for and often found Indians whom they had known and employed before 1894, when the last of them had been forced onto reservations.

Indians were awarded prizes in such contests as "best old-time costume," "best trained dog and travois," tepee raising "for squaws," and the "best medicine pipe in possession of a full-blooded Indian delegate." The remainder of the day was filled with band concerts, the baseball game, and dances held in Mondak's Great Northern Hotel, reopened for the occasion. Three prominent members of the expedition were adopted into Indian tribes, a popular conceit of the 1920s.[39]

The event was not flawless, however. The arrival reception put the program a hour behind schedule, largely because newsreel cameramen were allowed to reshoot scenes "spoiled by the milling crowds." Worse, before the speech making began, a strong west wind raised clouds of dust that obscured the sun and blinded the spectators. (In the purple prose of one reporter, wind-blown women resembled the Winged Victory of Samothrace.) Few concessionaires made a profit because the wind and dust damaged their wares.[40]

Budd was concerned that the weather might have reduced local fervor for the Fort Union project, but, returning through Williston at the end of the trip, he discovered that the enthusiasm of the business community remained undiminished. Budd's courting of regional governors and national figures such as Pierce Butler provided heady encouragement to the windswept upper Missouri. In a full-page newspaper ad, the Williston Commercial Club even described the town as the "Stopping Point for Visitors to Fort Union."[41]

Budd himself believed the trip had gone "wonderfully." Even before it ended, his friends had created a permanent organization to endorse similar annual excursions. To Louis Hill, Budd wrote that the trip had been a public relations bonanza with "the Governors and high class people traveling with us and in every way reflecting a very fine feeling towards the Great Northern Railway." Five days after the flag raising at Fort Union, Budd was already considering the sites for a trip in 1926. In 1927 he hoped to dedicate a statue to James J. Hill and then in 1928 return to Fort Union to dedicate its reconstructed walls and bastions on the centennial of its establishment. The North Dakota people, especially those near Williston, he wrote, "are so extremely anxious to restore Fort Union that I do not believe there is any doubt but that it can be managed."[42]

Not surprisingly, the Upper Missouri Historical Expedition was publicized in many newspaper and periodical articles, frequently illustrated with photographs. The railroad's clipping service collected 806 articles from papers along the Great Northern line and 398 elsewhere. The railroad also reprinted editorial comments in a booklet for distribution and underwrote the publication of a book by Agnes C. Laut, *The Blazed Trail of the Old Frontier: Being the Log of the Upper Missouri Historical Expedition* (1926).

Still, the expedition received less publicity than Budd might have anticipated. He could not have foreseen that it would take place during the Scopes "Monkey Trial," a media circus occurring simultaneously in Dayton, Tennessee. (One Indian chief asked an expedition member for some books on evolution.)[43] Furthermore, Fort Union coverage tended toward the sentimental or trivial, such as photographs of Indians with little context beyond nostalgia for the Wild West. The *New York Times,* for example, published four pictures of Indians at "Old Fort Union" without mentioning where "Old Fort Union" was. (Newspapers can be forgiven for locating the ceremonies in both North Dakota and Montana, but some of them put the event in "Washington," "eastern Washington," and even "near Seattle, Washington.") Few newspaper articles noted the reasons for Fort Union's importance or mentioned that its reconstruction was being considered. In other words, as a means of bringing Fort Union into the consciousness of the educated elite, the expedition was less successful than Budd had probably hoped.[44]

By March 1926 Orin Libby wondered if the Great Northern would be able to reconstruct Fort Union on its own and suggested to Budd that, "having made a fine beginning," he might now want to cooperate with the State Historical Society. Budd replied that if North Dakota and Montana could generate enough political pressure to obtain twenty-five thousand dollars from Congress, he "would be willing to undertake the work, so that there would be no risk . . . that the estimate would be exceeded and the work be left unfinished." Budd also revealed that he planned to repeat the 1925 celebration "in order to keep the historical importance of Fort Union before the public."[45]

During the Columbia River Historical Expedition of 1926 Budd did just that. Weinrich and Overson promoted the second Fort Union event as enthusiastically as they had the first. Again there was flag raising and speech making. The Indians were returned, and Hugh Scott again spoke to them in sign language. There were dances, Indian contests, band concerts, and, this time, three baseball games. Although the effort enjoyed modest success and several thousand people attended the events, the largest turnout—on Sunday after the train had left—was for a baseball game between the Williston team and the long-haired, long-whiskered vegetarians of the House of David religious cult.[46]

Budd was kept exceptionally busy in 1925 and 1926, and demands on his time continued to increase. Between 1926 and 1928 the Great Northern

Fig. 5. Observing Indian contests at the Fort Union site during the Columbia River Historical Expedition, 17 July 1926. Courtesy, State Historical Society of North Dakota, Bismarck.

Fig. 6. Ralph Budd, president of the Great Northern Railway, receives a peace pipe from Yakima chief Minninick during the Columbia River Historical Expedition (1926). Gen. Hugh Scott looks on. Great Northern Rwy Co. Records, Minnesota Historical Society, St. Paul.

built the Cascade Tunnel in Washington, the longest railroad tunnel in the Western Hemisphere. Simultaneously, Budd was bending every effort to merge the Great Northern and the Northern Pacific, an effort ultimately doomed by a hostile Interstate Commerce Commission and vigorous political opposition. Meanwhile, an increase in long-distance automobile travel, combined with the onset of the Great Depression, caused the number of passengers on the Great Northern to fall from 8.5 million in 1920 to little more than 1 million in 1931. It was "a bitter disappointment" for Budd, who each year had put hundreds of thousands of dollars into the advertising budget. Finally, near the close of 1931, Budd left the Great Northern to become president of the Burlington, a line with more track and new possibilities for the now-respected railroad executive. There were to be no more historical expeditions.[47]

Nevertheless, the reconstruction of Fort Union's walls and bastions was not a dream Budd abandoned easily. In November 1927, when asked by a Great Northern attorney if he wanted to return an option to purchase a lot in Mondak, Budd told him to "hold onto [it] for awhile." Even in 1940, as president of the Burlington, he retained interest in the project. Budd also remained proud of his two historical excursions. When he visited the Great Northern's museum in 1949 and discovered that it did not have examples of the invitations, he donated his own framed copies.[48]

Aside from propagating a legend about an "old tunnel" at the fort—a minor nuisance to future interpreters—Budd's Upper Missouri Historical Expedition, along with the publicity and memories it generated, was entirely beneficial to the preservation of the site.[49] Given more time at the Great Northern, Budd might even have found a way to obtain federal funding for his Fort Union project. After all, in 1928 Congress appropriated $1.74 million for a monument to George Rogers Clark at Vincennes, Indiana.[50] Yet if Budd had been successful in his quest, the archaeological remains of Fort Union would have been seriously compromised, if not destroyed, and it is less likely that the federal government could later have been induced to incorporate the property into the National Park System. Thus, both Budd's enthusiastic interest in Fort Union and his departure from the Great Northern helped preserve the historic site, even though no one who witnessed its neglect and near destruction during the next decade would have believed it.

5 | Depression Years

THE PLAINS STATES were devastated by the Great Depression, and North Dakota was one of the hardest hit. Western North Dakota and eastern Montana suffered even more than areas farther east because in the semiarid West the economic crisis was compounded by a severe dry cycle. Drought and dust blasted crops and destroyed livestock. Perhaps one-third of North Dakota's farmers lost their land through foreclosure. Relief became the state's biggest business, and the federal government donated $8 million in surplus food to North Dakota. (New York, a state with twenty times the population, received $10 million.) In the middle 1930s per capita personal income in North Dakota dropped to 47 percent of the national average. Residents of North Dakota and eastern Montana emigrated to California and Washington by the thousands.[1]

The Great Depression per se had a deleterious effect on historic preservation in North Dakota. The legislature cut the biennial appropriation for the State Historical Society from $25,000 in 1929 to $13,520 in 1933, and the society's journal ceased publication from 1934 to 1939. Nevertheless, the massive federal aid that poured into North Dakota with the coming of the New Deal helped expand and develop the state's historic resources.[2] Still, for the Fort Union site, the economic collapse proved immediately harmful while its benefits remained largely potential.

During the 1930s Fort Union probably gained a greater advantage from a two-part article in *Popular Science Monthly* by Clarence E. Mulford describing how to "modelize" the trading post. Mulford, the creator of Hopalong Cassidy, achieved comfortable wealth even before his fictional western hero was discovered by Paramount Pictures. A man of simple tastes, Mulford amused himself on his Maine estate by making models of stagecoaches, steamboats, and covered wagons. The steamboats led naturally to a model of Fort Union, built on a scale of 3/16 inch to a foot.[3]

Mulford constructed his model without visiting the site. (Although he wrote more than a hundred westerns, he made few trips west.) Nevertheless, his plans, based largely on Edwin Denig's description, provide a reasonably accurate representation of the fort as it existed before the midcentury enlargement of the Bourgeois House. On the negative side, Mulford misunderstood some of Denig's details and probably invented others. In one sentence about the history of the fort he made four factual errors. He also put the fort in Montana.[4]

The *Popular Science* model drawings may have introduced more Americans to Fort Union than any magazine article before or since. A National Park Service employee, writing to the Museum Division about Fort Union in 1938, assumed knowledge of the article. When the State Historical Society of North Dakota decided to build a model of the fort in 1934, it purchased the *Popular Science* blueprints. In 1941, when reconstruction of the fort was again mooted, the *Williston Herald* illustrated its announcement of the project with a *Popular Science* drawing.[5]

The reconstruction of Fort Union might easily have become a project of the Civilian Conservation Corps (CCC), a relief agency for unemployed youth that became one of the most widely respected of all New Deal agencies, especially in North Dakota. More than twenty camps operated in the state between 1933 and 1942, and the major complaint about them was that there were too few.[6]

Almost simultaneously with the creation of the CCC, President Franklin Roosevelt (at the suggestion of NPS director Horace Albright) transferred dozens of historic parks and monuments from the War Department to the National Park Service. Suddenly, in 1933, the National Park Service became the primary custodian of federally held historic properties in the United States. To develop these areas, the Park Service used CCC enrollees in archaeological and historical projects. At Gettysburg they built five hundred miles of period fencing, at Shiloh they restored the "Sunken Road," and at Ocmulgee National Monument they reconstructed an Indian council chamber.[7]

There were no national parks in North Dakota in the 1930s, and most CCC enrollees in the state were employed in soil conservation or wildlife refuge development. Nevertheless, a considerable number of "boys" (as they were always called at the time) participated in state park construction, including historical restoration and reconstruction. During the 1930s Russell

Reid (1900–1967), a gifted, though largely self-taught, superintendent of the State Historical Society, bought acreage to expand existing parks and create new ones. He also cooperated closely with the National Park Service in locating the North Dakota CCC camps. Some were installed in western North Dakota, where the CCC extensively restored the Chateau de Mores in Medora and reconstructed block houses and Mandan earthlodges at Fort Abraham Lincoln near Bismarck.[8]

A similar reconstruction of Fort Union was easily imagined. The idea was promoted locally at least twice during the first two years of the agency's existence, most seriously in the late summer and early fall of 1934 when for a time there were nearly two hundred CCC boys in Williston. Acting through a committee of Williston Rotarians, W. B. Overson, the general chairman of the Great Northern's Fort Union celebration in 1925, attempted to involve the CCC in historical reconstruction at the confluence. His friend, businessman J. B. Lyon, who had also played a role in the 1925 celebration, visited Ralph Budd and received his blessing for the undertaking. Even at this stage Overson talked of Fort Union becoming a national park.[9] In Montana the drive for a CCC reconstruction was spearheaded by R. S. Nutt, a former resident of Mondak, a business acquaintance of Ralph Budd, and the manager of the Northland Seed Company in Sidney.[10]

Nothing came of any of this. No existing records indicate that the confluence was even considered as a possible CCC campsite. Perhaps Overson's campaign was mistimed. Two years later, when there was a sudden need to locate a new CCC camp in North Dakota for the benefit of the National Park Service, Russell Reid hardly knew where to put it on short notice.[11]

A larger problem was the one that had faced Budd a decade before. The Fort Union site was still the private property of Frank Weinrich, and Weinrich was in a less generous mood in 1934 than he had been a decade earlier. Like most other residents of North Dakota and eastern Montana, Weinrich struggled through the depression. At the time of the Great Northern's Historical Expedition he already had one mortgage on his confluence property. In 1935 he added another but was still unable to pay his taxes for the previous three years.[12]

Meanwhile, the Weinrich property beneath and around old Fort Union was increasing in value. The American Fur Company had built its fort above a gravel base that retarded erosion and stabilized the riverbank during the annual flooding of the Missouri. Now that gravel nearly destroyed the fort's archaeological record.

During the road-building boom of the 1930s (for which the New Deal can take nearly as much credit as for the CCC) most states found sufficient rock for road surfacing nearby. North Dakota was not among them. Its shales and soft sandstones were unsuitable for road construction because of their comparative weakness and instability. In North Dakota, gravel of glacial origin was virtually the only material appropriate for road building.[13] Although found throughout the state (except in the southwest corner), these glacial deposits were comparatively uncommon at the confluence of the Yellowstone and Missouri. Furthermore, the Fort Union gravel was of an exceptionally high quality because it was primarily composed of smaller stones that could be screened rather than larger ones that had to be crushed.[14]

Weinrich had planned to reserve his gravel beds even while he discussed the donation of the fort site to the Great Northern in 1924. Actual extraction of the gravel began even earlier, in 1919, west of the fort site in what later became a parking lot of the national historic site. By the 1930s mining had reached the few acres between the fort and the state line. Undoubtedly, many archaeological features and Indian burials were lost. The resultant quarrying scars were soon visible from the air and were noted as landmarks on topographic maps. Then sometime before the autumn of 1936 the foundations of the southwest bastion were undermined and its artifacts, mixed with its gravel, were carried away.[15]

Fig. 7. Fort Union site, 1924. Taken from the west near the North Dakota–Montana state line, this photograph, sent to Ralph Budd, shows the Missouri in spring flood and hugging the north bank as in the historic period. Great Northern Rwy Co. Records, Minnesota Historical Society, St. Paul.

Fig. 8. Fort Union site, 1937. Taken by Edward Hummel from roughly the same direction as the 1924 photograph but later in the year. (The clump of trees in both pictures provides orientation.) The Missouri has moved toward its south bank. Note the clear evidence of gravel mining that has undermined the southwest bastion. The flagpole raised by the Upper Missouri Historical Expedition in 1925 is evident, as are the remains of the earthlodge also erected for that occasion, visible between the trees. Courtesy, National Park Service.

Ironically, at nearly the same time that the foundations of the fort were being subverted, the National Park Service began to take an interest in the site, an interest that stemmed largely from the passage of the Historic Sites Act of 21 August 1935. The act provided legal authority for NPS supervision of state historic preservation efforts, something the Park Service had already been doing on an ad hoc basis through agencies such as the CCC. But the Historic Sites Act also envisioned federal acquisition of additional historic properties, especially those that reached beyond the prehistoric ruins and battlefield parks of which the National Park System was then composed.[16]

Shortly after the passage of the Historic Sites Act, the chief of the Museum Division, a fur trade buff, set a "junior historian" to work writing a report on Fort Union. In part, the information was intended to aid the building of a diorama of Fort Union for the Interior Department Museum. The resulting thirteen-page report was unexceptional—on the level of a good college term paper—but it provided a bibliography and raised a host of unanswered questions.[17]

By the summer of 1937 the National Park Service approved a full-dress review of the Fort Union site. The job of preparing it fell to Edward A. Hummel (1909–76), an energetic young historian, born and raised in Gackle, North Dakota, and fresh from a graduate program at the University of Minnesota. Hummel was based in Omaha, but his original assignment was to provide technical advice to all the CCC camps working on historical projects in the upper Midwest. Additionally, he was given the task of doing preliminary investigations of historic areas proposed as national monuments by members of Congress—sixty or eighty of them, as he recalled. Hummel eventually became superintendent of some of the largest units in the Park System and retired as an associate director. Nevertheless, in retirement he remembered his first seven years with the NPS as "great days" when he "never worked harder . . . and [never] enjoyed it more."[18]

Considering the time and resources available, Hummel's report was careful and literate. The twenty-eight-year-old historian made little use of manuscript sources, but he apparently discussed Fort Union with Ralph Budd before traveling to the confluence in the fall of 1937. Hummel evaluated the Fort Union site as the best example in the country—"with the possible exceptions of St. Louis and Mackinac Island"—of one of the Park Service's new thematic topics, "Exploitation of Natural Resources to 1870." Because there were excellent contemporary descriptions of the trading post, Hummel concluded that Fort Union might even be reconstructed, if "visitation would justify such extreme measures." Hummel's positive evaluation of Fort Union was especially weighty in light of his recommendation against NPS acquisition of Mount Rushmore, where, he said, the sculptures "defaced a beautiful part of that mountain."[19]

One goal of the Hummel report was to determine the location of Fort Union. Although for two generations its location had been no mystery to confluence residents, the question was still being debated in Washington into the late 1930s. Obviously, it would not do to build a diorama or urge incorporation of a historic site into the Park System without knowing whether the fort was in North Dakota or Montana.

In part, the problem arose from late-nineteenth-century military sources that referred to "Fort Union, M.T.," before the North Dakota–Montana boundary was surveyed in 1885. In part, the confusion was due to a century of shifts in the river channels that changed water distances between Union and Buford. Chittenden's now-famous fur trade history (not to mention Mulford's *Popular Science* article) identified the fort's location as Montana Territory. Even NPS director Arno Cammerer suspected that some ignorant error (or worse) had occurred in the identification of the North Dakota ruins as Fort Union. In August 1937 Russell Reid, with a hint of frustration, wrote Acting Assistant Director (and soon to be Chief Historian) Ronald Lee that the Fort Union site was "so clearly defined on the ground that a person would have no difficulty in accurately locating practically all of the buildings."[20] Hummel's 1938 report effectively silenced the eastern skeptics—although not the Federal Writers' Project history of Montana, which in the following year, in both map and text, implied that the ruins were west of the border.[21]

While examining the Fort Union site, Hummel took photographs and noted the impending destruction of the southwest bastion by gravel mining. He also commented on the depredations of souvenir hunters who had found the site a source for "old hinges, locks, harness buckles, arrowheads, shelves [?], pieces of tools, and other artifacts."[22] There had also been some fear during the 1920s and early 1930s that the Missouri might claim the ruins, but by the time of Hummel's visit the river had begun to move back toward the south bank. Nevertheless, it seemed that the combination of graveling and souvenir hunting would eventually achieve a comparable destruction.[23]

Most depredation at the site was, of course, anonymous, but the documented story of the Fort Union "anvil post" may conveniently represent the gamut of casual destruction during the period. In 1925 Ralph Budd was warned that a large wooden post, the last piece of original wood at the Fort Union site, was being destroyed by "curiosity seekers." Budd asked Frank Weinrich to remove and store it for safekeeping. Weinrich replied that the post had not been damaged but that he would "keep an eye on it and see that nothing happens to it." By 1932 the aboveground portion of the wood had been almost obliterated, and Weinrich allowed the remainder—a timber 4 1/2 feet by 20 inches in diameter—to be divided between the Williston High School shop and the man who dug it up.[24]

Even before Hummel completed his report, Russell Reid had decided to try to save what remained of the Fort Union site. By March 1937 he reported to Ronald Lee at National Park Service headquarters that although the state had not yet been able to purchase the property, it was "continuing the negotiations."[25] Reid's bargaining position was seriously handicapped by the Historical Society's lack of money, and he expressed his need to the North Dakota Federation of Women's Clubs. Its state treasurer, Nellie Johnson Hydle, a prominent Willistonite, spearheaded the drive to purchase the site.[26] Although the first contribution of twenty-five dollars was given by the Pioneer Daughters of North Dakota in December 1937, it took more than five years for the Federated Clubs to raise the five-hundred-dollar purchase price. Fearing the site would be lost before that amount could be accumulated, the State Historical Society advanced the money and purchased a crucial 10.46 acres on 6 August 1938. From land estimated by Edward Hummel to be worth fifteen dollars an acre, Frank Weinrich realized nearly forty-eight dollars an acre.[27]

Both Hummel and Reid almost certainly anticipated that once the Fort Union site became state property, the National Park Service, operating through one or another New Deal relief agency, would improve the site. In 1935 the North Dakota legislature passed a companion measure to the federal Historic Sites Act, allowing the State Historical Society to administer any new state parks, "when so authorized, as an agent of the National Park Service." An agency that had to go hat in hand to North Dakota women's clubs for five hundred dollars was a poor candidate to improve new park property. Reid himself stated frankly in 1940 that he could have done little for his state parks without aid from federal agencies.[28]

It seems unlikely that the National Park Service planned to incorporate the Fort Union site into the federal system. Hummel's report was advisory only, and what little evidence of contemporary Park Service intent exists suggests a lack of interest in turning the fort into a national historic site. For instance, a letter from Chief Historian Ronald Lee to Russell Reid in 1939 implied that Lee, at least, had a greater interest in helping the state develop Fort Abraham Lincoln than the Fort Union site.[29]

In any case, the most important question for the principals was not whether title to Fort Union should be held by the state or the federal government but how federal relief funds could be channeled into state preservation and reconstruction. The State Historical Society and the National Park Service had worked together closely for five years. (How closely is illustrated by a letter from Hummel to an employee of the State Historical Society, asking him to drop what he was doing and prepare a Fort Union bibliography, unless Reid objected "too strenuously.")[30] Both sides anticipated that this symbiotic relationship would continue indefinitely.

Even before Weinrich signed over the property, an official of the National Farm Loan Association suggested reconstructing the fort.[31] In February 1941 the *Williston Herald* announced that the state had appropriated funds to start the work. Ralph Budd promised his assistance. The Williston Chamber of Commerce, energized by W. B. Overson and J. B. Lyon, pledged its cooperation. Russell Reid arranged to obtain the necessary timber from the Farm Security Administration and prepared to ask the Great Northern to donate materials and to assume the cost of transportation. The state office of the Works Progress Administration (WPA) was "much interested in the proposed restoration" and approved a small project to begin the construction. The only immediate difficulty was that in 1941 the wpa labor force was at work on the nearby Buford-Trenton irrigation project.[32]

Of course, the attack on Pearl Harbor brushed aside these plans as if they had never existed. Especially in poorer states such as North Dakota, the war was a calamity for historic preservation. The financial tie that had bound the National Park Service to state agencies was, in the event, forever severed, with a consequent loss of professionalism and planning. According to State Historical Society superintendent Ray Mattison, development of North Dakota "historic sites practically came to an end."[33]

Yet if a New Deal agency had reconstructed the fort, any archaeological excavations would probably have been casual at best, poorly funded, and sketchily conducted, at least by modern standards. As late as the 1960s nps chief historian Robert Utley considered the Fort Union site barren and lacking in integrity.[34] If in the prewar period a conjectural reconstruction had been built or a shoddy archaeological dig had been conducted, opponents of the fort might have succeeded in excluding it from the federal system. After 1941 the Fort Union ruins still had to pass through another twenty-five years of uncertainty and depredation, but in the end North Dakota's temporary loss resulted in gain for both Fort Union and the nation.

6 | State Ownership

ALTHOUGH the purchase of the Fort Union site by the State Historical Society of North Dakota saved it from gradual destruction by gravel mining, the site remained unmarked, unfenced, and virtually unprotected for almost twenty years. The state made no improvements at the site until after World War II. Occasionally, someone from the society checked up on the property. In August 1939, for instance, trustee Dana Wright visited it while camping on the Missouri River with six boys. Wright noted that there was no sign of gravel extraction on state property and that the boys "had the luck to pick up a couple gun flints and some trade beads." A state crew may also have visited the site in 1941 to measure the ruins and remove trash from the bastions.[1]

Despite—or perhaps because of—the state's casual interest, in 1942 the Williston Chamber of Commerce urged the Historical Society to reconstruct the fort. Not surprisingly, the society's State Park Committee concluded that reconstruction without federal funds was impossible. It did agree to fence and mark the site and approved five hundred dollars to initiate the work. Nevertheless, this money was to be shared with the Fort Buford site, to which the society had administratively joined Fort Union.[2]

A depression-era pledge of federal assistance only increased the state's reluctance to spend its own money at Buford-Union. Although the state park budget for 1943 included a biennial appropriation of two thousand dollars for the sites, no money was expended because "promised Federal help did not materialize." Nevertheless, the Historical Society hoped that the fort sites could be improved "with the cooperation of the local communities."[3] Perhaps as an experiment, the society appointed a nine-member "local park board" composed of Williston community leaders, most of whom (like W. B. Overson and Nellie Hydle) had been involved in earlier attempts to preserve the forts. The committee seems never to have functioned as such, although some of its members retained an interest in the sites.[4]

It took the Historical Society more than ten years just to put a fence around Fort Union. Superintendent Russell Reid thought the project was under way in 1946. Three years later he discovered that fencing materials had still not arrived in Williston. Only in September 1954 was he able to report that the society's "field man" had enclosed the area.[5]

Legislative appropriations to the Historical Society increased from $52,000 in 1945 to $389,000 in 1963, but these funds were grossly inadequate to upgrade the North Dakota park system, especially since eighteen new historical parks had been acquired by the state between 1940 and 1965.[6] Despite Reid's careful management and his recognition that Fort Union was "a unique historic site," there was little he could do to protect much less improve it. Before the fence was installed—and to a lesser extent afterward as well—the site was, in the words of Dana Wright, "overrun with vandals."[7] During the major archaeological investigation of Fort Union in the mid-1980s archaeologists found "pot-hunter" trash from the 1950s buried under two feet of fill. Visitors more than once told the chief archaeologist about relic-hunting acquaintances who had carried away buckets of artifacts from the site.[8]

As late as 1959 Wright noted that a "well-traveled trail" ran across the site, which was "grown up to weeds and [was] certainly a shabby looking place." At least, he said, "the weeds hide the surface of the fort and there are few signs of digging." Car bodies were still piled in the ice house depression.[9]

Outside state property the situation was worse. In the late 1950s the fields surrounding the fort were leveled for irrigated farming. This leveling probably obliterated the remains of outbuildings, the fort cemetery, and much of the archaeological evidence from Crow-Flies-High village.[10] Gravel extraction continued into the 1960s in the area west of the fort and as late as 1970 in a newer pit to the east. Indian graves were not infrequently unearthed by the excavations. In 1960, when three graves were discovered and reported to the Indian agency at Fort Berthold, North Dakota, the gravel pit operator was told that unless the remains had names, the agency had no jurisdiction. The burials were summarily bulldozed except for some beads and bracelets and a skull that was mounted on a tractor.[11]

Ironically, the rural isolation that encouraged depredation and neglect during the middle decades of the century eventually proved an asset.

Throughout the 1950s many historic properties in more populated areas of the country were destroyed by interstate highway construction, urban redevelopment programs, and rising land values—often with the financial blessing of the federal government.[12] Meanwhile, the Fort Union site remained twenty-five miles from the nearest market town, surrounded by a nearly pristine landscape. A subdivision or an industrial park near Fort Union was unimaginable in the 1950s, and there was a consensus among area residents that preservation of the site and reconstruction of the fort would be the most profitable use of the property. In other words, the Fort Union site never became a focus of land-use conflicts like those that divided other American communities into preservationists and developers.

Nevertheless, support for preserving and reconstructing Fort Union was like the Missouri River in summer, broad but shallow. One obstacle to more dedicated community support was a lack of popular information about the fort. Preservationists are frequently challenged by local myths and romanticized notions that have grown up around historic sites; but in the 1940s and 1950s Fort Union might have benefited from some local romance. Williston schools did not teach the history of Fort Union.[13] There were no field trips to the site. One former resident half-jokingly recalled that local history began with the coming of the Norwegians.

Textbooks on North Dakota history provided little information about the fort, and what they did provide was unlikely to inspire enthusiasm among the community members most inclined to support historic preservation. The standard elementary and junior high text, *Our State North Dakota* (1953), spent one paragraph on the fort's location, another longer one on the sale of alcohol to the Indians, and two final sentences on the fort's destruction. Erling N. Rolfsrud's *Story of North Dakota* (1963), a popularized history for adults, used fifteen of its twenty-one paragraphs about Fort Union to describe the fort's liquor trade in lurid detail.[14]

Another impediment to the development of the Fort Union site was the discovery of oil in 1951. Fort Union lies at the center of a geological feature called the Williston Basin, a saucer-like depression of 130,000 square miles, rich in fossil fuels, which extends from northwest South Dakota into Manitoba and Saskatchewan and from central North Dakota to northeastern Montana. Fortunately for both the historic fabric and the natural environment, most early oil exploration was conducted at least forty miles from the fort site. Nevertheless, the discovery well was drilled in Williams County, of which Williston is the county seat. Williston began to advertise itself as the "center of the largest oil basin in the world." There was talk of North Dakota becoming the next Texas or Oklahoma. Within a year the population of Williston had grown from seventy-four hundred to nine thousand, and in 1953 the town had eight hundred people living in trailers. An influx of promoters, drillers, geologists, and brokers contributed to the boomtown psychology and undoubtedly dampened interest in developing the confluence forts for their tourist potential.[15]

Oil production diversified the North Dakota economy, but it also added a new boom-and-bust cycle to the one ordained by the climate on agriculture. By the late 1950s there was a worldwide surplus of oil, and the state government imposed production quotas on North Dakota wells. The state's comparative lack of refineries and pipelines also reduced the competitiveness of its petroleum products.[16]

Interest in the confluence forts revived with the waning of the oil boom, but between them, Fort Buford had a significant local advantage. Buford had been abandoned in 1895, within living memory of the oldest residents. Further, it already had enjoyed a considerable reputation as a historic site. In 1895 John Mercer, the fort's quartermaster clerk, purchased the commanding officer's twenty-room mansion for three hundred dollars, a fraction of its true value. For forty years the Mercer family lived in the house they called "Villa Militaire," turning it into a virtual museum of Fort Buford memorabilia. On occasion local money was raised to help preserve the house, and admissions were sometimes charged for tours conducted by the Mercers' eldest daughter, Sarah.[17]

Villa Militaire burned in 1937, and nearly all its contents were destroyed. Nevertheless, the loss of the mansion did not seem to dampen local interest in restoring Fort Buford. Even when the Bureau of Reclamation ran the main ditch of the Buford-Trenton irrigation project diagonally across a corner of the old post, the Williston Rotary Club continued to discuss a restoration. Two original buildings remained at the site, and one of them, the "field officer's quarters," was early recognized as the possible location for a small museum.[18]

The catalyst for community action appeared, surprisingly enough, in Fargo, more than four hundred miles away. In 1957 James B. Connolly (1915–81), the director of the North Dakota Automobile Association and an avocational historian, discovered that national automobile clubs had deleted Fort Union from their maps. The omission annoyed Connolly, who had talked of writing a history of the confluence. What energized him to action, however, was a *New York Times* editorial about national parks in November 1958. A few days after reading the opinion piece Connolly wrote a four-page, single-spaced letter to the author, boosting the area as possibly "the most exciting spot in the winning of the west."[19]

As Connolly admitted, there was "only a remote connection" between the *Times* article and his burden, the development of confluence historic sites.[20] It is doubtful the editorialist even acknowledged Connolly's extended history lesson. Nevertheless, Connolly duplicated it for the tourist committee of the Greater North Dakota Association, a statewide chamber of commerce. A copy made its way to Williston, where a group of civic leaders was again discussing restoration of Buford-Union. Within a month the Williston law firm of Bjella, Jestrab & Neff had distributed Connolly's letter to local political, business, and educational leaders along with a plea for federal development aid. For the first time, Willistonites proposed that the federal government take twenty square miles of confluence property, including "the sites of Fort Buford, Fort Union, and the old town of Mondak, and that steps be taken either by the state or by a public corporation formed for the purpose, to reconstruct Fort Union and possibly Fort Buford and Mondak."[21]

The time was propitious. Mass tourism based on good roads and national prosperity expanded dramatically during the 1950s and 1960s. Historic sites more than shared in that boom. Paid attendance at Colonial Williamsburg rose from 166,000 in 1947 to nearly 710,000 in 1967. Between 1960 and 1962 attendance at all historic sites in Massachusetts grew by 50 percent; in 1964 tourism was one of the three largest industries in twenty-nine states. One commentator in the early 1960s declared that history had "become a cash crop as eagerly tended as the hope for industrial plants."[22]

North Dakota was no exception. Tourism became increasingly important to the state's economy, especially after the state hard-surfaced most of its highways in the 1950s. Visitation at Theodore Roosevelt National Memorial Park—the North Dakota Badlands—more than tripled between 1951 and 1961. North Dakota's new Economic Development Commission was in the process of requesting an appropriation for tourist promotion just as Connolly and his Williston allies began urging development of the confluence forts.[23]

At the legislative session of 1959 state senator Frank Wenstrom (1903–97), a Williston banker and able politician, proposed the creation of a commission to preserve the historic sites at the confluence. The legislature passed the measure, creating an awkwardly named Yellowstone–Missouri–Fort Union Commission. The commission was composed of five ex officio members: the governor (as chairman), the president of the senate, the speaker of the house, the director of the State Historical Society (Russell Reid), and the director of the Economic Development Commission, along with five citizens appointed by the governor. Included in the latter were

Wenstrom, himself, and Connolly, who became commission secretary. LaVern C. Neff, a young Williston lawyer and chamber of commerce president who had been active in earlier efforts to develop the confluence, was named vice chairman. R. S. Nutt, the former Mondak banker and now aging businessman from Sidney, was appointed by the Montana governor as his state's representative.[24]

The legislature voted the Confluence Commission appropriations of one thousand dollars in each of five biennial legislative sessions, only part of which was spent, and then largely for postage and travel expenses. Nevertheless, the activity of the commission sparked local volunteer efforts that, with minimal direction from the State Historical Society, largely benefited Fort Buford. Neff effected a transfer of land that enlarged and squared off the Buford property, and local civic organizations repaired the existing buildings, developed a picnic area and parking lot, and refenced the post cemetery. The county also surfaced the road from Williston to Trenton, a hamlet about ten miles from the confluence.[25]

Little was done for Fort Union, and that was largely to the good. Talk of reconstructing the palisades with old utility poles fortunately came to nothing. One commission adviser, with more passion than propriety, suggested building a tower with elevator, observation deck, and blinking lights "as a Living Memorial to the Pioneers."[26] The Montana commissioner (who, in Connolly's words, had a case of "road-itis") wanted a Missouri River bridge on the state line, a few hundred yards from the fort site. Connolly entertained a brief enthusiasm for "sponsored signs," markers donated by professional, religious, or other interest groups that would commemorate visits to Fort Union by men of similar profession or persuasion.[27] The National Audubon Society submitted a proposal for such a sign; and in 1966, just before transfer of the property to the federal government, the Knights of Columbus built a considerable marker memorializing "Catholic Pioneers."[28]

Nevertheless, by 1961 it was clear to most members of the commission that little of consequence could be accomplished at Fort Union with the limited resources available from state and local governments. Therefore, the commission's most important contribution to the reconstruction of Fort Union was bringing political pressure to bear on the National Park Service at a felicitous moment.

In the late 1950s the Park Service had embarked on Mission 66, a developmental and promotional program that reflected the dramatic increase in the use of the national parks. As part of the plan, the Park Service reactivated the National Survey of Historic Sites and Buildings, a legacy of the

New Deal. In 1961 the survey examined Fort Union under "Theme XVI: Westward Expansion and the Extension of National Boundaries" and two of its subthemes, "The Fur Trade" and "Indian and Military Affairs." It decided that Fort Union had "exceptional value" in both the latter categories. These "exceptional value" designations were announced through two 1961 press releases—but in such a low-key fashion that Connolly did not hear of them until the following year.[29]

The double designation was unusual (though not unique), and the Park Service itself might have eventually taken the first steps toward incorporating Fort Union into the system. The process was expedited, however, when North Dakota senator Quentin Burdick (1908–92), who had grown up in Williston, began to perform constituent service for the Confluence Commission.

Burdick, a liberal Democrat and a member of both the appropriations and interior committees, wielded considerable influence during the Kennedy-Johnson era.[30] During an appropriations subcommittee meeting in March 1962 Burdick pointedly asked the director of the National Park Service, Conrad L. Wirth, about the status of Fort Union. As it happened, the Park Service was still embarrassed about a misunderstanding with Burdick that had occurred the previous year.

Russell Reid, in perhaps his last major contribution to the fort's preservation, had convinced the Confluence Commission that an archaeological study of Fort Union (which he estimated would cost ten thousand dollars) was necessary before any sort of reconstruction could take place. The lobbyist for the Greater North Dakota Association then had the North Dakota congressional delegation insert a five-thousand-dollar appropriation in the Interior Department budget for Fort Union archaeology. After questioning Wirth in the spring of 1961, however, Burdick became convinced that the Park Service already had "ample funds . . . without additional appropriations" and had the money removed from the budget bill. Then, when it was too late, Burdick discovered that he had been mistaken.

Consequently, NPS historian Roy Appleman advised Wirth not only to give Burdick "clear and accurate knowledge of the Service's work at Fort Union" but also to request a feasibility study from the regional office in Omaha to decide if Fort Union should be incorporated into the park system. Wirth authorized the study on the same day, 5 March 1962.[31]

Comparatively little needed to be done. Ray H. Mattison, the regional historian for the Historic Sites Survey and an expert on the fur trade era, had just completed the first scholarly history of Fort Union, which appeared in the Historical Society's journal.[32] Not surprisingly, the NPS report of September 1962 judged Fort Union to be "clearly of national significance" and urged the site's inclusion in the park system. At the same time, the report asserted that Fort Buford had "no special claim to national importance," and Mondak "no claim to commemoration" at all.[33]

About reconstruction of Fort Union the report was ambiguous. In one sentence it allowed that a comprehensive archaeological excavation, "coupled with the extensive documentary and pictorial information available, would permit a very accurate reconstruction of the Fort." In the next it asserted that a reconstruction would be too expensive and that interpretation of the site ought to be confined to "a modest Visitor Center" with perhaps a reconstruction of "part of the stockade and the exhibit of features uncovered during archeological excavations."[34]

Publication of the report changed the perception of Fort Union at both the state and federal level. The state parks director all but washed his hands of the property, declaring that until he received "positive information from the National Park Service," North Dakota would "do nothing with the site." The Park Service, in contrast, began to exhibit a proprietary interest. By the end of 1962 Roy Appleman expressed concern about a proposed Missouri River bridge that might be located on the state line and warned that the NPS would "oppose this if it is meant literally." More than a year before the creation of the park, the Service also insisted that the site be called "Fort Union Trading Post." Although this name had never been used during the historic period, the Park System already had a Fort Union in New Mexico, a former army post on the Santa Fe Trail.[35]

There was no organized opposition to federal acquisition of the fort site, and there were prominent supporters. The principal landowner, Ben Nordell, was described as eager to sell even though he would lose his gravel mining operation. Important allies, such as John Budd—son of Ralph Budd and himself now president of the Great Northern Railroad—used their influence in Washington to promote acquisition.[36] Nevertheless, it took nearly four years to pass a bill establishing the park.

Hearings before the Subcommittee on Public Lands of the Interior Committee were held on 2 August 1963. Since Senator Burdick was himself a member of the Interior Committee, it was a friendly session. Burdick and Director Wirth testified to the historic value of the site. The meandering questions from subcommittee members touched on—among other topics—North Dakota weather, the roads in Yellowstone National Park, the possibility of having to condemn private land at the confluence, and the current cost to the government of operating parks of a size similar to the one proposed. None of the senators, except Burdick, seems to have had prior knowledge of the fort. Even Burdick inexplicably asserted that the gravel mining mentioned in a Park Service report was being conducted at the "Fort Buford site a few miles away."[37]

Wirth explicitly stated that the Park Service did not intend to reconstruct the fort, but it is unclear if this message was comprehended by the senators. When asked by subcommittee chairman Alan Bible what would "completely develop" the site, Wirth responded that the Park Service was prepared to repeat what "we did in Jamestown": do archaeology, build a visitor center, and tell the park story with artifacts recovered—"not by reconstruction of the fort." Later Burdick returned to Wirth's comments about Jamestown and noted that he was "very impressed with the way Jamestown is portrayed."[38]

Perhaps Burdick understood Wirth and was simply being politic. Or Burdick may have been thinking of Jamestown Festival Park, a Virginia state operation adjoining the Jamestown unit of Colonial National Historical Park, which included speculative reconstructions of James Fort and three seventeenth-century ships. In any case, Burdick's constituent mailings referred to his "bill to restore Ft. Union"; and once the measure finally passed, Burdick wrote Connolly that he had always intended to press for "the complete restoration of the Fort."[39]

The bill to establish the park was reported favorably by the Interior Committee and was passed by the Senate in June 1964. Getting action in the House of Representatives proved more difficult. The representative from North Dakota's Second Congressional District was a conservative Republican of limited influence. Near the end of the session Interior Committee chairman Wayne Aspinall refused to schedule additional hearings for the national parks subcommittee on the ground that many congressmen had already left Washington.[40]

Burdick reintroduced the bill authorizing the establishment of Fort Union in January 1965, and Rolland Redlin, the district's new Democratic congressman, introduced companion legislation in the House. Connolly urged members of the Confluence Commission and its advisers to back the legislation with letters to Congress. The director of North Dakota's Economic Development Commission wrote chambers of commerce and civic clubs requesting resolutions of support. One commission adviser, who had grown up at the confluence, urged Montana senator Mike Mansfield to support the legislation, noting in explanation for his enthusiasm that Fort Union had served "me and my family [as] a hunting ground for historic artifacts."[41]

Again there was no opposition to the bill in congressional committees. In the House Subcommittee on National Parks and Recreation, historian

Roy Appleman helped new National Park Service director George B. Hartzog deflect the interest of two committee members in incorporating Fort Buford into the proposed park.[42]

Again there was considerable ambiguity about whether the National Park Service would reconstruct the fort—and if so, whether in whole or in part. In a formal report to the Senate Interior Committee, Under Secretary of the Interior John A. Carver followed the 1962 NPS proposal. Development would consist of an archaeological investigation, the building of a "modest" visitor center and administrative office, and the "reconstruction of part of the stockade."[43] Director Hartzog, the principal witness for the Department of the Interior at the House committee sessions, did not mention reconstruction. Representative Redlin in commenting on his bill said that its intent was "not to rebuild the Fort as such." Conversely, Rep. James F. Battin of Montana, who had introduced similar legislation, declared that the "restored Fort . . . would be an unusual tourist attraction."[44]

At the Senate hearings Chair Alan Bible of Nevada and Senator Clinton Anderson of New Mexico both, at different times, asked whether the fort would be reconstructed. Assistant Secretary of the Interior Stanley Cain repeated the Jamestown comparison: the Park Service would expose foundations and erect suitable interpretive signs. Roy Appleman later commented that "the exchanges on this subject led me to feel that Senators Bible and Anderson were not satisfied, although they did not press it." To further confuse the issue, Appleman himself testified that a "full scale replica . . . offered the best means of interesting and informing visitors" but that the question of reconstruction of Fort Union ought "to be held in abeyance" until archaeological, historical, and interpretive studies had been completed.[45]

On 8 June 1966 the authorization passed the Senate and four days later the House. President Johnson signed the bill creating Fort Union Trading Post National Historic Site on 20 June.[46] The same week, Connolly was cited for his work (and given a coonskin cap) by the Publicity Committee of the Greater North Dakota Association. Although many Willistonites undoubtedly believed that a reconstructed fort would rise from the Missouri riverbank in short order, Connolly was more realistic. To Vern Neff he prophesied that although the National Park Service would eventually "do the right kind of job at Fort Union," working with the agency would be "a frustrating thing."[47]

7 | **A New National Historic Site**

SHORTLY AFTER accepting Fort Union into the National Park System, Congress passed the Historic Preservation Act of 1966. In part a reaction against the wholesale destruction of historic properties during the postwar era, the measure authorized creation of the National Register of Historic Places, provided matching grants for state surveys and acquisitions of historic properties, and established procedures for protecting registered areas from projects of the federal government itself. Responsibility for carrying out the act fell to the National Park Service. During the same period—between 1964 and 1968—twenty-three new historical units were added to the park system. The historical section of the Park Service, having previously "played second fiddle to the natural wing," now came into its own.[1]

NPS administrators responded enthusiastically to their growing professional authority by issuing a new, systematic outline of American history to serve as a guideline for the agency. Published in 1972, the outline sought to encourage inclusion of even more historic sites in the system while dampening congressional enthusiasm for pork-barrel parks. To former chief historian Ronald Lee, the plan provided "the historic preservation program with an underlying framework."[2] Thus, NPS historical administrators increasingly combined assertions of professional competence with a proclivity toward preservationism. Within this larger framework occurred the development—or rather, the nondevelopment—of Fort Union Trading Post National Historic Site.

The 1967 master plan for the Fort Union site was more quickly approved than any that followed it, and most of its recommendations were eventually achieved. In May 1966, a month *before* President Johnson signed the park authorization bill, NPS planners examined the site. Drafts of the planning document had been circulating even earlier. Because at the time no federal requirements mandated public involvement, the drafts were quickly critiqued within the Park Service and by the following May a final version was approved by the acting director.[3]

The 1967 plan was thoughtfully conceived, contained valuable maps, and (considering the genre) was well written. Significantly, the plan considered partial reconstruction of the trading post a "primary management objective." Reconstructed structures at the site were to include palisades, bastions, the trade house, and the Bourgeois House—the structures actually rebuilt between 1986 and 1991. The facade of the Bourgeois House was to be historically accurate, but the interior was to serve as a visitor center. The plan even recommended replanting native grasses and creating a cooperating association.[4]

Commentary on the plan by NPS historian Roy Appleman (1904–93), who took a sympathetic interest in the site, focused appropriately on the issue of reconstruction. In a seven-page, single-spaced review the chief of the Branch of Park History Studies wrote that although he did not "necessarily think [reconstruction] bad or objectionable," he urged that reference to it be excluded from NPS plans until the historical, and possibly the archaeological, research had been completed. The Service, he said, should wait until it was certain enough evidence remained on which to base an "authentic replica."[5]

To discover what information did survive, Appleman assigned his subordinate, Erwin "T" Thompson (1926–98), to write Fort Union's "Historic Structures Report." In retirement, Thompson called his Fort Union study the most exciting project of his career. Although at first taken aback by the graveling scars and the mounds of trash thrown over the far bank of the Missouri, Thompson was soon captivated by the site. Reading his notes near the location of the original flagpole, he felt "the presence of the past around."[6]

Thompson discovered so many written and pictorial descriptions of Fort Union that he became a staunch supporter of reconstruction. In fact, he argued that the master plan was too conservative. Eventually, he wrote in 1970, "the decision will have to be made to reconstruct the greater portion of the fort, if not all." And Appleton agreed with him.[7]

Acquiring the four hundred acres of land authorized by Congress and delineated in the master plan took ten years and considerable haggling. Of course, North Dakota was more than willing to donate the State Historical

Society's tract of ten acres, and a private ceremony at the governor's office on 7 June 1967 effected that transfer. The Confluence Commission ceased operation on the same day.[8]

Purchasing the private land was another matter. The largest landowners were the Nordell family, whose spokesman, Ben G. Nordell, was the president of the First Union Bank of Sidney, Montana. Nordell's negotiations over possible land exchanges and sale prices were complex, shrewd, and unblinkingly focused on the bottom line. In 1963 the Park Service believed that 380 acres might be purchased for $30,000. In the 1967 master plan the same acreage was believed to be worth $48,000. Less than a year later Nordell was estimating the value of his family's land at $780 per acre.[9]

Nordell threatened that if the Park Service did not purchase his land before 2 June 1976, he would attempt to derive "the maximum in material benefits" from it, which, he implied, might include opening new gravel pits. The superintendent of Theodore Roosevelt National Memorial Park (to whom administrative supervision of Fort Union had been assigned) responded by attempting to initiate condemnation proceedings. Shortly thereafter Nordell and the Park Service agreed that the Service would approve three land appraisers, Nordell would choose one, and, unless that appraiser's figure was outrageous, the Park Service would purchase the land at his appraised value. The appraisal came in at about 50 percent higher than the amount Nordell had been willing to accept earlier, but the Park Service bought the property anyway.[10]

In August 1966 the superintendent of Theodore Roosevelt warned James Connolly that it would be premature to set a target date for the Fort Union reconstruction because both land acquisition and the necessary archaeological excavation might be "time-consuming."[11] He was right on both counts. The Park Service conducted at Fort Union one of the largest archaeological investigations it would ever undertake—twenty years later.

The 1967 master plan mandated archaeological research, and excavations took place seasonally in 1968, 1969, 1970, and 1972. Nevertheless, within a few years these early digs were criticized in language that virtually accused the supervising archaeologists of incompetence.[12] It is necessary, therefore, to review the circumstances under which these excavations were conducted.

First, no one (with the possible exception of Roy Appleman) realized how big a project Fort Union might be.[13] Despite decades of farming outside the walls and pothunting within, the density of archaeological features and the sheer number of surviving artifacts that remained to the fort were beyond the ken of the early planners. The first archaeological excavations were also handicapped by erratic funding and by the failure of the Park Service to appoint a director who would see the project through. Four archaeologists were assigned to the site during the first five years of the program. If small-scale projects in the 1970s are included, the number of supervisory archaeologists at Fort Union before 1980 rises to six or seven. Even with the most careful record keeping, there might have been confusion.[14]

Second, the archaeology originally contemplated at Fort Union was of the traditional sort practiced by the Park Service at sites such as Jamestown and Fort Necessity National Battlefield. As the master plan stated, the purpose of excavation was "to provide precise structural data for restoration purposes and to collect artifacts." Archaeology was viewed forthrightly as the handmaiden of history and historic architecture, not of anthropology—a perspective soon out of fashion with most professional archaeologists.[15]

Third, "historical archaeology," the study of archaeological sites from the colonial period forward, lacked the status of prehistoric archaeology, in which nearly all contemporary archaeologists had been trained. A Society for Historical Archaeology was not even organized until 1967. Sometimes historical archaeology was less rigorously pursued than prehistoric archaeology because documents supposedly revealed much of what a researcher wished to glean from a historic site anyway. For instance, screening excavated soil for small artifacts, a typical practice among contemporary prehistorians, was not always employed by historical archaeologists of the period.[16]

Even before a spadeful of earth had been turned, the archaeological project at Fort Union was trammeled by a personality conflict masquerading as an interagency dispute. NPS archaeologist Jackson W. "Smokey" Moore was sent temporarily to the confluence largely to ensure that the Park Service, rather than the Smithsonian Institution's River Basin Surveys, would conduct the excavations. Yet even though Moore, who was being treated for acute gout, was a somewhat unwilling project supervisor, his selection was not arbitrary. Moore had done a considerable amount of historical archaeology, and he had recently completed a major dig at Bent's Old Fort in eastern Colorado, another important mid-nineteenth-century fur trading post.[17]

Moore arrived at Fort Union in early June 1968 with a crew of six students. During a two-month stay he laid out grids, dug test trenches, and delineated elements of the palisades, the bastions, and the Bourgeois House. Moore was under no illusion that he was truly excavating the fort. It was an "investigation," he told the Fargo newspaper, "strictly a construction-related project." Yet artifacts came out of almost every hole, even the one he intended as a latrine. "The biggest blow," he wrote to his supervisor in Omaha, "is the realization of how *big* this site is!" Unfortunately, Moore's documentation was sketchy and his final report a memo three pages long.[18]

The following year Moore became assistant to the chief of the new Midwest Archeological Center (MWAC), into which the River Basin Surveys had by now been transformed. Wilfred M. Husted, Moore's successor at Fort Union for the next two seasons, considered himself a prehistoric archaeologist. Nevertheless, he had had considerable experience with surveys and test excavations, the sort of background believed necessary at Fort Union.[19]

In June 1969 Moore oriented Husted to the site and left after some backfilled units were reopened. Others, hidden by the tall grass, were discovered by Husted's crew when they stumbled into them. Artifacts again appeared everywhere: broken glass and dishes, iron hooks and rings, gun flints, and Indian pipe bowls. Beads were ubiquitous, and nails became "boring to find."[20]

In two summers of excavation Husted investigated the Bourgeois House and kitchen, the blacksmith shop, the trade house, and the area around the main gate. Progress on other features was hampered by an unusual amount of rain in 1969 and by the discovery of four Indian skeletons in the ice house near the end of the 1970 season. Husted's record keeping was superior to Moore's, and his report provided helpful photographs. Husted removed Moore's grid stakes, however, because his crew was tripping over them. The Fort Union project, Husted later recalled, "was interesting and fun, but I really didn't know what I was doing."[21]

There were no excavations in 1971. An archaeologist under contract to the NPS backfilled several trenches from the previous year because they were considered hazardous to visitors. In 1972 Husted hired another crew but was transferred to the Northeast Region before the season began. The National Park Service then contracted the work to an anthropology professor at the University of Colorado, who in turn made his graduate student, David Gillio, field supervisor for the project.[22]

Although Gillio tried to work within a grid and to use uniform sizes for his excavation units, he caused unnecessary confusion, both by creating a new and eccentric system of unit naming and by starting over with the artifact cataloging sequence. His excavation was also hindered by a short season and heavy rains. Gillio believed he would be allowed to analyze the plethora of recovered materials for his dissertation, but once he completed his maps and report, MWAC demanded the artifacts.[23]

By this time Adrienne B. Anderson, an MWAC archaeologist and a part-time instructor at the University of Nebraska-Lincoln, had been assigned to the Fort Union project. Anderson, who held titular responsibility for the site from 1972 to 1976, had great plans, little time, and no funding. She visited the site twice, assigned undergraduates to write introductory papers about the artifacts, and criticized the work of her predecessors. On her final visit in May 1976 she monitored the excavation of a well and trenches for water and power lines. Although some archaeological features from the post-fort period were briefly investigated, their exact location is uncertain because no maps were made to accompany the memo describing them. Shortly after Anderson completed her doctoral dissertation, she was transferred to the Rocky Mountain Regional Office.[24]

After that, no large-scale archaeological projects were conducted at the Fort Union site until the major excavation began in 1986. Small tasks, such as conducting a magnetic survey, studying infrared aerial photography, and monitoring the installation of the interim visitor center, were completed by 1978.[25]

The course of Fort Union archaeology in the 1960s and 1970s is a striking example of how such a project ought not be undertaken. The National Park Service grossly underestimated the archaeological resources remaining at the site, underfunded the excavations, and at best remained unconcerned about the turnover of personnel that contributed to the project's lack of continuity. The erratic archaeological excavations further postponed the planned reconstruction, pushing it into a more hostile era and thus ensuring that developing the fort site would be more difficult and costly to accomplish.

Nevertheless, it is probable that these less-than-perfect archaeological investigations resulted in no significant loss of historical or anthropological knowledge. Before directing the major excavations of the late 1980s, William J. Hunt located the vast majority of the earlier excavation units on a master map of the site; and his intensive excavations, comparatively well financed by the Park Service, more than atoned for past deficiencies. Although order and clarity are always to be preferred to disorder and obscurity, it is likely that in the future only theorists will be exercised by the fact that the first archaeologists did not dot their i's and cross their t's.

The early archaeological investigations also unintentionally helped bring the first Park Service rangers to Fort Union. During the first three years of Park Service ownership the NPS had virtually no uniformed presence at the site. Park headquarters in Medora, 150 miles away, arranged for the land to be hayed, and a neighboring farmer was hired to check on the site. Undoubtedly, some casual pothunting continued. Husted had to gently dissuade some bead collectors who began to scrutinize the site right before his eyes.[26]

Publicity given the archaeological investigations stimulated visitation, and crew members rarely stayed at Fort Union overnight or on weekends. (Husted noted a "surprising" number of visitors in June 1970: fourteen on one day and twelve the next.)[27] Both Moore and Husted experienced incidents of vandalism, the first occurring two weeks into the first season.[28] The most serious took place in the spring of 1969, before Husted's arrival, when a Williston man dug up and carried off a nearly complete human skeleton from the fort site. The theft was reported to the U.S. district attorney, who treated it blithely as the work of an "amateur archaeologist . . . on a Sunday excursion." Apparently, the FBI agreed to drop charges in exchange for the remains—except that the "amateur archaeologist" was allowed to keep the skull.[29]

After another incident in June 1970 and the discovery of the ice house burials in July the Park Service finally put a seasonal ranger on site for the remainder of the summer. Another followed in 1971.[30] In the summer of 1972 the Park Service assigned the first area manager to the Fort Union site, Sylvester Putnam. Putnam could not recall a single incident of pothunting or vandalism during his two-year tenure, and his successor, William Wellman, had more serious problems with deer poachers.[31]

Both Putnam and Wellman were well known and well liked. Putnam had the advantage of being an African American, a curiosity in northwestern North Dakota, and Wellman's North Carolina background and low-key manner, combined with his growing knowledge of the fur trade, gained him local appreciation as well. What local residents could not understand was why the National Park Service was taking so long to reconstruct Fort Union. Although Jim Connolly complained about the slow pace of the archaeology as early as 1971, it took most area residents another few years to realize that Park Service ownership of Fort Union did not mean expeditious development.[32]

Local interest in Fort Union remained strong. In 1972, when the Park Service asked its units to commemorate the centennial of Yellowstone National Park, a flag-raising ceremony at Fort Union on 6 August 1972 assumed a larger significance. Putnam considered it "sort of a rededication of the site." More than twelve hundred people from counties on both sides of the state line came to enjoy the day's activities, which included a look at David Gillio's trenches and performances by a drum-and-bugle corps and a square-dance club. A model of the fort, built by Sidney Junior High School students, was displayed "so those in attendance could more clearly visualize how the reconstructed site would look."[33]

James Connolly addressed the crowd in his role as secretary of the Confluence Commission, deftly employing the career of geologist F. V. Hayden to tie the history of Fort Union with that of Yellowstone. Connolly praised the late Russell Reid for saving the Fort Union site during the depression and then spent much of the remainder of his speech recounting Fort Union's historical greatness and urging his hearers to political action. The Park Service "does wonders in enhancing the areas it acquires," said Connolly, but it takes "its own sweet time." He urged his listeners to let their congressmen know how important reconstructing Fort Union was to them, not only for the sake of history but also to "boost the economy of the state and particularly of this western section."[34]

8 | Winning Congressional Authorization

ALTHOUGH Connolly never lost interest in Fort Union, an even more effective champion of the historical site emerged during the 1970s, Ben Innis Jr. (1920–85). Without the congressional authorization for which Innis worked diligently in the 1970s, Fort Union almost certainly could not have been reconstructed during the 1980s.[1]

Ben Innis had grown up in Williston, and he spent much of his adult life there selling insurance and working as a radio and television newsman. His interest in history appeared early and ran deep. As a child, he and a friend raced to see who would be the first to read all the history books in the Williston library. As an adult, Innis researched his gun collection, only to become so engrossed in the research that he sold the guns to buy more microfilm. He planned family vacations around historic sites and dyed plumes for uniform reproductions on the kitchen stove.[2] Ben Innis became the quintessential buff.

Blessed with a fine voice and a charismatic personality, Innis magnified his influence through those whom he persuaded to support his causes. Sometimes community leaders raised eyebrows at his enthusiasms, and occasionally his zeal outran political prudence—as when he proposed that Williston be renamed "Sitting Bull." Nevertheless, he remained a superb motivator, especially among like-minded younger men.[3]

Innis was introduced to Fort Union in the eighth grade, but he was unable to gratify his growing preoccupation with confluence history until he returned to Williston in his forties. In 1962 he founded the Fort Buford Sixth Infantry Regiment Association, an Indian Wars reenactment group, which was named North Dakota's official delegation to the 1964 New York

Fig. 9. Ben Innis, near the end of his life, as sergeant major of the Fort Buford Sixth Infantry Regiment. Photo by Tom Cantarine.

World's Fair. The frontier army remained Innis's first love, but his interest easily lapped over into the earlier fur trade era. Innis had participated in the successful drive to have the Fort Union site incorporated into the National Park System, and the Fort Buford Sixth Infantry took part in the flag-raising ceremony of August 1972.[4]

In October 1975 Innis organized what soon became the Fort Union–Fort Buford Council, a group dedicated to promoting "the restoration" of Fort Union. Membership was never large, and the budget was minuscule. (In 1976 a vote of the council board allowed Innis to buy two hundred postage stamps.)[5] Fortunately, Innis did not appreciate the strength of the opposition. He believed the Fort Union reconstruction faced only National Park Service indifference and procrastination. In fact, it faced hostility.

During the controversy that surrounded the appropriateness of reconstructing Fort Union, proponents and opponents of reconstruction exhibited roughly equal strengths. Opponents of reconstruction were largely cultural resource managers in the Washington office of the National Park Service. They had developed a reasoned preservationist philosophy and were knowledgeable in the ways of bureaucracy. As professionals, they were paid to consider such questions, and they were eager to defend their expertise. Since inertia was an easy option, opponents of reconstruction could rely on general apathy and a reluctance to commit tax dollars to an obscure site in a sparsely populated area of the country.

Supporters of the reconstruction were typically history buffs. Sometimes they were assisted by local businesses in search of tourist dollars, sometimes by area Park Service personnel, and sometimes by NPS specialists, such as historical architects and archaeologists, whose professional skills might be employed in achieving such a project. A reconstruction of Fort Union promised obvious psychological and financial benefits for the community. Nevertheless, reconstruction enthusiasts were amateurs for whom lobbying could be only a part-time affair. Their knowledge of governmental power was imperfect, their funds were limited, and they could be discouraged by determined resistance from the Washington professionals. The greatest chance for local success lay in a perseverance that attracted attention from members of their congressional delegation—especially those with an interest in history or with a committee membership that provided leverage with the Park Service.

In 1969, three years after the publication of the first master plan for Fort Union, Congress passed the National Environmental Policy Act. The measure mandated examination of management alternatives and required public involvement in the planning process of all federal projects.[6] The Public Involvement Program sent Park Service officials back to the confluence communities three times within a decade, and the results were the same each time. Since there were no alternate uses for the Fort Union site besides gravel extraction, an overwhelming majority of local residents and community leaders preferred reconstruction. One resident said he would take as much reconstruction as the Park Service would provide, "the more the better." Another was baffled by the NPS declaration that "virtually all historic resources would be irretrievably lost" through reconstruction. When he realized that these historic resources were only building materials moldering in the ground, he proposed measuring, then destroying, them.[7]

In contrast, the NPS Washington office had opposed even incorporating Fort Union into the park system. To Robert Utley, the site was barren and lacked integrity. In 1974 a member of Utley's staff provided him with a thoughtful response to the park master plan that included nearly all the arguments that could be marshaled against reconstruction. The memo held that reconstruction had not been contemplated by Congress and was not "*essential* to public understanding." It would destroy historic fabric and freeze interpretation to a historic period of lesser significance. It would be conjectural and expensive to maintain.[8]

To Utley, Willistonites were a "constantly buzzing nuisance." Fort Union had hardly entered the Park System before Ben Innis began a persistent, if unfocused, attempt to have Fort Buford transferred from the state to the

NPS. Despite unequivocal rebuffs and discouragement at every turn, Innis somehow convinced himself that the Park Service had a "strong interest" in joining Buford to Union. James Connolly counseled that although Buford was important, reconstruction of Fort Union was the priority. By at least the mid-1970s Innis embraced this view himself.[9]

Innis created the Fort Union–Fort Buford Council during the local exhilaration that followed the naming of Thomas S. Kleppe, a North Dakotan, as secretary of the interior by President Ford in September 1975. Innis believed—simplistically and wrongly—that the reconstruction of Fort Union and the transfer of Fort Buford stood a better chance of success during Kleppe's administration. (As it turned out, Kleppe had no interest in the confluence forts and turned over most of his correspondence about Fort Union to Park Service personnel, who concocted stiffly polite replies.)[10] Innis followed other will-o'-the-wisps, such as devoting considerable effort to extracting a letter of support from the regional representative of the National Audubon Society, whom he considered "a powerful ally."[11]

Nevertheless, Innis had considerable experience at orchestrating media publicity. He ensured that council meetings were well covered in the local press, organized petition drives in Williston, and drew up fill-in-the-blank resolutions of support for passage by local governments. Innis also had the backing of Bill Wellman, the site manager, and his superior, Theodore Roosevelt National Memorial Park superintendent John O. Lancaster, both of whom supported reconstruction.[12]

The political culture of North Dakota nearly guaranteed that supporters of reconstruction would receive a respectful hearing from their congressional delegation. North Dakotans traditionally emphasized parochial over national issues and maintained what one political scientist called a high "pork-oriented expectation." During the 1970s all three members of the North Dakota delegation were masters at bringing home the bacon.[13] Unfortunately for Innis, the intensity of their support for the Fort Union reconstruction was in inverse proportion to their immediate political clout.

Milton R. Young (1897–1983), the senior senator, was a Republican who had never lost an election and had already served more than twenty years on the Senate Appropriations Committee. Young was proud of his ability to direct farm-oriented federal projects to North Dakota. In 1954 he also successfully campaigned to have the interior of Ford's Theater restored to its appearance at the time of Lincoln's assassination. Young should have been an enthusiast for Fort Union development, but he was not. By the mid-1970s he was serving his last term in the Senate and was nearing eighty. His support for the Fort Union project remained, at best, perfunctory.[14]

Quentin Burdick (1908–92), the junior senator (although well into his sixties), had engineered Fort Union's entrance into the Park System. He retained membership on the Interior appropriations subcommittee, relished constituent service, and maintained an interest in regional history. (His father, Congressman Usher Burdick, had been a respectable amateur historian who had owned twelve thousand books on the West.) During the reconstruction period Burdick was an articulate spokesman for the reconstruction project. On the negative side, he had a low-key personality and sometimes proved absentminded.[15]

The most diligent supporter of Fort Union development was Mark Andrews (1926–), North Dakota's only congressman, a member of the House Appropriations Committee, a farmer, and a liberal Republican from the opposite end of the state. Along with his dedication to the political game, Andrews early demonstrated an interest in North Dakota's history. For instance, he unsuccessfully attempted to incorporate Fort Totten, an army post in eastern North Dakota, into the Park System. Park Service rejection of Fort Totten was an unusual defeat for Andrews because his prowess at pork-barrel politics was legendary. "I got a lot of criticism during my political career," Andrews later recalled, "but nobody ever said I wasn't effective."[16]

Andrews's letters to Innis often went beyond mere formality as the congressman coached him in the workings of the political process. Andrews respected Innis's "genuine passion" for the Fort Union project and understood that the goals of both could be more easily achieved if Innis's enthusiasm were properly channeled. For instance, Innis tended to believe that whoever signed NPS documents unfavorable to reconstruction was a personal enemy of the project. Andrews tried to warn him off such rabbit trails, advising that "who shot John is not particularly important to us except to understand that we must overcome this resistance in the Park Service."[17]

The spring of 1976 seemed an opportune moment to push for congressional authorization of the Fort Union project. Public meetings held the previous winter for the Park Service's "environmental assessment" had reinvigorated local interest in both the historic fort and the boost to tourism that might accompany its rebuilding. Membership in the Fort Union–Fort Buford Council rose from zero to two hundred within a few months. Burdick and Andrews were also campaigning for reelection that year. Not coincidentally, both introduced reconstruction bills in their respective houses of Congress.[18]

Andrews believed that the authorization stood a good chance of passage. In late May he had a staff member call one of Innis's less sanguine supporters to assure her "that everything would turn out all right." Innis himself was exhilarated. In attempting to energize his lieutenants for what he thought would be the last push toward realizing the goals of the council, he wrote, "Let's get to work! Then just imagine! Four or five years from now we can walk the ramparts of the stockade[,] . . . wind our minds back 150 years, and say (inwardly), 'So this is what it was like!' I don't know about you, but I find it darned tough to wait!"[19]

Unfortunately for Innis, his reverie was spoiled by bureaucratic politics. Robert Utley, now assistant director for park historic preservation and an opponent of Fort Union reconstruction on philosophical grounds, had for two years waged a personal battle to prevent a conjectural reconstruction at Fort Smith, Arkansas. Fort Smith was an undertaking of the powerful John McClellan, chairman of the Senate Appropriations Committee, and it was only with "some very intricate political dancing" that Utley and his allies were able to scuttle the project. Near the end of this fight the Fort Union reconstruction seemed likely to be approved. To have allowed the North Dakota delegation to prevail would have "utterly doomed the impending victory in the Fort Smith battle." McClellan could not have been expected to accept the rejection of his fort while he watched another built for Milton Young, the committee's ranking Republican.[20]

Utley persuaded Park Service director Gary Everhardt to derail the Fort Union bill as well. On 23 July the Park Service requested the Senate Interior committee to "defer action" on the measure until the Service could "thoroughly review all the alternatives." Although the NPS letter admitted that the local public overwhelmingly favored total reconstruction, it estimated that the project would cost $8.1 million and so argued for "less expensive ways" of interpreting the site.[21]

The Park Service announcement caught Andrews by surprise. The congressman had been encouraged by Park Service reaction to his reconstruction proposal little more than a month before. An exasperated John Lancaster complained in a three-page letter to his regional director that Fort Union had "been studied to death" and warned that the local public, whose participation had been so carefully solicited, would surely lose faith in the Park Service's planning system. (Three master plans for Fort Union had been developed within ten years, although the second was abandoned after the Fort Union site was transferred from the Midwest to the Rocky Mountain Region in December 1973.)[22]

Ben Innis was shaken. Publicly, he assured members of the Fort Union–Fort Buford Council that there was still hope for the reconstruction. Privately, he wrote Jim Connolly that promoting Fort Union development had been "excruciatingly frustrating and heartbreaking" and that after "this round, regardless of the outcome, I quit."[23]

The Park Service's attempt to derail the Fort Union project ultimately had little consequence, but a different outcome was altogether possible. Had Andrews and Burdick lost their elections or had Utley stayed in the Park Service or had Innis remained discouraged, the reconstruction authorization might have been delayed indefinitely. Despite Park Service opposition, Burdick's bill passed the Senate at the end of the session (although it was never considered by the House). Mark Andrews kept after the Park Service to provide its promised alternatives to reconstruction, and the chief of the Rocky Mountain regional planning division continued to recommend reconstruction "to the extent practical."[24]

By September, Innis had regained his composure and had worked up a twenty-one-point list touting Fort Union's past and present importance to the region. In February 1977 he wrote, produced, and narrated an eighteen-minute slide show promoting the reconstruction. Above the strains of "This Land Is Your Land" his production concluded with the question, "Would you like to help?"[25]

In January, Senator Burdick reintroduced the Fort Union bill. A few weeks later Representative Andrews reintroduced his measure as well, charging Innis with the task of maintaining "broad-based public support." Innis and his allies arranged for resolutions from town and county governments and from the legislatures of North Dakota and Montana. Andrews also asked Innis for a petition requesting hearings on his bill to be sent to the chairman of the House national park subcommittee. Innis had the forms delivered to "every possible bank and business place that [would] accept them" and wrote radio and television spots to promote the drive for signatures.[26]

Meanwhile, Andrews believed that he had obtained the "solid backing" of the lame-duck NPS director, Gary Everhardt. At the beginning of 1977 Robert Utley had left the Park Service because of fundamental disagreements with his chief on cultural resource issues. Nevertheless, Everhardt was at best ambivalent about the Fort Union reconstruction. In a memo of 24 June (titled "Some SOB Never Gets the Word . . ."), the now former director wrote a top NPS official that although he "wholly endorse[d] . . . some acceptable alternative to reconstruction," he also believed the Park Service's current position had been compromised. Its own Fort Union brochure announced long-term plans for "complete reconstruction." "Could it be," Everhardt concluded, "that Speaking with a Forked Tongue is the living history theme at Fort Union?"[27]

Before appropriate congressional committees the Park Service recommended enactment of the Fort Union bill only if it authorized a development ceiling of $4.1 million, rather than the more than $8 million requested by Burdick and Andrews—calculating that the lower figure would be enough to develop the site with everything *but* a reconstruction. In the spring the Senate repassed Burdick's bill with the $8.5 million intact, but the House version, first passed in July, followed the Park Service recommendation, and Andrews was unable to restore the higher funding limit.[28]

By the summer of 1978 passage of a final authorization bill seemed likely. Nevertheless, the Fort Union bill was approved with a touch of drama and a small contribution to legislative history. Subsumed in an omnibus parks bill brokered by Representative Phil Burton, a master politician from San Francisco, the Fort Union measure came close to expiring during the closing days of the 95th Congress. Nevertheless, Burton had packed his bill with authorizations for more than a hundred parks, eventually generating enough votes to immobilize the opposition. ("We'll pork out," he boasted.) Maneuvering adroitly, he then passed the same bill four times, shuttling between House and Senate to negotiate and resolve differences. At one point Burton attached most of the important provisions of his monstrous conglomeration to the Fort Union measure, so that for a time it nearly *was* the omnibus bill. Burton's log rolling resulted in the largest parks bill in history, authorizing $1.2 billion in federal spending to be spread among scores of congressional districts. It also created the phrase "park barrel."[29]

Although the $1.2 billion park appropriation was inconsequential in comparison with an $18.7 billion tax cut also approved by Congress at the end of the legislative session, an accelerating inflation rate had become a campaign issue. On 24 October President Carter announced a new anti-inflation program that included the promise of lower budget deficits, and he waited until 10 November 1978, a few days after the midterm election, to sign the omnibus bill.[30]

The Fort Union section raised the authorized size of the park from four hundred to four hundred fifty acres—land for which the National Park Service now anticipated paying two thousand dollars an acre. (Roy Appleman had advised his superiors more than a decade before to purchase rights on the south bank of the Missouri in order to protect the historic scene, but the Service waited until the cottonwood screen on the south bank was partially obliterated.) The total authorized for both acquisition of land and the development of the park—minus the $280,400 already spent—came to about $4.4 million. Also included in the bill was a directive to the secretary of the interior to study the possible reconstruction of the fort and report his recommendation to Congress within a year.[31]

Unlike the period following the site's entrance into the Park System in 1966, this time no one thought the battle for reconstruction won. Even before passage of the omnibus bill Andrews warned that "authorization" did not mean "appropriation," and Innis promised that the Fort Union–Fort Buford Council would "start chasing that money down" as soon as the bill was approved.[32] Nevertheless, Andrews and Innis underestimated the continued antagonism of the Park Service's Washington office and the amount of local involvement that would prove necessary to wrest the appropriation from Congress.

9 | Reenergizing the Project

SO MANY obstacles stood between the congressional authorization to rebuild Fort Union in 1978 and the first appropriation to fund it in 1985 that reconstruction supporters recalled its accomplishment as something of a marvel. One proponent wondered at aspects of the effort that seemed to be the result of "blind faith" or "dumb luck." Another recalled that "the timing was perfect . . . like it was meant to happen."[1]

Congress authorized the reconstruction of Fort Union just as the national economy entered a period of "stagflation," inflation combined with high unemployment. By 1978 the economic crisis became President Jimmy Carter's most serious domestic problem. For the remainder of his presidency, Carter opposed spending increases and even suggested balancing the federal budget. The Senate went further, cutting an additional $4.3 billion from the president's recommendations for domestic spending, including $11 million for the National Park Service.[2]

During this inauspicious period, in August 1978, the Park Service finally approved a much delayed General Management Plan (GMP) for Fort Union Trading Post. Despite Robert Utley's departure from the Park Service, philosophical opponents of historical reconstruction remained ascendant in the Cultural Resource Management (CRM) Division, including its new chief, F. Ross Holland, and his subordinates Harry Pfanz and Barry Mackintosh. An earlier draft of the management plan, submitted by a regional planning team in the spring of 1977, had been rejected by the Washington office because it advocated reconstruction despite Park Service guidelines.[3] CRM reminded the planners that they had not proved reconstruction of the fort "*essential* for public understanding," especially given the needs of "original historic resources" elsewhere in the system. The Washington office also argued that Congress had considered interpretation of Fort Union "feasible and comprehensible without a full-scale reconstruction." Finally, CRM put the regional planners on the horns of a dilemma. To comply with NPS guidelines for a reconstruction, their management plan would have to prove the existence of sufficient archaeological evidence to allow an accurate reconstruction. But if they uncovered such evidence, a reconstruction would then likely violate the guideline that prohibited destruction of "significant preservable remains."4

Unlike CRM officials in Washington, the thirteen-member planning team from the Rocky Mountain Region actually visited the Fort Union site. There it was easier to appreciate the historic landscape, the interpretative void at the park, and the impatience of local communities for development. (By the late 1970s backfilling from the archaeological digs had rendered even the outline of fort structures difficult for the casual visitor to discern.) Wishing neither to abandon reconstruction nor to engage the Washington office in futile debate, the planning team tried to find a middle way. The team proposed that a partial reconstruction be accomplished in stages. A scale model could be built as research information accumulated, and the full-size reconstruction could wait until each of the proposed elements was tied to "scientific evidence."5

CRM officials in Washington were unhappy with this proposal. In a memo written for the signature of Ross Holland, Barry Mackintosh warned that if a phased reconstruction were begun, the incomplete elements would themselves generate pressure for completion. Then either accuracy would suffer or the reconstructed components, lacking context, would become interpretively misleading. The Washington office also insisted that the planning team qualify or delete any suggestion that reconstruction of the fort was inevitable. Exhibits, models, and other traditional interpretative techniques were to be given a "fair trial." Any other course, wrote Mackintosh, would impugn the professional talents of Park Service interpreters and "the intelligence and imagination of the public."6

CRM made one unstated concession. It tacitly agreed that rebuilding part of the stockade would not be considered reconstruction, perhaps because there was clear congressional intent for at least that much development. Nevertheless, the final version of the General Management Plan, released in August 1978, pushed beyond this allowance by asserting that sufficient evidence existed to reconstruct the entire palisade and, "with minor conjecture," the bastions. Yet so ambiguously worded was the "management objective" concerning future development that the report could be interpreted as both advocating and opposing reconstruction.[7]

With pressure from Chief Historical Architect Henry Judd, a strong opponent of reconstruction, the final plan recommended an underground visitor center in the southwest corner of the fort site and the building of a scale model. The planners suggested (perhaps waggishly) that the model might someday be used to "explain how an authentic reconstruction of the fort was made possible." John Lancaster, supervisor of all North Dakota national parks and a member of the team, jokingly told a Williston audience that his group had tried to have the Park Service build the scale model full size.[8]

In fact, the planning team considered constructing the model on a fairly large scale. One possibility was to build it in the gravel pit west of the site (now the handicap parking area), through which visitors would rise to the level of the fort. Another proposal envisioned a model at the same height as the archaeological site. Visitors would first see the model at eye level, climb a spiral ramp to get a bird's-eye view, and finally look from the top of the structure toward the fort site.[9]

None of these innovative suggestions was included in the management plan. Instead, it was filled out with innocuous information such as how visitors would be warned about the "dangers of cactus and the rarely sighted prairie rattlesnake and the potential for exhaustion and frostbite." Considering the number of man-hours spent, the compromises negotiated, and the amount of public opinion solicited and ignored, the GMP of 1978 was a failure, the sort of planning document that, in Dwight Rettie's words, might as well have been "put on a shelf somewhere and forgotten."[10] Until the question of reconstruction could be decided, management planning at Fort Union Trading Post would continue to be little more than costly wheel spinning.

Despite hints in the General Management Plan that rebuilding Fort Union might be an eventual possibility, Washington seemed to have won the round. It had added the requirement of a model to the other criteria that would be necessary to justify a historical reconstruction. Although not disheartened by the GMP, Superintendents John Lancaster and Bill Wellman understood that winning an appropriation might take quite a few years— "sometime in our lifetime," Lancaster wryly predicted. Meanwhile, the clock was running on the authorized funding amount. If the project waited a decade for an appropriation, the contemporary inflation rate would ravage the value of the authorization, and $4.5 million would no longer pay for even a partial reconstruction.[11]

Further historical investigation of the Fort Union site might have been postponed indefinitely had it not been for the requirement, inserted in the omnibus bill by Representative Andrews, that the Interior Department "transmit to the Congress, within one year of the enactment of this Act, a recommendation on the reconstruction of the fort based on historic documentation."[12] The NPS delegated responsibility for this study, called the *Fort Union Reconstruction Analysis,* to the Regional Historic Preservation Team of the Rocky Mountain Regional Office in Denver. Erwin Thompson had earlier written a history of Fort Union and had come away an enthusiastic supporter of reconstruction. At least two of the three archaeologists who had surveyed the site had done the same.[13] Now it was the turn of the historical architects. Rodd L. Wheaton (1945–), who was to direct the *Reconstruction Analysis,* had visited the Fort Union site in July 1975 and at that time had recommended an off-site reconstruction, even though it would require a reexamination of Park Service policy. Wheaton noted that the rear elevation of the Bourgeois House was unknown and that therefore a "totally accurate" reconstruction would be "impossible."[14]

Four years later the data accumulated by Thompson, the archaeologists, and the preservation team itself proved far stronger than Wheaton had earlier anticipated. An 1851 drawing by Rudolph Kurz, discovered in Bern, Switzerland, provided a partial glimpse of the rear of the Bourgeois House and accurately established the location of the fort's bell tower. Written descriptions, period drawings, and evidence from the archaeological surveys furnished the historical architects with a surprising amount of information about both the measurements of the fort and the materials used to build it.[15]

The *Reconstruction Analysis* was composed mainly of large architectural drawings—some unusually fine—with notations for each building that explained how much of the design was based on hard evidence, how much was assumed, and how much more information would be required for a relatively accurate reconstruction. Wheaton's interdisciplinary group was determined to avoid the mistake made during the reconstruction of Bent's Old Fort when the designer failed to distinguish between what was known about the historic structure and what was a product of his own imagination. Although minor errors were detected in the *Reconstruction Analysis* after subsequent archaeological excavation, the drawings were so detailed that the team agreed that building a scale model of the fort would be superfluous. The team rejected total reconstruction, but the "partial reconstruction" it did recommend embraced all important structures of the 1851 fort, including several not reconstructed during the 1980s.[16]

The CRM Division in Washington immediately charged the preservation team with exceeding its mandate. Its job, wrote Harry Pfanz, had been to "provide a basis for a decision," not to endorse reconstruction. Not surprisingly, CRM, joined by the Division of Interpretation, strongly opposed the team's recommendation, a decision it claimed was based partly on policy grounds and partly on the belief that the Park Service ought not be committed to the "costs of such a project in these times." Ross Holland asserted that it would be "the height of stupidity and irresponsibility to expend so much of the taxpayers' money to do such a reconstruction in so isolated a place," especially since the reconstructions at Bent's Old Fort and Fort Vancouver had "turned out badly and [had] proved to be maintenance burdens out of proportion to their usefulness as interpretive devices." Congress, he wrote, should be warned that reconstructions were of questionable authenticity and would project a "romantic view of history." Holland further grumbled that when it came to proposed reconstructions, the Park Service was too "quick to lie down when the first Yahoo threatens rape."[17]

To fulfill the mandate of the omnibus bill, the National Park Service issued a two-paragraph statement to Congress. The official communication declared that although the preservation team had found partial reconstruction "feasible," no provision for reconstruction of Fort Union had been made or, "in light of other considerations," *would* be made, at least for the immediate future. The letter satisfied neither friend nor foe of the Fort Union project. On the one hand, Ross Holland thought the statement irresolute, providing "an invitation for the concerned congressmen . . . to get the project funded." On the other hand, Mark Andrews (one of those concerned congressmen) described the transmittal letter as "not very encouraging" and warned Ben Innis that there would be "little or no chance" of funding during the next few years.[18] As if to underscore the point, two of the more vocal opponents of Fort Union reconstruction published an article that month in the Park Service's in-house journal, CRM Bulletin, attacking historical reconstructions as "expensive, life-size toys."[19]

Nevertheless, what appeared to be a stalemate was actually a victory for the advocates of reconstruction. Not only had the Park Service team—the fourth in twelve years—endorsed partial reconstruction on the basis of unimpeachable research, it had issued its report in response to a request by Congress for the opinion of the Service. Congress had asked only if Fort

Union *could* be reconstructed, but after that question was answered positively, it was (as Holland feared) much easier for Congress to decide that the fort *should* be reconstructed. Once that happened, congressional legislation would trump Park Service guidelines.

Nonetheless, formidable obstacles to reconstruction remained. One from the larger world was the election of Ronald Reagan as president in 1980. Though in reality the National Park Service "fared rather well" during the Reagan administration, Reagan's supposed enthusiasm for draconian cuts in federal spending discouraged Great Society liberals from advocating further growth in the Park System and forced them into a defensive posture to preserve earlier gains. The administration's bark was worse than its bite, but the barking was not without effect. Master politician Phil Burton relinquished the chairmanship of the House parks subcommittee to better protect the interest of labor unions. "I'd rather spend my time passing laws," Burton told a reporter. "But people like me can hardly expect much progress in the next few years, so I guess the effort is to hold the fort."[20]

Reagan had little personal interest in the Department of the Interior and appointed as its secretary James Watt, a Colorado lawyer who had ostentatiously opposed the environmental movement. Watt ordered the Park Service to halt the acquisition of more land for national parks, purged the department of career employees whom he believed would thwart the development of natural resources, and talked of "cannibalizing" senior managers in the Park Service for reassignment to other Interior agencies.[21] "I will err on the side of public use versus preservation," Watt told a conference of park concessionaires in 1981. Cultural resource managers were justifiably irked when he put this philosophy into practice by holding two private Christmas parties at Arlington House, the antebellum home of Robert E. Lee and a Park Service unit that happened to overlook the Washington skyline.[22]

Supporters of reconstructing Fort Union were, of course, gratified that its strongest proponent, Mark Andrews, had been elected to the Senate seat vacated by Milton Young. Andrews, who had long served on the House Appropriations Committee, now took a seat on the corresponding Senate committee. North Dakota thus had two senators on the same powerful panel. As a senator, Andrews continued to channel respectable amounts of federal money to North Dakota while maneuvering to protect the committee from the effects of Reagan's budget cuts.[23]

Unfortunately for advocates of Fort Union reconstruction, Andrews's enthusiasm for the project had been chilled in 1979 by a miscommunication that originated in the NPS legislative office. The North Dakota congressional delegation often provided extra money for North Dakota parks through "add-ons," funds provided in the two appropriation committees outside the formal budget process. When Andrews asked the North Dakota supervisors for appropriate projects that might be funded by add-ons, Superintendents Lancaster and Wellman suggested more archaeology at the Fort Union site, something that would have to be done in any case before reconstruction could begin. Wellman wrote the questions for the senator to ask during the appropriate committee hearing along with the responses the Park Service representative was supposed to make. But when Andrews asked in open session if more money were needed for Fort Union, the NPS representative answered no. It proved to be a costly misunderstanding. Andrews forcefully expressed to Lancaster his embarrassment and his annoyance at Park Service incompetence. Although Andrews never lost interest in Fort Union, his zeal for the reconstruction project waned during the next few years.[24]

During the same period, the Fort Union site faced another threat to the integrity of its historic scene. The Snowden Bridge over the Missouri River, which Ralph Budd had first planked for the Upper Missouri Historical Expedition of 1925, was coming to the end of its usefulness as a combination rail and vehicular span. In June 1977 the Burlington Northern publicized its intention to exclude vehicles from the bridge. Shortly thereafter the corporation posted an ambiguous warning sign on the structure, then insisted that the Montana counties on either side of the river assume full legal liability for any mishap.[25]

Few doubted that another bridge for motor vehicles was needed, and Mark Andrews found much of the funding for it at the Federal Highway Administration. It took time to develop a plan that would fit into federal categories and then find the remaining money in two state budgets, but the most difficult decision was where to locate the new bridge. Early in the selection process there were three proposed sites: in Montana, near the Snowden Bridge; in North Dakota, somewhere between Forts Union and Buford; and on the state line, a few hundred yards from Fort Union.[26]

As early as 1963 the National Park Service expressed concern when R. S. Nutt, a member of the Yellowstone–Missouri–Fort Union Commission, recommended a bridge on the state line. At that time the director of North Dakota State Parks assured the NPS regional director that North Dakota

Fig. 10. Snowden Bridge, designed by J. A. L. Waddell and built across the Missouri in 1913; at the time, its 296-foot vertical lift span was the largest in the world. Jet Lowe for the Historic American Engineering Record, National Park Service.

would never build a bridge there. Yet as late as 1981 a few area residents continued to believe that the state line would make a fine place for the new bridge—including one gentleman who envisioned motorists peering down on a reconstructed Fort Union before they crossed the Missouri.[27]

As a practical matter, the federal government would not permit a bridge to be constructed on the state line once the Park Service had acquired the land. The real question was how close to federal property the new bridge would come. A new bridge next to the old one would be invisible from the fort but would add eleven miles between Williston and Sidney for the North Dakota sugar beet farmers who were its chief proponents. Several alternate routes west of Fort Buford would be more of an intrusion on the historic scene, but they could be nearly concealed from view by tree screening.[28]

Unfortunately, the farmers preferred "Alternate B," which approached through Garden Coulee and nearly touched the southeastern corner of the current park property. Wellman warned the North Dakota engineering supervisor that the National Park Service would strongly oppose such a route because it would destroy the integrity of the historic scene and "nullify" planned development at the site. Supporters of Alternate B seemed unable to comprehend the basis for Park Service opposition. Fred Gardner, president of the MonDak Bridge Association and leader of the beet farmers, argued that any damage to the park would be offset by a twenty-fold increase in tourists who would visit the site. Another area farmer claimed that since Alternate B would bring more visitors to the park, the federal government would have an even greater incentive to reconstruct the fort. Even a Williston city planner recalled that at the time he could not understand why the Park Service was making such a fuss over aesthetics.[29]

Emotions heated quickly. One landowner refused access to a survey crew investigating another route. A petition attacking Wellman as a hostile bureaucrat circulated. An anonymous letter to Senator Andrews castigated the opponents of Alternate B as "self-styled demigods," "power mongers in the Park Service who are tax consumers and not producers."[30]

Supporters of Alternate B also mustered considerable political clout. The North Dakota highway commissioner, a potent individual in state politics, both supported Alternate B and had a son-in-law who was an area beet farmer. The State Historical Society of North Dakota, which had earlier recommended another route, found it politic to back away from its endorsement; the superintendent of the society shifted his support to Alternate B. Vern Neff, a Williston lawyer who had helped create the park in the 1960s, now warned Ben Innis that if he opposed Alternate B, the legal action might consume "thousands of dollars" and would probably cost Fort Union and the Park Service every friend they had in the region. Neff refused to take such a brief himself, citing his close ties with the highway commissioner and other interested parties.[31]

Innis plunged ahead anyway. In July and August 1982 he mobilized the few active members of the Fort Union–Fort Buford Council and gained the support of Williams County Historical Society president Greg Hennessy, the sympathy of longtime Fort Union supporter and state senator Frank Wenstrom, and the enmity of the highway commissioner.[32]

Even Innis was surprised when, in October, the MonDak Bridge Association abruptly conceded. Fred Gardner advised Innis that the farmers had decided to back Alternate D, the route supported by the Fort Union–Fort Buford Council. In return Gardner asked Innis to help "speed [the bridge] project along." Within a week the Federal Highway Administration approved Alternate D as the location, and within a month test borings were being taken in the river. Apparently, like the Wizard of Oz with his megaphone, Innis had succeeded in magnifying his voice, encouraging the beet farmers to consider whether the advantages of Alternate B were worth the price of a possible delay in construction.[33]

Although the approach road of the approved route passed within eight hundred feet of Fort Buford State Historic Site, the compromise location proved more than satisfactory to defenders of Fort Union's historic scene. The bridge itself was situated around a river bend about a mile east of the fort site and thus was inconspicuous to Fort Union visitors unless they made a deliberate attempt to find it. Furthermore, the navigational clearance required for Snowden Bridge in 1912 was waived for the new structure so that it could be designed with a low profile.[34] Had Alternate B been selected, reconstruction of the fort might have been permanently quashed. At the least, further studies of the site would have followed such a serious degradation of the historic scene.

With the successful conclusion of the bridge controversy, three additional advantages accrued to the supporters of reconstruction. First, in 1983 North Dakota paved the gravel road leading to the bridge—and therefore to the fort site as well. Second, the new span, completed in 1985, opened a second paved access to the park. Finally, the spirit of cooperation between the states augured well for future joint projects: Montana had shared equally with North Dakota the 20 percent of the $2.8 million cost not funded by the federal government, even though the bridge was located completely in North Dakota.[35]

During the period when it still seemed the Park Service might lose the bridge dispute, Superintendent Bill Wellman, who had served Fort Union for seven years, moved on to Timpanogos Cave National Monument, Utah. His successor, Earle B. Kittleman, was a singular choice. After graduating from Cornell, Kittleman had worked at journalism and public relations in Chicago and Washington and as publications and interpretive staff specialist at the NPS Rocky Mountain Regional Office in Denver. He had never been an interpreter or a supervisor at a park. It was unusual for Park Service staff at headquarters or a regional office to take a field position, but for personal reasons Kittleman chose to assume the Fort Union superintendency.

Williston and Fort Union's isolated visitor center—a double-wide trailer—provided a more dramatic change of scenery than the new superintendent had anticipated. Despite interest in his new environment, Kittleman found that the gap between his experience and the complexities of the park were too great to bridge during his short stay. Nevertheless, the reconstruction effort was not hindered during Kittleman's tenure. In fact, the opposite was true. Kittleman had no preconceptions about his responsibilities as a superintendent, no loyalties to the past, no proposals for the future. He was therefore highly receptive to suggestions made by local history buffs and his two full-time staff members.[36]

One of the most important of these suggestions resulted in the creation of an annual event called Rendezvous, the first of which attracted one hundred twenty buckskin-clad fur trade–era reenactors and more than three thousand spectators during the first week of July 1983. During that week the number of visitors to Fort Union equaled the visitation for the previous six months. Kittleman knew little enough about the fur trade era, but he had no difficulty recognizing that more visitors would increase support for the park. Congress, he said, could authorize historic sites, but it took people to "energize them."[37]

What a few energized people might mean to the reconstruction of Fort Union was amply demonstrated a few months later. Senator Mark Andrews, now chairman of the Senate Transportation Committee, had arranged for Secretary of Transportation Elizabeth Dole to speak at the annual business conference of the Greater North Dakota Association, held that year in Williston on 27 October. Sensing a public relations opportunity, the Fort Buford Sixth Infantry Association decided to name Dole its honorary "wagonmaster." Ben Innis wrote a florid script for the occasion that included a list of Sixth Infantry achievements. Failing health made it impossible for him to make the presentation, and he passed that responsibility to Richard Collin (1955–), a young radio broadcaster and history buff who had moved to North Dakota barely a year before and who had been a member of the Sixth Infantry for only six months.

Unexpectedly, Senator Andrews himself appeared at the convention and was present when Collin declaimed that the Sixth Infantry had "supported congressional legislation which authorized, but failed to appropriate—repeat, authorized but failed to appropriate—four million, four hundred thousand dollars for reconstruction of the Fort Union Trading Post." The crowd laughed even before Collin completed the sentence, and the laughter grew and ended with applause when he repeated the dollar figure. Later Collin asked Andrews (who had laughed as loudly as any) what it would take to get a congressional appropriation. The senator encouraged him to write a letter outlining the reasons why Fort Union should be restored.[38]

Wondering if the request were simply politic courtesy, Collin conferred with Andrea Winkjer (1954–), an acquaintance who had worked in Andrews's Washington office. The daughter of a prominent Williston family, Winkjer had tired of the capital after two years and returned to Williston, where she edited two small publications. Winkjer assured Collin that if Andrews had asked for a letter, he was serious about aiding the reconstruction.

Fig. 11. Rick Collin (*left*) confers honorary membership in the Fort Buford Sixth Infantry Association on Governor Allen Olson (*center*) and Secretary of Transportation Elizabeth Dole by providing them with appropriate hats. Collin's brief conversation with Senator Mark Andrews (*second from right*) during the October 1983 annual meeting of the Greater North Dakota Association initiated a new, and ultimately successful, effort to gain congressional appropriation for the Fort Union reconstruction.
Courtesy, Greater North Dakota Association.

Andrews, she believed, would be looking for an appropriate project in the northwestern part of the state where his potential challenger in the next election was comparatively strong. Within two weeks Collin and Winkjer collaborated on the letter to Andrews.[39]

Not having been frustrated by previous efforts to rebuild the fort, Collin and Winkjer considered a new reconstruction campaign something of a lark. "Why not give it a try?" Collin wrote in his diary. Furthermore, both Winkjer and Collin held jobs that made it easy to promote the cause. Winkjer could champion the fort in her publications. As a radio news director, Collin could call virtually anyone in his role as a reporter. He could even spend some of each working day on the Fort Union project with the blessing of the station owners, who considered its promotion a community service.

The collaboration of Collin and Winkjer had several long-term consequences, not the least of which was that they eventually married. Senator Andrews resumed making inquiries about the fort to the National Park Service, and he discussed development of the park at local news conferences, where Collin frequently asked the relevant questions. Meanwhile, Collin and Winkjer began the process of organizing a new advocacy group for the park, the "Friends of Fort Union." In December they met with Superintendent Kittleman and Williston's tourism director to discuss the idea. By February a six-member "steering committee" had been elected at public meetings in Williston and Sidney.[40]

Some older civic leaders lacked enthusiasm for the initiative, and a few openly deprecated the project. But Ben Innis was not among them, even though he might have been jealous of upstarts who had ignored his Fort Union–Fort Buford Council and created a new organization. Innis provided as much support to the Friends of Fort Union as he was physically able. In the spring of 1984 he expressed the hope that with "better weather and a change in medication" he might attend a Friends meeting himself. "Before I die," he told Collin, "I'd give anything to be able to stand inside the reconstructed fort and just get a sense of what they felt a hundred and fifty years ago." It was not to be. Ben Innis succumbed to pneumonia in April 1985. He had done his best, but as Collin recalled, "it just wasn't the right time."[41]

10 | Winning the Appropriation

DURING the energy crisis of the 1970s, North Dakota oil production nearly doubled, and the Williston Basin became a center of North American oil exploration. Oil-induced euphoria enticed the town of Williston to build a million-dollar firehouse and a million-dollar library. Unwise business decisions were made in almost every sector of the private economy. Then, in 1982, dissension among OPEC nations flooded the world with oil, and the petroleum market collapsed almost overnight. The number of drilling rigs in the North Dakota portion of the Williston Basin fell from 122 to 46 in less than a year. About two thousand people—nearly an eighth of the population—left town within six months. Houses that could not have been obtained for any price the previous year now sat vacant. Simultaneously, northwestern North Dakota entered a severe agricultural depression exacerbated, as in the thirties, by another dry cycle.[1]

Before the crash North Dakotans in general and Williston civic leaders in particular were relatively indifferent to tourism. In 1980, at the height of the boom, the superintendent of Theodore Roosevelt National Park complained to his regional director that only "a mere murmur" could be roused from the local media about the development of Fort Union Trading Post, whereas the discovery of salt-water intrusion in the governor's oil property was "front-page material."[2] Only after the simultaneous downturn in energy and agriculture did North Dakotans begin to appreciate the comparative stability of tourist dollars. During the late 1980s the state tourism office created the "American Legacy Tour," a cluster of mostly historical attractions in the western part of the state, intended to turn North Dakota into a destination as well as a stop on vacationers' treks to Yellowstone and Glacier National Parks.³

The prerequisites for another effort to reconstruct Fort Union had now largely fallen in place: the sanction of scholarly research, revitalized grassroots activism, the attention of influential politicians, and an economic rationale that aroused civic leaders indifferent to history. Only lacking was a catalyst to unify these elements. As if on cue, Paul L. Hedren (1949–) appeared in April 1984. Some months earlier Earle Kittleman had taken a job at NPS headquarters better suited to his background and abilities, and Hedren successfully applied for the vacant superintendency.⁴

A native of southwestern Minnesota, Hedren began his Park Service career even before graduation from St. Cloud State College in 1972. First employed as a seasonal employee at Fort Laramie National Historic Site, he rose to chief ranger at Golden Spike NHS by 1984. Hedren was a capable and ambitious young man, determined to "make a lasting imprint" wherever he worked. A competent interpreter and a careful observer of his superiors' managerial decisions, Hedren arrived at Fort Union with a good understanding of how the Park Service operated in practice. At Golden Spike, for instance, Hedren noted how local activists had used political pressure (including a lobbying trip to Washington) to prod the Service into providing two locomotive reproductions it had earlier promised the park.⁵

Hedren had considerable organizational ability and a gift for finding and motivating people who could help him achieve his goals. Like most other effective leaders, he was generous in giving credit to others for shared accomplishments. Hedren also had a flair for public relations, and at each stage of the Fort Union project he organized ceremonies such as ribbon cuttings that attracted media attention and maintained momentum. Hedren's hobby of writing books about the Great Sioux War (1876–77)—considered a harmless idiosyncrasy by some of his superiors—heightened his ability to speak as an equal with NPS specialists who held advanced degrees. In a 1991 memo Chief Historian Edwin C. Bearss described Hedren as "a rare bird," a park superintendent who possessed the combined talents "of a good manager, an excellent interpreter, and a historian who commands the respect of his peers both within and outside the service."⁶

When Andrea Winkjer interviewed the new superintendent shortly after his arrival in Williston, Hedren "straddled the fence" when asked his views about reconstructing the fort. He had come to the confluence tending to support the Park Service guidelines that virtually precluded historical reconstructions. Within a few months, however, Hedren took "the pulse of the community," thought "the issue through," and became a staunch supporter of the Fort Union reconstruction—or as he called it—"development."[7]

Hedren later argued that during the early 1980s "Fort Union supporters would have gladly accepted a well-designed interpretive facility . . . in lieu of a reconstructed fort." He contended that if the Washington office had championed another sort of development at the site—perhaps a first-rate museum and a walking tour of the archaeological site (as at Knife River Indian Villages)—the Park Service might have avoided the local "bitterness and frustration" that eventually took the decision out of the agency's hands and delivered it to the politicians.[8]

Although it is difficult to imagine Ben Innis conceding to the offer of a museum, no matter how grand, it is possible that he and other buffs could have been marginalized by a more adroit response from the Park Service after the completion of the 1979 *Reconstruction Analysis*. Nevertheless, the National Park Service was a bureaucracy and made its decisions bureaucratically. Unlike Phil Burton or Mark Andrews, the agency could not easily cut deals; it had too many centers of power. Park Service officials at all levels found it easier simply to veto objectionable projects through what Robert Utley called "the stall." Politicians were soothed, investigations were made, reports were written and rewritten; and in due course, enthusiasm usually waned and the political threat disappeared. Furthermore, even if the Park Service had been able to trade a museum for a reconstruction during the 1980s, there could be no assurance that some future campaign might not reconstruct the fort.[9]

Even before Winkjer's interview Hedren received a phone call from Williston's economic development director, Thomas C. Rolfstad. A former professor had asked Rolfstad to scout a summer internship for a graduate student, Auggaphol "Duke" Brickshawana, a Thai architect studying tourism planning at North Dakota State University in Fargo. Rolfstad could find nothing for him in Williston, but he remembered Fort Union's new superintendent. Could the park use an architectural model or display of some sort? Not surprisingly, Hedren jumped at the chance to acquire a replica of the fort.[10]

Brickshawana shortly crafted a 1/8 :1' scale model of the 1851 Fort Union based on the architectural drawings of the *Reconstruction Analysis*. The model immediately became a valuable interpretive tool at the site and an exciting visual aid for the civic groups and elected officials to whom the Friends of Fort Union began appealing for support. There was, of course, a pleasant irony in the use of a scale model to promote reconstruction, since only a few years earlier Park Service officials had tried to require the building of a model to retard development.[11]

At least as important as the model itself was the friendship that developed between Rolfstad and Hedren from a contact Rolfstad described as "pure coincidence." As economic development director, Rolfstad worked with Williston Jobs & Industries, a semiprivate business organization that sought to improve the local economy. In effect, Rolfstad could tap economic development funds. Brickshawana's model of Fort Union was followed by one of the first Fort Buford, and Williston Jobs & Industries paid for them both. Rolfstad also arranged a twenty-thousand-dollar loan from Jobs & Industries to publish Ben Innis's *Sagas of the Smoky-Water*, a series of historical sketches about the confluence during the nineteenth century. Published in 1985, in anticipation of Williston's centennial, the book further stressed Fort Union's historical importance to local residents. At a time when the Friends of Fort Union had virtually no funds of their own, Jobs & Industries provided the loaves and fishes with which later miracles were performed.[12]

Although Rolfstad had comparatively little interest in history, he had an insider's understanding of Williston and a sense of how to develop broad-based community support for the Fort Union project. The Friends' bylaws provided that its board include representatives of other local historical groups: the Fort Union–Fort Buford Council, the Fort Union Muzzle Loaders, and the Fort Buford Sixth Infantry Association. Nevertheless, Hedren and Rolfstad ensured that most board members were not partisans of the older groups. Similarly, they tried to keep the board as apolitical as possible to avoid having Democrats view the project as a Republican effort.[13]

Rolfstad also convinced Hedren that certain influential residents of Williston were potential "legitimizers" who, if enlisted early in the Fort Union effort, would carry the rest of the community with them. As the project gained momentum, the number of middle-class buffs among the Friends' leadership declined and the number of upper-middle-class professionals increased. It would be easy to exaggerate this change. Buckskinners and black-powder enthusiasts continued to make real contributions to the project, and nearly all the newly enlisted members of the local elite had an energetic interest in history as well. Money per se was not the issue either. Rather, Rolfstad and Hedren realized that educated professionals brought two additional assets to the effort. First, they had enough discretionary income to assume what amounted to an additional unpaid job; second, they more often had the vision to pursue the millions necessary to reconstruct the fort. Some buffs, in contrast, persisted in a "bake sale" mentality and could imagine only long-range, small-scale improvements at the site.[14]

The evolution in Friends leadership illustrates this general trend. The group's first chairman was the affable Mike Jones, an amateur genealogist and a neighbor and close friend of Ben Innis. Born in Illinois, Jones had graduated from high school in Charleston, South Carolina. He lived in Williston only seven years before being elected president of the Muzzle Loaders. Jones could not be faulted for lack of vision even if his strategy for turning plans into reality was vague. He contemplated extensive development at the Fort Union site, including a separate, underground visitor center; he even talked of compelling the Corps of Engineers to bring the Missouri back to the north bank and obliging the Burlington Northern to move its tracks from between the fort and the Bodmer Overlook. To Jones, Hedren was a trimmer who perhaps had been sent by the Park Service to derail local efforts to rebuild the fort. Not surprisingly, the two men did not get on well. Fortunately, when Jones perceived that his presence might undermine the Friends' efforts, he resigned as chairman.[15]

In mid-September 1985 Rick Collin took his place. Collin brought to the post a degree in history, considerable organizational ability, and time to invest in the project. He could speak both to reenactors and to the chamber of commerce. Yet Collin was comparatively young, and he had arrived only recently in Williston.

When Collin took a job in Bismarck the following May, the chairmanship of the Friends was shouldered by Dr. Edward J. "Bud" Hagan (1916–), a quintessential community "legitimizer." Hagan was the son of pioneer Willistonites for whom a local elementary school had been named. After heroic service in the Pacific theater during World War II, Hagan came home to practice medicine as his father had before him. Doctor, bank director, and civic leader, Hagan was enormously respected. He had long been an enthusiast of history and a collector of Western Americana. Once retired from his medical practice, Hagan invested himself fully in the work of the Friends. In a period in which some local leaders hesitated to join a new effort to rebuild the fort, Hagan lent the project the finest sort of credibility.[16]

To promote local tourism in general and the tourist potential of a reconstructed Fort Union specifically, Rolfstad conceived a promotional dinner held at the confluence forts on 13 September 1984. Called "Evening at the Confluence," the invitation-only affair was underwritten by Williston Jobs & Industries and attracted more than two hundred civic leaders and their spouses from a six-county area on both sides of the state line. Cocktails were served at Fort Buford followed by a buffalo steak barbecue at Fort Union. (Guests had to pass Brickshawana's model before they could get their dinner.) After the meal Hedren showed a film about the reconstruction of Bent's Old Fort, announced the official formation of the Friends of Fort Union, and invited everyone to contribute ten dollars and join.[17]

The evening's keynote speaker was Harold Schafer, the founder of Gold Seal cleaning products—a North Dakota success story—and the developer of Medora, a major tourist attraction adjoining the South Unit of Theodore Roosevelt National Park. Rolfstad had hoped for a stem-winding address celebrating the economic benefits of tourism, but by all accounts Schafer's low-key blessing of the Fort Union project proved even more effective. Schafer advised that reconstructing the fort would not be easy, but he wished his listeners "happiness in this project" and "some fun in trying."[18]

The "Evening at the Confluence" and its aftermath brought two other influential Willistonites to the project, Greg W. Hennessy and Marvin L. Kaiser. Hennessy (1952–), a childhood friend of Rolfstad's, a young supporter of Ben Innis, and a former president of the Williams County Historical Society, became treasurer of the Friends during the heart of the reconstruction effort. Then he assumed the presidency when Hagan retired from the post in 1992. A liberal and a Democrat, Hennessy helped balance the Republican bent of Williston.[19]

Kaiser (1943–) was another significant asset to the project. An influential Williston businessman and lawyer, Kaiser was a seasoned promoter of North Dakota entrepreneurship and an accomplished fundraiser who had recently served as president of the local United Way campaign. Kaiser had visited Colonial Williamsburg shortly before attending the 1984 Rendezvous at Fort Union and had contemplated the historical and economic potential of a reconstructed Fort Union to the local economy. The idea of reconstructing the fort challenged his creativity and provided emotional satisfaction as well. Kaiser and Hedren quickly developed a mutual admiration for each other's talents, and Kaiser agreed to become the Friends' finance chairman. He refused to become a board member, however, so as not to interfere with his golf game.[20]

The Friends spent the winter of 1984–85 solidifying the organization and debating how it might raise the eight to ten million dollars that reconstruction was estimated to cost. Representatives of the group promoted the project to local chambers of commerce, working with special diligence to maintain interest among Montanans—especially because leadership had now clearly fallen to Willistonites.[21] In the spring the Friends began publishing a newsletter, *Confluence News*, and delegations visited both state capitols. The Friends easily garnered resolutions of support from the legislatures—they asked for no state money—and in Collin's words, "the media ate it up." Businessmen in suits and Hedren in his uniform were always accompanied by fully accoutered buckskinners.[22]

Similarly, whenever members of the North Dakota congressional delegation visited Williston, buckskinners joined the welcome. In 1985 representatives of the Friends met twice with North Dakota congressman Byron Dorgan, twice with Senator Burdick, and four times with Senator Andrews. On 1 June both senators visited the fort, where they were lobbied by the Friends' leadership and were photographed together viewing the model.[23]

Although the congressional delegation promised its collective support for the project, the Friends could not feel reasonably certain of ultimate success until after two important events of 1985: a successful lobbying trip to Washington and the reconstruction of the fort's historic flagpole. The trip

Fig. 12. Supporters of reconstruction lobby in Bismarck, 12 March 1985. On that day the state legislature unanimously approved a resolution calling for the reconstruction of Fort Union. *Left to right:* Muzzle Loader Jim Gunderson; Blake Krabseth, Williston Convention and Visitors Bureau director; Governor George Sinner; Superintendent Paul Hedren; Rick Collin, Friends of Fort Union legislative chairman; Muzzle Loaders Bob Evans and Orville Loomer. Courtesy, Rick Collin.

to Washington in June followed an invitation from Mark Andrews to promote their project among some of his senatorial colleagues. Although the Friends had almost no money, they wisely decided to send a delegation and bill the organization. Marv Kaiser later raised more than enough to cover expenses.[24]

Not only did five members of the Interior Appropriations Subcommittee and Robert Byrd (D-WV), the Senate minority leader, attend the meeting, but the new director of the National Park Service, William Penn Mott, also appeared. One of Mott's assistants later told Hedren that Park Service officials were stunned when they were asked to send representatives to a meeting about a little park in western North Dakota that had aroused the interest of six influential senators.[25]

Again fortune smiled on the Friends. A few months earlier Russell Dickenson, the previous director, had clearly opposed the reconstruction. In a blunt response to the executive vice president of the Williston Chamber of Commerce, Dickenson suggested that reconstruction of the fort, and even the building of a visitor center, remained "well off into the future." If the chamber wanted development, the director advised that it work with the Park Service to find "alternative ways to interpret this site."[26]

Unlike Dickenson, who was chosen by Jimmy Carter from within NPS ranks, William Penn Mott (1909–92) was an outsider, selected by Ronald Reagan because of his prior service as director of the California Department of Parks and Recreation. Having been on the job for only a few weeks, Mott brought to the Fort Union meeting no Park Service prejudices about historical reconstructions. Indeed, one of Mott's proudest achievements was his creation of Children's Fairyland, the nation's first theme park and a model for Disneyland. Mott admired those who, like himself, desired to turn dreams about parks into reality, and he sincerely believed in the benefits of community volunteerism, especially in the raising of private funds to foster park development.[27]

The Friends' delegation had prepared diligently for the meeting, and Andrews enjoyed putting the enthusiasm of his constituents on display.[28] Nevertheless, there was more than a little political theater to the meeting. If a deal had not been struck before the session, one was at least in progress before the senators arrived. Part way through the half-hour session Senator Byrd arose, praised the project, pledged his support, and left.[29] Andrews, chairman of the Transportation Subcommittee, later enjoyed recalling Byrd's passion for a West Virginia Amtrak train called the *Cardinal*. "How well the *Cardinal* did," Andrews remembered, "and how well North Dakota did."[30]

At least as important as the Washington meeting in quickening the Fort Union project was the reconstruction of the historic flagpole during the spring and summer of 1985. Unlike the almost spur-of-the-moment lobbying session in Washington, re-erecting the flagpole had been discussed even before Hedren arrived at the confluence. The instigators were a group of black-powder enthusiasts who called themselves the Fort Union Muzzle Loaders.[31] After a shooting match in 1983 discussion turned to how the group might initiate reconstruction of the fort. The Muzzle Loaders decided that if they could reconstruct something—anything—without Park Service assistance, the NPS would then be forced to embrace the project. A replica of the original flagpole was an obvious choice both because of its symbolism and because of its comparative ease of construction.[32]

Hedren endorsed the Muzzle Loaders' proposal but cautioned that the reconstruction would have to be preceded by detailed planning. Fortunately, Edwin Denig had described the flagpole and a small garden that surrounded it in 1843, and several sketches of the original sixty-three-foot structure were extant, including a fine one by Rudolph Kurz (1852). Richard Cronenberger (1956–), a historical architect at the Rocky Mountain Regional Office in Denver, produced detailed construction drawings of the Fort Union flagpole based partially on a pole reconstructed a few years earlier at Fort Larned NHS, Kansas. His design also included subsurface features necessary to ensure that it remained standing in the North Dakota wind.[33]

Meanwhile, the Muzzle Loaders solicited donations for the hundreds of components necessary to build the pole, which at completion was valued at twenty thousand dollars. Cronenberger encouraged club members to help design the details because their knowledge of period craftsmanship was often superior to his. But he refused to let them raise the pole with horses (as the original had been) on grounds that the reconstructed pole was too heavy and too valuable to risk.[34] Because the area around the flagpole had already been excavated in 1972, the archaeology necessary to fulfill the requirements of the National Historic Preservation Act was conducted in only three days at the end of April,[35] and the flagpole was raised into position on 17 May.[36]

Despite a strong wind and temperatures over a hundred degrees, more than fifteen hundred people attended the flag raising on 6 July. In a scene reminiscent of Budd's 1925 Historical Expedition, held at the same spot sixty years before to the month, Assiniboine dancers were paid to entertain the crowd. Dignitaries spoke, and Muzzle Loaders hoisted the reproduction fourteen-by-twenty-four-foot, thirty-star flag into a stiff breeze.[37] The main speaker, Senator Andrews, expounded a clever, politically sensitive argument for reconstruction: that Fort Union was unique because it had been not a military fort intended to "wreak vengeance on the Indian" but a meeting place "where white settler and the Native American worked side by side, traded in peace, and enjoyed each other's heritage." Andrews also came close to pledging that he would find money for the reconstruction project during the next appropriation cycle.[38]

"Make a success of that flagpole," Theodore Roosevelt superintendent Harvey Wickware had told Hedren, "and next year we'll build a bastion." The reconstruction did not happen quite that quickly, but Wickware's instincts were true. Erection of the flagpole got the project off the ground, figuratively as well as literally. The Denver regional office had cooperated in the design, a minor archaeological dig had broken something of a taboo about resuming excavation, and the volunteerism that had created the flagpole gave Andrews a political advantage in a period in which private funding for national park projects was strongly encouraged. Nor should the psychological boost provided by flying a huge flag over the site be underestimated. A letter of greetings extracted from the White House and signed by President Reagan thanked the participants "for keeping the history of this Nation in your hearts and for raising Old Glory high." Hedren later wrote that re-erecting the flagpole "resolved the reconstruction issue in one gentle step." Part of Fort Union had already been reconstructed.[39]

On 18 September 1985 Andrews struck a deal with Appropriations Subcommittee chairman McClure that provided nearly a million dollars in federal funds to continue the project. Andrews performed a few legislative maneuvers to protect the appropriation through four rounds of budget cuts, and a bill containing $988,000 for Fort Union Trading Post NHS was signed by the president on 19 December. Collin, who interviewed the senator on the radio the following day, could hardly believe that the appropriation would not somehow disappear. Although the project still faced obstacles, Hedren correctly concluded that once the reconstruction was funded, it could not be easily derailed. "This is it," he told a reporter after the appropriations bill had passed.[40] A combination of enthusiasm, hard work, and improbable serendipity had finally initiated the project envisioned by Ralph Budd sixty years earlier.

11 | Groundwork for the Reconstruction

BETWEEN 1985 and 1991 Fort Union Trading Post National Historic Site was transformed from an open prairie with a few low mounds into an impressive, though partial, recreation of the historic fort. During these half-dozen years anti-reconstructionists made final efforts to derail the project, a fundraising effort marketed an English lord, and the National Park Service conducted the most intensive archaeological investigation it had ever initiated.

Planning for the Fort Union reconstruction began at the Rocky Mountain Regional Office in 1985, even before the new thirty-star flag flew over the historic site. Although Director Mott had endorsed the Fort Union project, the Rocky Mountain Regional Office might have delayed the reconstruction indefinitely had it chosen to do so. Instead, the regional office in Denver defended the project against its opponents both within and without the Service and then successfully maneuvered to supervise the reconstruction itself.

One of the project's strongest proponents was Deputy Regional Director Jack Neckels. Neckels, a native of western North Dakota, had grown up on a ranch between the North and South units of Theodore Roosevelt National Park. After Neckels had been assigned to the Interior Department's legislative division in Washington, the governor of North Dakota asked that he be detailed back to his home state to serve as director of its planning division. By the time the burly Neckels arrived at the Denver office in 1984, he was well acquainted with the politics of both North Dakota and the National Park Service. Superintendent Paul Hedren and the leaders of the Friends of

Fort Union quickly forged an important working relationship with the deputy regional director.[1]

Not surprisingly, regional-office planning for the Fort Union reconstruction aroused preservationist ire. Within the NPS Washington office another attempt was made to thwart the reconstruction by reducing the project budget to a level at which only token elements—perhaps a palisade or two—could be rebuilt. Although the plan to limit funds was presented to Director Mott as an economy measure, it was clearly intended to prevent another historical reconstruction from slipping through Park Service guidelines.[2]

At nearly the same time, Adrienne Anderson, the regional archaeologist, as well as preservationists outside the Park Service, began to argue that any reconstruction of the fort should be rebuilt next to, rather than on top of, the historic site in order to save its archaeological remains. Preservationists were well aware that the province of Ontario had reconstructed a magnificent Old Fort William off site. A similar off-site reconstruction of Fort Union would have been comparatively easy to accomplish on the flat, open land to its east.

Neither the rebuilding of token elements nor an off-site reconstruction was an unthinkable alternative for developing the Fort Union site, but neither possibility had been seriously considered during the earlier stages of the debate. Reconstructionists viewed both proposals as attempts to derail the project. In a letter to the director, Jack Neckels carefully delineated the disadvantages of an off-site reconstruction. He warned, for instance, that local political pressure might turn an off-site structure into a "complete reconstruction" that would incorporate conjectural components. The planned "partial reconstruction," however, would incorporate ghosted elements of the sort popular among cultural resource managers. After noting that a reconstructed flagpole had already been erected on its historic location, Neckels further argued that if the fort's archaeological remains were to be preserved, they would have to be stabilized at a significant cost, even though the accuracy of the reconstruction (wherever its location) would depend on intensive excavation of those very remains. Finally, Neckels maintained that locating the fort on its historic foundations was necessary in order to interpret the site accurately to visitors. Neckels judiciously neglected to mention that NPS guidelines prohibited off-site reconstructions.[3]

Fiscal limitations that might have restricted development to only token elements of the fort were effectively overcome by the redirected congressional appropriation signed by the president on 19 December. And on the following day Senator Mark Andrews twice declared that Congress intended its money to be used for reconstruction of the fort *on* its historic site.[4]

Some Park Service officials were undoubtedly vexed by the decision to proceed, but formal NPS opposition to the reconstruction ceased with the congressional appropriation. Nevertheless, preservationists outside the Park Service continued to challenge it. Section 106 of the National Historic Preservation Act of 1966 had established an Advisory Council on Historic Preservation (ACHP), charging it with the authority to "comment" on any proposed federal spending that affected a historic site. The council's administrative rules transferred responsibility for the initial review to State Historic Preservation Officers (SHPOs), usually officials of state historical agencies appointed by their governors.[5]

In October 1985 Jack Neckels officially notified the Advisory Council and the preservation officers of North Dakota and Montana that the proposed partial reconstruction of Fort Union would "constitute an adverse effect" by destroying the archaeological remains of the Bourgeois House, kitchen, bell tower, palisades, and bastions. Although the planned reconstruction was no surprise to the council and the SHPOs, replies to Neckel's letter were formal and frosty. Both the Advisory Council and the Montana preservation officer challenged the propriety of any historical reconstruction at the site, and all three groups attempted to reopen the reconstruction debate. ACHP official Thomas King maintained that reconstructions were difficult to "justify in terms of national and international historic preservation policies." That is, they were professionally unfashionable. With greater reason the preservation officers and the Advisory Council complained that the Park Service had submitted the project review despite having already decided to reconstruct the fort.[6]

The Advisory Council's official recommendation of May 1986 accused the National Park Service of violating its own guidelines and urged it to stop spending money on the reconstruction. Unfortunately for the preservationists, the council lacked veto power. NPS associate director Jerry Rogers (who personally opposed the reconstruction) first attempted to find a "palatable" answer to the council's letter and then decided to end the debate with a simple declaration of the Park Service's intent to rebuild the fort. Thomas King expressed the sentiment of the letter succinctly, "We told them to look at alternatives. Their response was, 'Get lost.'"[7]

Although the Advisory Council had successfully challenged formidable economic and political forces in the past, in this case preservationists lacked necessary support outside their own offices. A potent North Dakota congressional delegation had furnished an appropriation of nearly a million dollars to inaugurate the project, local public opinion firmly supported it, and there were no land-use controversies that might have created private-sector allies to oppose the undertaking. "We know and the Council knows," Rogers wrote the director, "that this particular decision to reconstruct was made outside the system we would normally use to make such decisions."[8]

Staunch local support also bolstered the fundraising effort on which the Fort Union project was predicated. Although Director Mott had approved reconstruction, he wisely scaled back the estimate of the General Management Plan of $8 to $10 million to the approximately $4.25 million for which the reconstructed fort was actually built. Further, he and the Friends' delegation agreed that some part of that cost would be raised privately. The decision to limit federal funds to the 1978 congressional authorization and to require a local fundraising effort saved the taxpayers several million dollars. Not only were nonappropriated funds not spent, but the belief that federal money would be limited turned the Rocky Mountain Regional Office and the Friends of Fort Union into financial watchdogs of the project.

Solicitation of private donations to aid the National Park System was an innovation of the Reagan administration and one enthusiastically embraced by William Penn Mott. At the June 1985 meeting in Washington, Mott promised that if local communities could raise roughly a hundred thousand dollars, the Park Service would find matching private funds at a rate of perhaps seven-to-one or more.[9]

Once Congress passed its first appropriation, Friends' president Rick Collin sensed Willistonites coming "out of the woodwork" to aid the project.[10] To those still reluctant to participate, the Friends pitched the economic benefits and civic pride that would certainly follow the creation of a handsome national park unit nearby. Although some local residents understood only "gas, meals, and motel rooms," leaders of the Friends of Fort Union were not primarily motivated by their own, or even by their community's, economic interest. The Friends leadership contributed significant amounts of money, office time, and uncompensated labor to the project without regard to financial benefit. Furthermore, although the Friends encouraged local businessmen to view the reconstruction in the light of economic self-interest, the latter would have had neither the vision nor the perseverance to organize the reconstruction effort themselves, especially during an economic recession.[11]

Local fundraising included mass mailings, the redemption of grocery coupons, and an "adopt-a-log" program. Nevertheless, most of the money was raised by a handful of Friends—especially Hagan and Kaiser—who knew whom to ask for large contributions. Hagan importuned the board chairman of a Williston bank, a childhood friend, for five thousand dollars. Kaiser then visited a competing bank and persuaded its officers to match that donation. Friends' treasurer Greg Hennessy approached local lawyers; Hagan and Kaiser called on the doctors. The North Dakota fundraising goal of one hundred thousand dollars was reached by February 1987. Including in-kind donations, the Friends' contribution to the project ultimately amounted to perhaps half a million dollars.[12]

As it turned out, the National Park Service's efforts to raise private funds proved inconsequential, netting no more than fifty thousand dollars rather than the hundreds of thousands Mott had all but promised. The director's fundraising plan was well intentioned but beyond the ability of his office to execute effectively.[13] Mott had hoped that the National Park Foundation, the official nonprofit partner of the NPS, would sponsor a fundraising drive. But in a March 1986 meeting with Friends' representatives the foundation's director announced that although he was prepared to accept contributions, he would certainly do no fundraising. In the end, deficiencies of the failed national drive were rectified with Park Service appropriations.[14]

Still, Mott's vision benefited the project significantly (if indirectly) by effecting a fortuitous contact with Lord John Jacob Astor VIII, third baron Astor of Hever (1946–). Mott had entrusted the national fund drive to his special assistant, Priscilla R. Baker, a former professional fundraiser, and Baker believed that since the historic Fort Union had been built at the command of John Jacob Astor, one of his descendants might aid its reconstruction. She soon learned that John Astor, a British corporation director, had a considerable interest in his family's history. A deliberately worded letter led to a meeting in Washington at which the two hit it off. Astor enthusiastically enlisted in the fundraising effort and contributed a considerable amount of time to the project.[15]

On 7 August 1986 Astor visited the fort and toured the archaeological dig in progress. His presence was a public relations bonanza for the local fund drive and lent increased credibility to the project. For instance, as early as Ben Innis's creation of the Fort Union–Fort Buford Council, community leaders had tried, with virtually no success, to interest local Indians in the reconstruction. But during Astor's visit the chairman of the Assiniboine tribe at Fort Peck, Montana, presented the English lord with a quilt and promised tribal support for the rebuilding effort.[16]

Nevertheless, an attempt to raise large family and corporate contributions by capitalizing on Astor's name was a dismal failure. On 15 Sep-

Fig. 13. Archaeologist Bill Hunt (*left*) gives a tour of the Fort Union site to Lord Astor (*right*), 7 August 1986. Courtesy, Rick Cronenberger.

tember 1987 Astor appeared at a New York reception arranged by Priscilla Baker. The Waldorf Astoria, eager to have the Astor name again associated with the hotel, agreed to host (that is, pay for) the affair, and representatives of the American Astors and major corporations were invited to attend.

Unfortunately, Director Mott arrived at the reception an hour and half late, and after his presentation he neglected to press for contributions on the spot. Several Astors promised Baker their assistance in the indefinite future, but none actually made a contribution. The reception was viewed as a triumph in North Dakota, but it soon became clear that reconstruction boosters had (in Paul Hedren's words) entertained "graciously and pointlessly."[17]

Still, John Astor's participation aided the reconstruction financially in two other ways. First, Astor became so enamored of the project that he commissioned a large oil painting of historic Fort Union from Robert Back, an English painter of sailing ships and seascapes. After Baker found out about the painting, Astor readily approved making copies as a fundraiser.

Baker negotiated bureaucratic obstacles at the National Park Foundation and Park Service headquarters and then arranged for the production of a limited-edition print, which sold for about a hundred dollars, as well as an inexpensive poster reproduced in larger quantities. Prints and posters raised nearly twenty thousand dollars.[18]

The other financial benefit of Astor's involvement was totally serendipitous. At their first meeting Astor and Baker discovered a mutual friend in John Bennison, the executive vice president of the American Society of Travel Agents and its chief lobbyist. Bennison chanced to be a native of North Dakota, and he pledged to use his contacts on Capitol Hill to benefit the project. Bennison soon introduced Baker to Senator Burdick, who had once been his next-door neighbor in Fargo. After "a little private chat" between the men Bennison assured Baker that whatever money was needed for the Fort Union reconstruction would be forthcoming from Congress. As a federal employee, Baker was forbidden to lobby Congress, but each year she let Bennison know how much money was needed for the Fort Union project, and he provided that figure to Burdick, reinforcing the requests for funds that came through more formal channels.[19]

Fig. 14. Entertaining "graciously and pointlessly." Influential promoters of the Fort Union reconstruction meet for a fundraising reception at the Waldorf Astoria in New York City, 15 September 1987. *Left to right*: Marv Kaiser, Paul Hedren, John Jacob Astor VIII, Lady Astor, William Penn Mott Jr., and Dr. Edward "Bud" Hagan. Courtesy, Fort Union Trading Post NHS.

Nearly $3.3 million in federal money, far exceeding any amount that could have been raised by local supporters, was appropriated in four installments. Senator Mark Andrews served as political godfather for the project, and despite the wariness with which NPS employees traditionally approached political activity, even Superintendent Hedren volunteered to work in Andrews's 1986 campaign. Then Andrews lost the election.

Andrews had promised reconstruction proponents that once the first appropriation was voted and the project was under way, additional federal funds would almost certainly follow until the partial reconstruction was complete. Despite initial apprehension on the part of Hedren and the Friends, Andrews's assurances proved correct. After Andrews's defeat Senator Burdick again took the lead in directing federal funds to the project, and the newly elected senator Kent Conrad also emerged as an effective advocate. Congressman Byron Dorgan and the Montana senators lent the weight of their offices to the effort as well.[20]

Meanwhile, the large-scale archaeological excavation of the Fort Union site, necessary before any reconstruction could begin, was initiated during the summer of 1986 by the Midwest Archeological Center of Lincoln, Nebraska. Chosen to direct the dig were Thomas D. Thiessen (1947–) and William J. Hunt Jr. (1947–), both of whom had Fort Union experience. Thiessen, a veteran NPS employee, had monitored the installation of a temporary visitor center and a waterline trench that exposed remains of Crow-Flies-High village in 1977. Hunt, a Ph.D. candidate in historical archaeology at the University of Pennsylvania, not only had considerable archaeological experience but also had made a critical analysis of the earlier Fort Union excavations and the preliminary artifact reports.[21]

Anticipating passage of the 1985 Fort Union appropriation, MWAC archaeologists drafted an excavation plan and a budget for a single season, even though they realized from the beginning that it would be nearly impossible to excavate such a large and complicated site in that amount of time. Shortly thereafter Thiessen and Hunt discovered that a gravel layer, at which previous archaeologists had ended their investigation, masked many features of an earlier Fort Union below. Consequently, it became necessary to re-excavate areas of the fort site thought to have been completed earlier.

During the first summer Thiessen and Hunt enlisted a paid crew of eleven and five to eight volunteers per week. Because the Bourgeois House was scheduled for reconstruction in the fall of 1986, that area was excavated first. The archaeologists then planned the second and third seasons—which largely investigated the palisades, the bastions, and the Indian trade house—from what had been learned about the complexity of the site in 1986. Much larger crews of thirty-five to fifty were employed during the last two summers, and Hunt was forced to become something of an administrator, a role he found less congenial.

In three field seasons the archaeologists excavated approximately forty thousand square feet of the park. The Fort Union dig became the largest excavation ever supervised by MWAC on a single site, it employed larger crews than any other archaeological project in North America during the same years, and it was the most intense excavation ever conducted at any unit of the National Park System. A project that might have taken up to twenty seasons on a schedule comfortable to archaeologists was squeezed into less than thirteen months to accommodate the reconstruction.[22]

Several techniques, uncommon at the time, were used to increase work efficiency. Archaeologists typically employed manually operated shaker screens to recover small artifacts from excavated soil. At Fort Union, Thiessen and Hunt introduced large, motorized grain cleaners to accomplish the same task in about a tenth the time with no more damage to fragile objects than would have been caused by the shaker screens. The proximity of the Missouri River also permitted water screening (with a hose called "George the Water Boa") of approximately 12 percent of the soil samples, an innovative technique at the time. By pumping water over clumps of excavated soil on small mesh screens, the archaeologists revealed and preserved embedded artifacts such as small beads.[23]

Although the Fort Union excavation was not the first to employ computers on site, it was one of the first to do so systematically. Laptop computers with twenty-four kilobytes of memory were used to catalog artifacts and to log photographs in the field; larger machines were used to prepare reports. Because archaeological data could be entered on site in nearly final form, notes did not have to be transcribed by a typist. This procedure at least ensured that no additional errors were introduced in the transcription process. The only serious drawback to field use of computers, besides their expense, was that keyboards became useless when dirty.

In the summer of 1988 a larger computer with a forty-megabyte hard drive was installed in the basement of the newly completed Bourgeois House. With computer-aided drafting (CAD) software, it produced site maps showing the location of all the excavations and their cultural features. Drawing site maps by hand, usually from field notes during the off-season, had previously been a time-consuming task for every serious archaeological investigation. Computer-aided drafting allowed complex maps of high quality to be produced on site with only a three-day delay from excavation to documentation, a boon not only to the archaeologists but to the historical architects who were designing the reconstruction in their wake. Moreover, archaeologists could investigate possible mapping errors simply by talking to the excavator or by going outside and taking a look for themselves.[24]

More than 150 crew members were volunteers, most recruited by park press releases and media stories about the excavation. Volunteers came from around the country to spend a week doing manual labor—often under a glaring sun—while providing their own meals and lodging. Since few had any archaeological experience, they were given a brief orientation and were then supervised by archaeologists for the remainder of their stint. Training amateurs slowed the archaeologists at the beginning of each week, but the enthusiasm and dedication of the volunteers more than compensated for the time expended. Volunteers saved the Fort Union project more than fifty thousand dollars while they acquired a better understanding of both archaeology and the historic fort. An additional benefit was the media attention that volunteers attracted. A couple of reporters even signed on themselves.[25]

One volunteer, describing her week's experience to a reporter, said that as she concentrated on her area, she sometimes looked up to find "a bunch of people staring down" at her. Conservatively, the Fort Union excavation increased visitation at the park by 60 percent, and more people on average came to see the archaeologists dig than viewed the reconstructed fort a half-dozen years later. The attention of regional media stimulated tourism, and the Friends of Fort Union also publicized the project with billboard advertising along major North Dakota highways.[26]

The archaeologists' priority was to provide information that would aid the reconstruction, but MWAC excavations also uncovered the remains of many structures for which historical information was limited or nonexistent.[27] Most significant was evidence of the smaller, 1828 Fort Union, the existence of which (at least as "Fort Union") had previously been questioned. Artifacts, recovered by the tens of thousands, spanned the centuries from prehistoric Indians to twentieth-century pothunters.[28]

The MWAC archaeologists were at first well received, in part because their presence meant that the long-awaited reconstruction would shortly follow. During the 1986 season Marv Kaiser brought soft drinks and snacks to the crew and reported to Senator Andrews that the excavation had raised the spirits of reconstruction proponents to "a new high." By fall, however, Kaiser was less sanguine. Despite his praise for Thiessen and Hunt as "outstanding worksite personnel," Kaiser complained to Jack Neckels that the project was beginning to look like "a complete dig of each and every spoonful of dirt on the Fort site."[29] In retrospect, it is easy to understand why friction developed between the archaeologists and the reconstruction boosters. Given their differing perspectives, it is more surprising that the discord did not end in either a shoddy excavation or a delay of the reconstruction.

To MWAC, the Fort Union project was something of a pact with the devil. Although the dig provided exciting research opportunities for its archaeologists, much of the Fort Union site had to be excavated quickly to satisfy what many of them believed to be an interpretive folly. (MWAC archaeologists, including Hunt, had argued for an off-site reconstruction.) The excavation smacked of a salvage effort mandated by politics rather than the more leisurely and (therefore presumably) more scholarly investigation that the archaeologists would have preferred. Furthermore, the Fort Union project reinforced a view of the profession that many federal archaeologists rejected: that archaeology served chiefly as a "handmaiden to history," providing architectural details for reconstructions and artifacts for museum displays. Finally, because the Fort Union project was funded outside the normal fiscal conventions, with appropriations provided as budget add-ons, the archaeologists did not receive a typical cushion of funds from which they could analyze the excavated artifacts once the fieldwork was complete. This analysis, the archaeologists argued, was necessary to meet Park Service standards for archaeological investigations.[30]

The archaeologists' ambivalence was revealed in a speech written by Tom Thiessen and delivered by Bill Hunt at the conclusion of the Bourgeois House excavation in October 1986. Thiessen titled his remarks "Requiem for an Edifice" and called the occasion a "sad day." "You and I, friends," wrote Thiessen, "have participated in [the building's] final obliteration. . . . Hail and farewell, great building!"[31]

To the Friends and the park staff, however, excavating the historic fort was largely a legal necessity, an impediment to be removed before reconstruction could begin. Reconstruction proponents believed that project funds were limited, and they became agitated as substantial portions of the money they had raised or wangled from their congressional delegation were funneled into archaeology rather than construction. "We were just basically ignorant," Kaiser recalled. "But we were very worried. . . . Our sense was that the project was funded at a certain dollar level. We weren't presuming that we could go back to Congress and say, 'Now we need another million dollars because they spent it on archaeology.'"[32]

The feeling grew among reconstruction supporters that time constraints had forced the park to accept MWAC's services when a better bargain might have been struck with a university. Whenever MWAC archaeologists seemed not to be behaving as handmaidens to history—as for instance (in Hedren's words), when the archaeologists followed "every nuance in soil coloration to no place"—the Friends tended to view them as impediments to progress. As for post-excavation research, Hedren argued that the responsibility of the Park Service should end with the completion of field reports.[33]

Besides the misunderstandings and philosophical differences, there were the petty annoyances that might have been expected to accompany any group of young people temporarily employed at an isolated location. The archaeological crews did not receive housing or per diem expenses, and most crew members had to commute fifty miles a day, round trip, to the park. Furthermore, after May 1987 the weather was mostly hot and dry. Two specialists Hunt had hired for the 1987 season proved incompetent, and although he considered firing them, he had no available replacements. Hunt's marriage also failed that summer. Meanwhile, the park mainte-

Fig. 15. Superintendent Paul Hedren gives National Park Service director William Penn Mott a walking tour of the Fort Union site a few minutes before Mott threatened the pace of the reconstruction by berating archaeologist Bill Hunt. *Minot Daily News*, 10 June 1987. Courtesy, Eloise Ogden.

nance staff took a dim view of the crew's general messiness, especially when combined with lectures on the near sacrilege of reconstructing the fort. On one occasion a drinking party at Bodmer Overlook ended with quantities of broken glass at that potential archaeological site.³⁴

Thiessen chose not to return after the first season, both for personal reasons and because he felt he had been publicly praised and privately criticized by the local boosters.³⁵ Nevertheless, an accommodation between the Friends and the archaeologists might have been reached had it not been for the rambunctious personality of Park Service director William Penn Mott. When Mott appeared for the dedication of the Bourgeois House on 7 June 1987, Hedren took the opportunity of a tour around the grounds to convey the discontent of the Friends with the pace and expense of the excavation. Hedren unwittingly put oil to fire; Mott disliked archaeology and archaeologists. By the time the director had circled the fort site and was introduced to the unsuspecting Hunt, he was "at a fever pitch." Mott launched into a tirade against Hunt, against the Fort Union excavation, and against Park Service archaeologists in general.³⁶

Mott's diatribe might have had even more serious consequences if nearby media representatives had reported his unprofessional outburst.³⁷ As it was, MWAC chief F. A. Calabrese, an opponent of the reconstruction and not one to tolerate fools gladly, took MWAC's case to Washington and sparked an investigation by the chief anthropologist and chief historian into the larger issues of the controversy. Their report essentially agreed with MWAC that the ongoing archaeology was "the minimum necessary," that the excavations were not overpriced, and that the Friends' conclusions about cost overruns were based on misunderstandings. Calabrese also attempted to extract a personal apology from Mott, but the director responded that Hunt should not have taken his criticism personally.³⁸

Thereafter communication between MWAC and the park was conducted with utmost formality, and the incident destroyed a budding friendship between Hedren and Hunt. Although Hunt himself had not been the target of the Friends' criticism, he not surprisingly concluded that there had been a "conspiracy . . . to try to bring the project to a halt."³⁹

Yet despite the ill will created by Mott's eruption, the quality and pace of the archaeological excavation were little affected. Hunt had invested too much of his career in Fort Union to abandon it at this juncture, and the boosters and park staff were anxious to have the archaeology completed as quickly as possible. Despite continuing tension between archaeologists and reconstruction proponents, Hedren and Hunt—both talented professionals—maintained a businesslike relationship for the duration.⁴⁰

12 | Reconstructing Fort Union

FORTUNATELY, both archaeologists and reconstruction supporters worked well with the Rocky Mountain Regional Office, the Park Service agency that supervised the actual construction. Their collaborative work eventually resulted in a historically accurate and aesthetically pleasing structure that avoided many pitfalls of previous reconstructions.

Normally, major Park Service projects were assigned to the Denver Service Center (DSC), an NPS office that provided professional planning and construction services for the Park Service nationwide. The DSC was a project-funded operation, however, sustaining itself on a percentage of funds from every assignment and inflating the cost of Park Service projects by 50 percent or more. The limited budget of the Fort Union project could not bear such surcharges.[1]

Furthermore, the Rocky Mountain Regional Office had conducted nearly all previous planning at Fort Union, including the *Reconstruction Analysis* of 1979. Excited by the professional challenge, veterans of the earlier project argued that allowing the base-funded regional office to do the reconstruction would save hundreds of thousands of dollars that would otherwise be consumed by DSC salaries and overhead. Furthermore, they contended that the *Reconstruction Analysis* had taught them much about the historic fort that would have to be relearned by the Denver Service Center. Not surprisingly, there was grumbling at the DSC, with which the regional office shared a building. Some service center staff ridiculed the idea that Fort Union could be reconstructed on such a small budget and gloatingly regretted the money that eventually would have to be spent to prove them right.[2]

Nevertheless, after the maintenance debacle at Bent's Old Fort, personnel at both the service center and the regional office remained leery of historical reconstructions. Even the Rocky Mountain Regional Office personnel engaged in the rebuilding paid lip service to the anti-reconstruction philosophy of the Park Service and insisted that by helping reconstruct Fort Union, they were not endorsing reconstructions per se—only this one in particular mandated by Congress. If the job had to be done, the regional office argued, it was the best equipped to do it.[3]

After some maneuvering by Regional Director Lorraine Mintzmyer, the Washington office approved the unusual arrangement. Rodd Wheaton, who had earlier directed the *Reconstruction Analysis,* became supervisory historical architect, and his subordinate, Richard J. Cronenberger, who had overseen the flagpole reconstruction, the project manager. Marcy Culpin, historian for the *Reconstruction Analysis,* served as historian for the reconstruction as well. Although Culpin made her major contribution to the project during the 1970s, she discovered another historically significant (though artistically primitive) view of the fort during the reconstruction period. The credibility of the reconstruction was strengthened by the quantity and quality of paintings, sketches, and verbal descriptions of Fort Union she collected.[4] Furthermore, inconsistencies in this evidence could be checked against three photographs of the aging fort taken in 1866, an advantage not available to those who had reconstructed Bent's Old Fort.[5]

The first stage of the Fort Union project, the reconstruction of the Bourgeois House, commenced during the winter of 1986-87 and concluded with the dedication of the building the following spring. Wheaton and Cronenberger considered doing the entire project in-house, but in part because of the tight construction schedule, they chose Yeater Hennings Ruff, a Fargo firm with experience in historic preservation, to perform architectural and engineering services.

Although the new Bourgeois House was built with modern construction techniques and the interior was designed as a visitor center and administrative office, the building's exterior was a faithful representation of its 1851 predecessor. The floor plan generally followed original spatial divisions, and when authentic hearth stones were uncovered by the archaeologists, they too were incorporated in the design.[6] The incongruity of a contemporary interior behind a nineteenth-century facade encouraged visitors to question the nature of the building. Probably fewer believed that they had entered an original structure than did, say, the average visitor to Louisbourg or the Capitol at Williamsburg.[7]

Since only the roof of the freestanding exterior kitchen could be documented, the architects chose to support a reconstructed gable on four, twelve-inch steel columns within the original foundation stones.[8] This partial "ghosting" was the most questionable architectural decision of the project. Visitors sometimes mistook the structure for a picnic shelter—an impression reinforced when employees took their breaks there. Nevertheless, in partial compensation for the missing elements, thoughtful visitors might more easily consider the nature of the structure they were viewing as well as the care taken by the historical architects not to reconstruct beyond evidence.

Yeater Hennings Ruff submitted the completed Bourgeois House for a design award, and a New York jury of architects praised the structure for its "authentic 19th century detail." Nevertheless, Wheaton and Cronenberger were dissatisfied with the firm's performance. Yeater had won the contract in part by claiming expertise in the new technique of computer-aided drawing, but the subordinate in charge of the process made serious design errors. Windows on the front of the House were misplaced, and the construction documents put two two-ton stone chimneys on the roof with no additional support. After the head of the firm wrote an impolitic letter implying that Cronenberger was professionally unqualified to supervise the project, the regional office dismissed the firm for its lack of "sensitivity [to] historical architectural details."[9]

At this point Cronenberger, who had overseen the contract for the Bourgeois House and corrected the architectural errors, began to take a larger role in the Fort Union project. Wheaton continued to involve himself with the political elements of the project and often tendered advice, but decision making thereafter rested with Cronenberger. Typically, the Park Service appointed committees to manage such complicated projects. Having a single project director saved time and money, but it was personally risky for Cronenberger. "They don't hang committees," he later reflected.[10]

Barely thirty years old, a graduate of the University of Miami who had never ridden a horse, Cronenberger appeared an unlikely candidate to reconstruct a historic fort in western North Dakota. Yet he proved unusually well suited to the task. Like Ralph Budd, Ben Innis, and other earlier advocates of the Fort Union site, Cronenberger reveled in the mystique of the place. Then, too, because he had no children at the time, he was able to devote his days (and sometimes sleepless nights) to the project.[11]

Most important, unlike the gifted but quick-tongued Wheaton, Cronenberger enjoyed putting buildings together, and he early demonstrated the ability to arouse enthusiasm in those whose expertise or industry might benefit the project. Cronenberger and project archaeologist Bill Hunt developed a close working relationship. Because archaeological excavation and construction design were taking place simultaneously, Hunt sent preliminary excavation reports to Cronenberger, and Cronenberger asked Hunt to keep an eye on building outlines and the size of construction members. When Hunt's crew discovered two previously unknown drains on the west side of the fort, Cronenberger added them to his construction documents. Cronenberger benefited from not having to interpret enigmatic archaeological reports, and Hunt profited from having a nonarchaeologist endorse the relevance of his archaeology. The greatest impediment to their cooperation was technical: the comparative difficulty of long-distance communication before the advent of e-mail and fax.

As a young man with comparatively little experience, Cronenberger carefully researched his potential construction problems and was proud to have consulted with "all the elders." To stimulate potential informants, he recounted Fort Union history and distributed the site's fundraising brochure, which he had helped design. He often coaxed important information from trade-group representatives for free. Nor did he overlook the expertise of other federal employees—even employees of the Denver Service Center—most of whom were more than willing to assist him.[12]

Cronenberger also maintained an excellent relationship with the major contractor, Edsall Construction of Bozeman, Montana, and its foreman at Fort Union, Perry Metcalf (who entered into the spirit of the project by becoming an enthusiast of fur trade history). Edsall subcontracted most of its three Fort Union projects to local businesses, and since federal wage rates were higher than local ones, the contractor could pick the most qualified craftsmen available.[13] Cronenberger wrote two days of "preservation training" into the construction contracts so that the men would be exposed to the unique nature of the project. When Hunt conducted half-hour readings of Larpenteur's journal for the archaeologists, Metcalf encouraged members of the construction crew to sit in as well.[14]

Normally, the contractor would have purchased his own construction materials, but to save money and maintain better quality control, Cronenberger bought the necessary wood and stone separately, writing detailed specifications for the materials to take advantage of bidding competition on the open market. The decision involved some risk, even after he had educated himself in the realities of timber grading and stonemasonry, a risk that was especially great in the case of the timber, which had to be stacked and air dried for a year before it could be used. Fortunately, Cronenberger found limestone in Kansas of a type very similar to the local original, and the timber-drying yard survived a nearby prairie fire during the summer of 1988.[15]

The cooperative atmosphere of the project stimulated pride among staff and craftsmen. Aware that drawings would not necessarily translate into accurate reproductions, Cronenberger gave George Ainslie, a talented historical blacksmith, the general designs for wrought-iron hardware and let him fill in the details from his own experience. Members of the park maintenance staff were also asked for their advice and were made responsible members of the reconstruction team. The contractor for the stone bastions called the Fort Union job one of the most difficult he had ever bid for and "one of the best in my thirty-three years in business." A specialized woodworker marveled at the architects' concern for detail and noted that he had been obliged to fabricate special tools to finish his job—"whatever we need to get it right.... It's been fun," he said, "but a challenge."[16]

During a preliminary visit to the Fort Union site in January 1986 Rodd Wheaton declared that his primary concern was for accuracy. "We are not trying to create a Disneyland on the Missouri," he told a reporter. "We won't guess at anything." Both Wheaton and Cronenberger did, in fact, try to make the reproduction as accurate as possible. Cronenberger worried about such things as the saw marks on palisade timbers and whether the new limestone would have fossil impressions like those of the original. Wheaton fussed over the millwork of the Bourgeois House facade, determined that molding profiles would remain true to nineteenth-century patterns.[17]

Nevertheless, the architects were just as concerned with future maintenance as with historical precision. The reconstructions at Fort Vancouver and Bent's Old Fort had combined historic and modern materials and building techniques. The result was a notorious maintenance problem at Bent's and the necessity of rebuilding the Vancouver palisade at more than twice the cost of the entire Fort Union reconstruction. Unlike many architects who worked for the Denver Service Center, Cronenberger regularly dealt with park maintenance issues. Some details in the original construction technique, such as joins in the palisade members and the design of its stone foundation, he modified unobtrusively in the interest of better maintenance. The North Dakota congressional delegation gently pressured him to rebuild the palisades with the original cottonwood because it could be supplied by a North Dakota firm, but Cronenberger held firm for more durable Douglas fir.[18]

Construction of the palisades and bastions began in the late summer of 1988, shortly after Hunt had completed the archaeological excavation. The palisade was built of approximately three hundred thousand board feet of timber—enough to construct a hundred three-bedroom houses—and was held together, as the original had been, with mortise and tenon joints and wooden pegs rather than nails or bolts. In contrast, the deep foundations were constructed with five feet of concrete capped with a foot of stone, virtually eliminating the effects of frost heave on the replicated walls.

Similarly, the bastions were built on concrete foundations with cores of concrete block heavily sheathed in perhaps two hundred tons of stone each. The concrete walls of their basements were two and a half feet thick at the base, and the stone was held together by mortar rather than by the mud-and-grass filler that had served the historic fort.[19] Nevertheless, none of this maintenance-saving durability was visible to the public. Finally, after the reconstruction was complete, both palisade and bastions were whitewashed, distressing workmen and local residents alike, who thought the stonework too beautiful to paint.[20]

Reflection on public misconceptions about the ghosted kitchen/picnic shelter convinced Cronenberger that despite legitimate concern with detail, it was not his mission to reconstruct the historic fort but to create "a stage set to interpret fur trade history." For instance, because there were no pictures of the interior of the bastions, they were originally to be finished in painted concrete block. Cronenberger urged a less "academic" approach. "We can guess what it looked like in there," he told Wheaton.[21]

The third and final phase of the reconstruction was a recreation of the Indian trade house, a "piece-on-piece" cabin of hand-hewn logs and sod roof. Begun in mid-1991, the structure was opened to the public two years later. There was so little evidence for the original's exterior appearance that Cronenberger feared a picture of the trade house might someday appear. Furthermore, although the trade house had an authentically recreated interior, the structure rested on a twenty-by-sixty-foot, nonhistoric basement vault intended to house the park's archaeological collection. (Although the nonauthentic basement vault was invisible to park visitors, its entrance was hidden behind a wooden door and shed typical of the period. Since there never was a door or shed at that particular location, these elements were some of the very few within the fort that falsely appeared to be reconstructions.)[22]

The remainder of the major historic fort buildings, including the dwelling range, store range, powder magazine, ice house, blacksmith shop, and dairy, were not reconstructed. The flagstones of the dairy were exposed, as was an original course of limestone in the southwest bastion foundation. Most of the other structures were represented only by cellar pits surrounded by wooden beams to mark their outlines. Despite seven seasons of archaeological activity, approximately half the acre enclosed by the palisade was never excavated to sterile soil.[23]

Meanwhile, the Friends of Fort Union developed a new park entrance and a new parking lot, making creative use of the gravel pits just west of the state line. Fortuitously, the old graveling scars largely concealed vehicles

RECONSTRUCTING FORT UNION 125

from the view of fort visitors while providing a riverside entrance similar to that of the historic fort. Public access to the palisade walkway was achieved by building modern stairs near the southwest bastion. An additional benefit of this access was that visitors walking from the parking lot got a better sense of the scale of the fort when they saw "little heads appearing over the walls."[24]

On 12–13 August 1989 the new Fort Union was celebrated with a Grand Dedication. Indians were again paid to entertain the crowds as they had during the Upper Missouri Historical Expedition sixty-four years earlier. Approximately five thousand people had attended the official opening of the Bourgeois House in 1987, but in response to extensive media promotion during North Dakota's statehood centennial, more than fifteen thousand welcomed the completion of the palisade and bastions. It was a larger number than had visited the park during all of 1984. Even *Time* magazine devoted a long paragraph to the reconstructed fort the week before the celebration.[25]

At the dedication ceremony the many advocates for the Fort Union reconstruction, as well as those who had made it physically possible, came together for the last time: politicians, state officials, former superintendents

Facing page

Fig. 16. Fort Union Trading Post: A Partial Reconstruction
To the casual visitor Fort Union Trading Post NHS might appear to be a complete recreation of the historic fort based on simple reproduction of historic structures. The bastion (*top, center*) and the palisades in these interior photographs are indeed grounded in considerable literary, artistic, and archaeological evidence. The trade house (*top, left, with sod roof*) is more conjectural, and the shed (*top, right*) is only typical of the temporary structures that appeared and disappeared throughout the historic period. Both the blacksmith shop (*top, center, with tent cover*) and the dwelling range (*top, right center*) are "ghost" buildings with logs outlining their foundations. No attempt was made to disguise a metal stair (*top, center*) that allows access to the palisade walkway, and a historic-looking shed to the side of the trade house (*bottom*), which has no historic basis, serves only to screen the entrance to an underground storage vault. All reconstructions, no matter how fastidiously researched and executed, are to some degree the product of professional debate, varied aesthetic taste, and differing interpretive goals. Photos by Carla Kelly, National Park Service.

Fig. 17. Original hearth stones relaid in the trade house reconstruction, April 1991. Courtesy, Rick Cronenberger.

Fig. 18. Members of the reconstruction team pose before the northeast bastion at the dedication of the reconstruction, August 1989. *Left to right*: Marcy Culpin, historian; Rick Cronenberger, historical architect; Adrienne Anderson, regional archeologist; Rodd Wheaton, chief, Division of Cultural Resources. Courtesy, Rick Cronenberger.

and park personnel, archaeologists, architects, contractors, craftsmen, and the leadership of the Friends of Fort Union. On an occasion when beauty queens and paid entertainers mingled with congressmen and clergymen, it was virtually impossible to properly recognize individual contributions, even of those who were present. But nearly forgotten were three men of great importance to the reconstruction of Fort Union who were not there that day: the late Ben Innis, who for years had persevered with his dream despite indifferent results; ex-senator Mark Andrews, whose political savvy provided the initial federal appropriation; and Ralph Budd, the modest railroad president who had first conceived of a reconstructed Fort Union.[26]

13 | The Business of a Park

THE PARTIAL reconstruction at Fort Union Trading Post National Historic Site will remain into the indefinite future the element of park history of greatest significance to most students of cultural resource management and historic preservation. Nevertheless, the story of the park's management—its true administrative history—is also worthy of examination. During the thirty years that followed congressional authorization of Fort Union Trading Post NHS the park confronted many of the same challenges in cultural and natural resource management faced by larger units of the system. Simultaneously, the influence of the park's local boosters, the Friends of Fort Union, grew to affect nearly every area of the site's administration.

In the late 1960s and early 1970s Fort Union Trading Post remained an unprepossessing unit of the Park System. A ranger at another park remembered it as "a relatively featureless grassy area with some cottonwoods down toward the river." A contemporary Williston reporter noted empty beer cans and broken bottles on the property that he thought, considering the currency of the fur trade, might "not be out of place as historical reminders."[1]

Of course, once Park Service personnel arrived, the trash was cleaned up. Nevertheless, the service left its own mark on the land. By 1974 there were three trailers within a few hundred feet of the fort site: quarters for the park manager and a seasonal employee and a combination office and visitors' center. When Bill Wellman approached the site for the first time, his wife, not realizing that they had reached their destination, remarked that the spot seemed like "an awful place for a trailer park."[2]

Visitor services were rustic. The park began with pit toilets and water trucked in from Williston. Since water lines were buried only eighteen inches below the ground, the park could stay open only so long as the lines could be kept from freezing, ordinarily from about April to November. In 1976 a well was dug, and in the following summer a modular visitors' center replaced the trailers, which were then moved into Garden Coulee. The new visitors' center was itself only a double-wide trailer, but compared with what had gone before, Wellman thought it "very nice."[3]

Visitors still had little to see. Even the fort's stone foundations, which had been partially visible before the archaeological digs, were backfilled to protect them. When the regional director visited during Wellman's first week on the job, the new acting manager had difficulty finding the outline of the fort. For his part, the regional director doubted that Fort Union had any future in the Park System and thought giving it back to North Dakota preferable to developing it.[4]

A few wayside exhibits were set up each spring and taken down in the fall. By 1972 a mimeographed leaflet with a rough ground plan of the fort was supplemented by an official, if somewhat rambling, Park Service brochure that touted "long term plans . . . for complete reconstruction." But any visitor who did brave the sometimes muddy gravel roads to reach the site was likely to get a private tour. And the superintendent himself might dismount a riding mower to give it.[5]

Sylvester Putnam displayed simple exhibit material sent from Jefferson National Expansion Memorial, such as a push-button exhibit that matched names and faces of famous Indian chiefs. But Wellman, his successor, spent more than eight years at the site and had a greater opportunity to make interpretive improvements. He organized the library, invited local hobbyists to do living history demonstrations on summer weekends, and, with little else to do during the winter months, developed a considerable expertise in the history of the fur trade era. Wellman occasionally wore trader outfits and slept in a tepee in freezing weather. He built bull boats until he got them to look like the ones in period drawings. (Because of a design flaw, he nearly sank on one of his first attempts to cross the Missouri.)[6]

Wellman's most significant interpretive innovation was the erection of a tepee village near the site. At one point there were fourteen tepees, the largest one a Blackfoot council lodge twenty-seven feet in diameter. The exhibit stimulated visitation, although keeping the tepees repaired and standing in the Dakota wind proved challenging.[7]

Completion of the reconstruction helped focus the interpretation. To some extent the reconstructed fort spoke for itself, even though its message was not altogether politically correct. Author Ian Frazier saw the "tall white walls [as] incredibly imposing.... like a spaceship that landed or something. It must have affected Indians like that."[8] But Carroll Van West, a noted professor of historic preservation, found it "troubling" that the reconstruction had "changed the visually perceived role of the Native Americans." Van West noted that before the reconstruction, the only visible structures were the tepees, "leaving little doubt as to the importance of the Native Americans in making that place possible and profitable." After reconstruction the tall, white walls shouted Euro-American achievement and technical superiority. Van West intuited this message as both "an interpretive burden for the staff" and a lack of responsiveness "to the needs of the present."[9]

The decision to use the interior of the Bourgeois House as the visitor center and park offices saved several million dollars and avoided a highly speculative restoration of its historic furnishings. Similarly, a fifty-car parking area created from the gravel pits to the west of the fort proved a satisfying means of salvaging an early-twentieth-century intrusion while virtually eliminating vehicles from the historic scene.[10] Nevertheless, an interpretive price was paid for both these decisions. At most historic units of the Park System visitors leave their cars near a visitor center before being oriented to the site. At Fort Union visitors parked more than a quarter-mile from the fort (literally in another state) and walked uphill to the structure—and often through the entire reconstruction—before opening the door to the Bourgeois House. Undoubtedly, many visitors were impressed by the magnificence of the reconstruction as they made their climb from the parking lot. Just as certainly, others, after a long drive over empty prairie, were anxious to find the restrooms.

Once inside the Bourgeois House some visitors were baffled by its unexplained contemporary appearance and by a stairway to park offices more conspicuous than the entrance to the park's two-room museum on their left. The museum itself contained a fine visual presentation of the site's history created by the Harpers Ferry Center featuring readable labels, archaeological artifacts, and even a pile of furs for hands-on examination. Nevertheless, the mounting of the display in such a restricted space made assimilating the information challenging, if not claustrophobic, if more than a half-dozen or so visitors shared the exhibit rooms. The Bourgeois House also had no space for a theater, and the park's only audiovisual interpretation was a three-minute, visitor-operated videodisk program displayed on a monitor in a corner of the museum.

After the completion of the reconstruction, park visitation tripled. Attendance grew from an average of fewer than ten thousand visitors a year in the ten years between 1976 and 1985 to an annual average of more than thirty-three thousand during the following decade. By necessity, though, ranger-led tours of the site became less frequent and more impersonal.

Another source of increased visitation was Rendezvous, the park's annual event, eventually held during the third week of June. Initiated in 1983 by the Fort Union Muzzle Loaders Association, Rendezvous featured a buckskinners' camp for fur trade reenactors, a traders' row, and craft demonstrations. Black powder shoots were early abandoned, but the event soon included talks on such topics as trade beads and period clothing as well as musical entertainment more or less appropriate to the period. In 1992 a "Rendezvous Run," a five-kilometer and ten-kilometer race sponsored by a local bank, was also inaugurated. Rendezvous was popular with both participants and park visitors. In 1993, for instance, the week of Rendezvous attracted more than six thousand visitors, more than the combined total for September through April. By the mid-1990s most expenses of the event were underwritten by Fort Union's support groups.

Of course, there had never been a historic rendezvous at Fort Union. Popular notions about early-nineteenth-century mountain men notwithstanding, the longest and most profitable fur trade of the historic period had been conducted with Indians at fixed posts such as Fort Union. Rather than delineate the difference between the two fur trading systems, the Fort Union Rendezvous tended to conflate them. Furthermore, the "Rendezvous Run" lacked any connection with the theme of the event beyond its name. Orville Loomer, a park maintenance worker and avid fur trade reenactor who had helped organize the original event, complained that Rendezvous was "a happening . . . not a rendezvous . . . [with] nothing authentic about it."[11]

Nevertheless, if the name *Rendezvous* was ignored, the "happening" was not difficult to defend. Balancing the sometimes egregious departures from historic accuracy in the camp and traders' row were scholarly lectures and craft demonstrations—blacksmithing, brain tanning, beaver skinning, fire starting, and the like—authentic to the period. "In effect," said Superintendent Hedren, "we had soft history outside the walls and hard history inside. We tried anyway." Even the Rendezvous Run was excusable as a trivial intrusion on the interpretive part of the event, and it lured a new and potentially receptive audience to the historic site.[12]

The interpretation of Fort Union's history—like the conduct of the historic fort's fur trading business—was necessarily shaped by the park's geographical remoteness and the harshness of winter on the northern Great Plains. For instance, in 1992 and 1993 two-thirds of park visitors arrived during three summer months and only 2.5 percent during three winter months. In the park's first thirty years the NPS assigned a total of only fifteen permanent employees to the site. Seasonal variation in visitation virtually ensured that the significance of the park would be interpreted to most visitors by temporary employees and volunteers.[13]

In the 1970s Fort Union was conveyed into the "living history" phase of Park Service interpretation. And, for better reasons than at many parks, costumed interpretation played an important (if seasonal) role there. Before the reconstruction costumed interpreters helped substitute for the near absence of anything else to see at the site.

After reconstruction costumed rangers continued to fill an interpretive void. Despite the fort's impressiveness from outside the palisades, the warehouses and employee quarters—the structures of greatest importance for the interpretation of daily life—were not reconstructed. The Bourgeois House was, of course, a facade. To humanize the wood and stone of the reconstruction, costumed interpretation was conducted in the Indian trade house. Furnished to the period on the basis of American Fur Company inventories and a fine interior sketch by Rudolph Kurz, the trade house was eventually provisioned with a large assortment of reproduced trade goods, from blankets and knives to tinware and face-painting pigments. Not only did the stock serve as an important interpretive device and hands-on display, but the trade items were sold to the public at a profit. To add to the visitors' sensory experience, the summer staff tried to conceal traces of the modern in the trade house and nearly always kept a small fire going in the fireplace.[14]

Attempts to involve nearby Indian tribes in that interpretation were mixed. Scott Eckberg, a ranger with a sustained interest in tribal participation at the park, inaugurated an annual "Intertribal Day" during which Assiniboines from the Fort Peck reservation were paid to present a program of traditional song, dance, and crafts. The event, in differing formats, was continued after his departure from the park. Eckberg's contact with Fort Peck also led to the hiring of two Indians as seasonal interpreters for one year and a token grant from the finance committee of the tribal government toward their salaries.

Another seasonal interpreter recruited at Fort Peck had to be fired during the 1992 season, however, and the distance of the park from the reservations made it difficult to retain Indians as employees. Paul Hedren reflected that the relationship of the park to the tribes was simply one of the challenges that came with the site, but he deemed it the park's responsibility to "at least extend the hand." Sometimes, he said, "you're going to win. [It's when] you stop trying [that] there's going to be trouble."[15]

A related challenge was interpreting the smallpox epidemic of 1837 and the equally destructive manufacture and sale of alcohol at the fort during the historic period. Unlike the abolition of slavery, the emancipation of women, and the civil rights movement, these controversial topics could not easily be transmuted into modern morality tales. During the smallpox epidemic the obscurantism and superstition of the Indians equaled the carelessness of the whites, and the Indians' craving for liquor could not be ignored by even the most exuberant censors of European rapaciousness. Fort Union's interpretive staff took a pragmatic approach, neither emphasizing nor totally ignoring these vexing issues. Both the liquor trade and the smallpox epidemic were mentioned in the park brochure and in books available for purchase. Nevertheless, Rodd Wheaton, chief of the RMRO Branch of Historic Preservation, successfully argued against alluding to the sale and consumption of alcohol in the museum display. It was, he said, "a social ill that is not really suitable for devoting space."[16]

Two more interpretive problems, common to all historical reconstructions, were aesthetic and philosophical rather than ideological. Should Fort Union be allowed to grow shabby, and should the odor of the original establishment be suggested to the visitors? Orville Loomer argued for "ratty" whitewash, faded paint, and "bones and wood chips all over" the place. "You could take road kills," he said, "and throw them in a corner of the fort. The smell should be brought to the public's attention."[17]

Paul Hedren thought otherwise. Although not a military veteran, he was a student of the frontier army and the sort of superintendent whose uniform was always neatly pressed. Hedren wanted a historic site that was "properly cleaned, painted, and shined." A tattered fur company flag, some flaking whitewash, and a quadrangle mowed but not manicured was as far as he wished to travel down the road toward shabbiness. Hedren's position was probably best for the site. Visitors would likely have attributed a messy park to the indifference of its caretakers. Moreover, as Daniel Boorstin has written, "fresh paint can be a useful warning of the unbridgeable gulf between past and present. . . . [It can] discomfit the romantic visitor."[18]

As for the Fort Union smell, the odors of the historic period from hides, horse manure, and human wastes would probably be so overpowering to modern visitors (who are aware of the need for sanitation as the historic inhabitants were not) that they would be loath to revisit such a place. Again, Boorstin has written that smells commonplace in the past "might seem more pungent and more offensive" in the present and "might actually destroy verisimilitude" for park visitors. Still, without making odor the interpretive theme of the park, park staff could have reminded visitors—in word if not in deed—that wood smoke was not the only aroma they would have encountered at the historic fort.[19]

Unlike park interpretation, which by definition communicates park themes to visitors, the curatorial functions of Fort Union Trading Post NHS were nearly invisible to the public. Before completion of the Bourgeois House museum, park personnel did their best to accession and catalog the objects on display at the park—mostly reproductions—as well as the ubiquitous surface finds. Unfortunately, the park's inventory of museum property was soon replete with discrepancies, double-numbering, and inaccurate descriptions. These lapses were not wholly the fault of the staff. The Park Service cataloging system was arcane, and the interpreters had neither the training nor the skills to catalog the collection properly.[20]

In 1992 Audrey L. Barnhart became Fort Union's first professional curator. In part, she was hired to order the existing Fort Union collection, as she had previously done for Agate Fossil Beds National Monument, Nebraska. But Barnhart's hiring also reflected a continuing struggle over the disposition of the site's archaeological artifacts, then held by the Midwest Archeological Center. In Paul Hedren's view the objects found during the seven seasons of archaeology at Fort Union should have been processed in some rudimentary fashion and then returned to Fort Union for cataloging by a resident curator. Hedren likened a collection of archaeological artifacts to an archive of books or documents. The Park Service, he believed, should not write every possible story from such a collection but merely maintain it, awaiting "such opportunistic storytellers as appear." MWAC archaeologists, however, insisted that NPS and Interior Department regulations forbade such a cursory treatment. They argued that the archaeological excavations remained incomplete and the damage to the historic site "unmitigated" until archaeologists had made a full analysis of the artifacts. Hundreds of thousands of dollars, directed either to MWAC or to the park, hung on how elaborate Park Service administrators believed the required reports ought to be.[21]

In 1993 the greater part of the "old" collection—approximately 131,000 objects recovered in the 1968–72 digs—was returned to Fort Union and stored in the twenty-by-sixty-foot concrete vault below the trade house. Most of these items were computer cataloged by Barnhart and seasonal museum aides during the summers of 1994–97, some twenty-five to thirty years after their excavation.[22] Nevertheless, MWAC was able to retain the 1986–88 material for further study. Its series of Material Culture Reports on the "old" collection proved helpful to the curator and to a handful of experts in fur trade archaeology, but they were frightfully expensive and of limited value to the park's interpretive staff. Further, although the reports created a host of questionable classifications, they did not attempt the sort of anthropological study of the artifacts favored by contemporary archaeologists.

In 1998 Barnhart estimated that the Fort Union collection (including the material still held at MWAC) comprised four to five hundred thousand items.[23] Most were fragments of bone, shards of glass, rusty nails, and scraps of metal. The collection contained many exhibition-quality artifacts, however, including locks, tools, buttons, and hand-carved pipe bowls. The quantity and quality of its trade beads were exceptional. Archaeologist and trade bead expert Lester Ross estimated that half of all trade beads ever found on the Great Plains had been recovered at Fort Union Trading Post. Because trade beads were of interest to hobbyists as well as to scholars, the Friends of Fort Union sponsored publication of archaeologist Steven DeVore's catalog of the 38,496 "old-collection" beads. The book sold remarkably well. Two boxloads were dispatched to a bookseller in Germany.[24]

In November 1990 an additional curatorial responsibility was created by the passage of the Native American Graves Protection and Repatriation Act (NAGPRA).[25] The law required all governmental agencies to identify the "cultural affiliation" of any aboriginal remains in their collections and attempt to return them and their associated funerary objects to the proper tribe. Five complete skeletons and two sets of partial remains had been discovered during the archaeological investigations at Fort Union. Unfortunately, experts could specify only that the remains were related to "Siouan-speaking populations of the Northern Plains"—a category broad enough to include nearly all nearby tribes, some historic enemies. Unfortunately as well, no tribe seemed to retain an oral tradition about the violent deaths of those exhumed, although it was estimated that they had been buried after 1867.[26]

Fulfilling the requirements of NAGPRA consumed time and paper, but the park staff was more than happy to be free of the human remains. Hedren viewed NAGPRA as an opportunity for the Park Service to gain "a certain amount of credibility" in the Indian community, "an opportunity to give back something that's emotional to somebody." Although the dead most likely had belonged to the Crow-Flies-High band of Hidatsa, the Three Affiliated Tribes (Arikara, Hidatsa, and Mandan) of North Dakota did not press their claim, and on 16 May 1997 the skeletal remains and associated funerary objects were "repatriated" to the Assiniboine Tribes of Fort Peck Indian Reservation in eastern Montana.[27]

Early site managers at Fort Union Trading Post made do with seasonal maintenance men. The park had no permanent maintenance worker until 1981 and was not authorized a second full-time position until 1989. Nevertheless, Orville Loomer and Dennis Borud, the only two men to hold those jobs during the site's first three decades, had been associated with Fort Union Trading Post for many years before as volunteers and temporary employees. Both were native North Dakotans and avid fur trade buffs, at least as qualified as the seasonal employees to interpret park history. Loomer discovered the remains of an Indian shrine painted by Karl Bodmer, and Borud's pride in his work was palpable. Both men regularly collected surface finds as they performed their duties.[28]

The maintenance staff made a concerted effort to restore a mixed-grass native prairie to park land that in the early twentieth century had been leveled and turned into a hay meadow. During the early 1980s limited attempts were made to burn the hay and treat it with herbicide in the hope that dormant native grasses would then reemerge. Results were uneven. Native grasses were returned to a dozen acres northwest of the fort, but in other areas identical restoration attempts proved unsuccessful. Borud reflected that trying to reestablish native grasses was like trying to save an endangered species—or to maintain one's lawn. Prairie restoration often had to be deferred while maintenance workers suppressed pesky exotics such as Canadian thistle and leafy spurge.[29]

Responding to a General Accounting Office survey on "External Threats to National Parks" in 1992, Paul Hedren cited "non-historic intrusions to the historic setting" as having caused the most significant injury to the park.[30] Yet despite some exasperating incidents, Fort Union Trading Post NHS was, in the end, largely successful in protecting the historic scene from development at its margins.

The park found it comparatively easy to check development instigated by other agencies of the federal government, notably a plan by the Corps of Engineers to aid the local irrigation district by channelizing the north bank floodplain.[31] More serious was the potential threat to the park from oil and gas drilling. The law of the United States allows mineral rights to be held separately from surface rights, and in North Dakota mineral rights were often retained by sellers of land. Therefore, mineral rights to some park land were not owned by the park. The National Park Service could prohibit drilling for oil and gas on its property, but it could not prevent "slant drilling" from outside park boundaries. In 1975 Amerada Hess drilled several expensive but profitable wells to extract oil from beneath Theodore Roosevelt National Park.[32]

During the second oil boom, drills appeared around the Fort Buford State Historic Site, and only the combined efforts of the Friends of Fort Union and the Confluence Commission prevented drilling inside state property. In 1985 a drilling rig was operating within a half-mile of Fort Union, although by that time the oil bust of the 1980s had effectively halted the threat to the park. In the future the National Park Service will undoubtedly challenge potential drillers, but improved technology should allow oil and gas to be removed with comparatively little impact on the historic scene, at least once the wells have been drilled.[33]

Ironically, the most serious "intrusions to the historic setting" resulted not from the actions of government agencies or large corporations but from small landholders enjoying their fee simple on the south bank of the Missouri. Worse, these annoyances could have been prevented had the National Park Service taken the advice of senior staff historian Roy Appleman more than a generation earlier. After visiting the Fort Union site in the summer of 1962, Appleman urged that a strip of land across from the fort be included in the park. His recommendation was ignored.[34]

Fifteen years later the Park Service realized its error, and the legislation of 1978 added more than forty acres south of the Missouri to the authorized boundaries. The properties were not purchased, however. Riverbank erosion continued, carrying away more cottonwood and ash. Other trees were cut by landowners.[35]

In 1984 Paul Hedren was vexed to discover that land just across the river was being turned into a "tacky tin trailer camp complete with sewage connections, 4th of July beer parties, a cut-bank boat launch, and vegetative disturbance, all on legislated park land." The new superintendent requested an emergency grant to purchase the property. Unfortunately, by the time the Rocky Mountain Regional Land Resources Division chief investigated the situation, development had ceased and the property was no longer eligible for purchase with emergency funds. Fifteen years later the "tacky tin trailer" was still visible to park visitors.[36]

Just before the Bourgeois House dedication in June 1987 another landowner created a private trash dump on a bank across from the fort and pushed a refrigerator halfway into the Missouri. Hedren complained to the owner, and when that protest had no effect, to the Army Corps of Engineers, whose jurisdiction extended to items in the water. The owner was annoyed at Hedren, but he cleaned up most of the refuse except the refrigerator. The park maintenance staff then managed to wrestle the eyesore from the silt. Still, the National Park Service did not buy the property.[37]

Four years later a third owner contracted to have cottonwood and cedar trees bulldozed to make way for irrigated sugar beet fields. When Hedren protested, the owner replied, "Make me an offer." Not surprisingly, the Park Service balked at paying twice the appraised value of the land, fearing that paying high prices to stop tree cutting would provide other landowners an incentive to *start* tree cutting. In September 1992 the Friends of Fort Union purchased part of the in-holding anyway, correctly believing that the Park Service would eventually reimburse it.

The Friends had also long coveted the property of the refrigerator dumper because it was directly across from the fort and had no tree screen. The Park Service and Friends' chairman Greg Hennessy, a Williston lawyer, patiently negotiated with the owner, who was both losing land to the Missouri and hoping to move into town—in Hennessy's words, being "jabbed from two directions: old age and Old Man River." As a negotiating ploy, the owner claimed that an abandoned house on the property had sentimental value. The final agreement required its removal. After selling his property, the owner burned down the house.[38]

North of the fort site, across the county road and railroad tracks, lay the undeveloped portion of the park known as the Bodmer Overlook. When the National Park Service contemplated creating the national historic site in the early 1960s, it decided to include an overlook with a panoramic view of Fort Union, Fort Buford, and the Missouri-Yellowstone confluence. A location nearer the confluence was first chosen, then abandoned after a visit by noted American artist Thomas Hart Benton (1889–1975) during the summer of 1965. Along with a party from the Corps of Engineers and the Park Service, Benton spent a full day trying to find where Karl Bodmer had drawn Fort Union in 1833. Eventually, he made his own sketch from the hill he thought best matched the perspective. The Park Service opted for Benton's choice of high points both because of the Bodmer association and because its proximity to the Fort Union site made it easier to protect the historic scene at both properties.[39]

The Bodmer Overlook was maintained largely with scenic easements, although a thirty-acre plot around the hill itself was purchased by the federal government. There were occasional awkward moments with neighboring farmers, but the area was not threatened by private development during the park's first thirty years. Neither the National Park Service nor the Friends of Fort Union took much interest in developing the property, and the potential accessibility to the Bodmer Overlook over a railroad grade crossing was transformed from an asset in the 1960s to a liability in the more litigious and safety-conscious 1990s.[40]

The activities of many national parks are supported by an associated nonprofit organization, usually described as a "friends group." A few such groups have been in existence for a half-century or more, but in general, they are a recent phenomenon. The Friends of Fort Union Trading Post was only twelve years old in 1996, but by then it was already older than half the friends groups in the country. Furthermore, the Friends of Fort Union Trading Post remained active even after the completion of the reconstruction, for which the organization could take considerable credit. In part because Fort Union Trading Post was such a small park, its dynamic friends group proved highly influential. In 1994 the National Park Foundation recognized the organization for its "outstanding contributions in partnership strategies and visionary leadership."[41]

The Friends of Fort Union donated microfilm of the American Fur Company papers to the park, published the Fort Union bead study, financially supported Rendezvous, and made an emergency purchase of park in-holdings. The Friends also raised funds or channeled contributions for the trade house timbers, a Red River cart,[42] a three-pounder cannon, and a buffalo-skin tepee. In 1990 and again in 2000 the Friends sponsored academic conferences, Fort Union Fur Trade Symposiums, and then published their proceedings. In 1993 it inaugurated an annual Fort Union Fellowship of one thousand dollars to support research "having the fort as a central theme." Meanwhile, the organization also contributed to similar activities and improvements at Fort Buford.[43]

By far the Friends' most innovative fundraising method was its collection and sale of paddlefish roe. The paddlefish, a large plankton feeder with a paddle-like bill, found the confluence an excellent place to spawn. Its eggs made such excellent caviar that the fish had been poached toward extinction in the southern United States. Paddlefish were nearly placed on the federal endangered species list, and until 1992 it was illegal to sell their roe in North Dakota.

Once the state was convinced that a legal harvest could be supported,

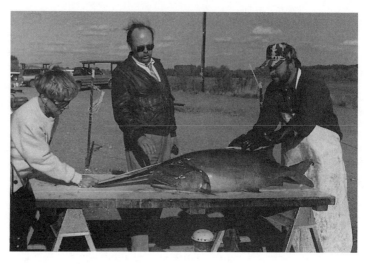

Fig. 19. Founder Greg Hennessy (*center*) oversees as members of the Gold Star Caviar management committee measure a paddlefish before its eggs are harvested. *The Gavel* (December–January 2000).

Greg Hennessy, the new Friends' chairman, suggested that profits from this unused resource might benefit Fort Union Trading Post. The president of the Williston Chamber of Commerce had a similar idea about using paddlefish caviar to aid nonprofit organizations in Williston. Rather than fight over the potential spoils, he and Hennessy joined forces. In 1993 the chamber and the Friends formed Gold Star Caviar, a corporation licensed to operate under the supervision of the North Dakota Game and Fish Department.

Through the season, Gold Star maintained a processing station where fishermen could have their legal limit of one paddlefish per year cleaned and filleted. The fishermen kept the meat, the skins were turned into boots and wallets, and the unused parts were ground into fertilizer. Gold Star took the roe. Happily, at the same time, consumption of caviar came back into fashion among trendsetters in New York and Hollywood. Hennessy was amused to find himself something of a successor to Kenneth McKenzie, "doing the beaver/buffalo thing" with a different product a century and a half later. After five years of operation Gold Star had profits of $248,000. Game and Fish took 25 percent, and there was some jockeying for control of the remainder. Ultimately, the Friends and the chamber reached an accommodation on how the money would be divided among local nonprofit organizations. Nearly all the special programming at Fort Union and Fort

Buford, such as Rendezvous and the Fort Buford Military Encampment, was eventually underwritten with caviar profits.[44]

Even before the paddlefish began to provide the Friends with a steady income, the organization began to lobby for the replacement of Fort Union's "cooperating association." Cooperating associations are neither friends groups nor concessionaires but nonprofit organizations chartered by the National Park Service to sell publications and other items that serve the park's interpretive program. Returns from sales are then donated to the park. Some cooperating associations, such as Eastern National Park and Monument Association, have become considerable businesses and operate sales outlets at many Park System units. In 1990 all the national parks in North Dakota were represented by Theodore Roosevelt Nature and History Association (TRNHA).[45]

During the reconstruction Fort Union Trading Post had experienced minor irritations in its relationship with TRNHA. For instance, the cooperating association would not approve an American Fur Company flag pin as a Fort Union sales item. Worse, when Paul Hedren's *Great Sioux War, 1876–77* (1991) was chosen as an alternate selection of the Military History Book Club, the book could not be sold at Fort Union because it had not yet been approved by the association. One TRNHA business manager proved so ineffectual that board dissatisfaction caused her resignation. More important, though, the Friends believed that TRNHA did not have the expertise to properly stock and maintain the long-planned, interactive trade store that the Friends intended to fund. Through an unwritten understanding, the Friends and the Rocky Mountain Regional Office agreed that the Friends would eventually create (or transform itself into) a cooperative association that would supersede TRNHA at Fort Union.[46]

The interest of the National Park Service, however, lay in reducing the number of cooperating associations, not increasing them. Furthermore, like all bureaucracies, the NPS preferred the status quo. An aggressive friends group, especially when combined with a park superintendent who had already displayed considerable independence, raised fears that a Fort Union cooperative association might try to dictate park policy. Unhelpful to Fort Union's case was a concurrent test of wills between the Park Service and Custer Battlefield Historical and Museum Association. The powerful Montana association opposed changing the name of the park to Little Bighorn Battlefield, refused to stock books requested by the Park Service, and generally resisted the park's new emphasis on Indian perspectives.[47]

The Friends' ambition to organize a new cooperating association broke old alliances. In June 1991 representatives from TRNHA, the Park Service, and the Friends of Fort Union met to discuss the proposed organization. Deputy Regional Director Jack Neckels and Pete Hart, superintendent of Theodore Roosevelt National Park, sided with TRNHA. Neckels, who had been a stalwart supporter of the Fort Union reconstruction, refused to admit that the RMRO had earlier agreed to allow Fort Union its own cooperating association—an about-face that stunned, then angered Marv Kaiser, the Friends' chief fundraiser.[48]

A few months later Neckels left Denver to become superintendent of Grand Teton National Park, and Regional Director Lorraine Mintzmyer was shortly replaced as well. Her successor, Robert M. Baker, heard Kaiser out, but he also declined to approve a new cooperative association. Baker assumed that after this rebuff the Friends would open their treasury to TRNHA. Kaiser and Hennessy insisted they would not. In April 1992 Baker visited the North Dakota parks, lunched with members of the Friends' board, and observed the new paddlefish operation. After listening to board members share accounts of their vision and previous success, Baker turned to Hart and said, "I don't know why we're saying no to these people." By fall he had agreed to the creation of the Fort Union Association. "We had the money," Hennessy recalled. "We had the power of the purse for once."[49]

Rather than dissolve itself, the Friends of Fort Union provided start-up capital for the Fort Union Association (FUA) with a long-term, low-interest loan of seventy thousand dollars so that it could buy out the TRNHA inventory and purchase the necessary replicated trade goods. A board was recruited, the FUA was incorporated as a 501(c)3 organization, and the new association became operational on 6 April 1993.[50]

Marv Kaiser agreed to take the chairmanship of the Fort Union Association and with it a great deal of the responsibility for establishing the new organization. The FUA board assumed that trade goods would become the association's greatest source of income, as had been the case at Bent's Old Fort. In fact, the bookstore in the Bourgeois House continued to outsell the trade house.[51] Attempts to market trade goods via mail order also netted little return.

In part, the low sales volume was the result of a perception that Fort Union products were overpriced. Unlike typical tourist souvenirs, however, these products were intended to be "absolutely authentic, museum quality trade goods." In some cases, such as tinware made from hand-dipped stock, custom-made chiefs' coats, certain kinds of blankets, and silver jewelry that copied Fort Union artifacts, the trade house reproductions were unobtainable elsewhere. At the very least, the high standards of the Fort Union Association allowed the park staff to interpret fur trade items to the public with considerable confidence in their authenticity.[52]

Kaiser introduced a computer and sophisticated accounting software to the park, and FUA operations at Fort Union were eventually linked by modem to his consulting firm and its office manager. The accounting system was complex, and supervisory ranger Scott Eckberg and the park's administrative clerk were provided with hundreds of dollars worth of formal training to master it. Unfortunately, Eckberg skipped a considerable portion of the training. The situation deteriorated when, in the late summer and early fall of 1993, the new accounting system caught the administrative clerk embezzling funds. After the clerk was fired, Eckberg floundered. Several seasonal employees with computer skills helped fill the gap during this stressful period, but another was so overwhelmed by the system that Eckberg had to relieve him of duty at the visitor center entirely. In 1995 Eckberg left Fort Union abruptly when a vacancy appeared at Grant-Kohrs Ranch NHS, Montana.[53]

Eckberg's successor as chief ranger, Randy Kane, was similarly baffled by the accounting software, although he confessed that he was eventually able to learn the basics of the system "after much pain." Fortunately, Mary Hale, the new administrative assistant, unraveled both its mysteries and the errors of her predecessors and relieved Kane of a great deal of the administrative burden. A significant difference between Eckberg and Kane, however, was that Eckberg considered FUA business an interruption of his other responsibilities, whereas Kane wisely made it a priority at a park in which the cooperating association played such an important role.[54]

Although the Fort Union Association was not as immediately successful as Kaiser had hoped, gross sales nearly doubled between 1994 and 1996. Gold Star Caviar helped close the financial gap by making substantial grants to the association. In its search for additional revenue the association also experimented with bookstore sales of commercial items, such as posters and cassette tapes of period music. A few eyebrows were raised when the park began selling Fort Union T-shirts, but Kaiser refused to compromise the integrity of the park or the association by peddling the "rubber tomahawks" of the tourist trade.[55]

The thirtieth anniversary of the park marked the end of an era in the internal history of Fort Union Trading Post National Historic Site. Near the close of 1996, after twelve years as supervisor, Paul Hedren announced his departure for Niobrara/Missouri National Scenic River, Nebraska. During his long tenure (four supervisory superintendents had served at Theodore Roosevelt National Park in the same period), Hedren had been given progressively more authority to do what he deemed best for his park.[56] Fort Union Trading Post had undergone a remarkable period of development during its first thirty years. It was now poised to join the ranks of mature units in the National Park System.

Conclusion

THE FORT UNION reconstruction was of life-changing significance to only a few area residents and scattered employees of the National Park Service. Development of an obscure park in a sparsely populated section of the country would have been of comparatively little consequence were it not for the larger issues that surrounded it.

Without doubt the Fort Union site possessed exceptional qualities as a prospective reconstruction. The historic fort was of undeniable national importance. For good and evil, the American Fur Company's trading center brought the Yellowstone and upper Missouri River basins into the orbit of Euro-American commerce, forever altering their previous natural and cultural environment. Furthermore, the artistic and literary men who ventured upriver to this outpost of European civilization left drawings and descriptions that provided unusually strong documentation for its rebuilding.[1]

Fort Union's attractiveness as a potential candidate for reconstruction was further strengthened by the chance preservation of its archaeological remains. The army might easily have obliterated the foundations of the trading post by building Fort Buford over it. Or if the ruins had remained outside the military reservation, the site could have become Williston. Or had the gravel bank on which Fort Union was constructed been located a few hundred yards to the west, the remnants of the fort might have been completely recycled into Mondak.

The Fort Union site was also fortunate to remain geographically isolated. Although many North American historical reconstructions have been built over original foundations, most are now surrounded by cities. Like Louisbourg in Nova Scotia, Fort Union Trading Post NHS has retained much of its historic scene. Comparatively few intrusions prevent a modern visitor from imagining how the surrounding countryside must have looked during the mid–nineteenth century.

One exception is the railroad. Yet because of the proximity of the fort's ruins to an important rail line, Fort Union attracted the attention of Great Northern president and amateur historian Ralph Budd. Budd's elaborate celebrations in 1925 and 1926 encouraged thousands of North Dakotans and Montanans to conclude that the remains of something worth rebuilding lay beneath those low mounds near the state line. Talk of rebuilding the fort with the assistance of one or another New Deal agency perpetuated Budd's vision into the 1930s. When the fort site was endangered by the value of the gravel that lay beneath it, regional interest enabled Russell Reid to put its most important ten acres under the protection of the State Historical Society of North Dakota.

The rise of mass tourism after World War II and lobbying by a new group of history buffs—especially the indefatigable Ben Innis—eventually brought the Fort Union site into the National Park System in 1966. Nearly all area residents and many local and regional NPS officials endorsed reconstruction of the fort as the preferred method of park development. Even Park Service archaeologists and historians who investigated the site during the 1960s came away supporters of a reconstruction.

Nevertheless, in the more preservation-minded 1970s and 1980s reconstruction of historic buildings provoked strong opposition from influential officials at NPS headquarters in Washington. Previous attempts by Congress to rebuild structures of secondary importance on the basis of limited evidence, as well as the maintenance fiasco at Bent's Old Fort, hardened attitudes against the Fort Union project. To authorize and fund the reconstruction over the objection of the preservationist community required a remarkable conjunction of people and events: an economic recession, a powerful North Dakota congressional delegation with an above-average interest in the history of the site, the catalyst of Superintendent Paul Hedren, appointment of William Penn Mott as NPS director, and a sophisticated public relations and fundraising effort managed by the Friends of Fort Union.

Although some of the circumstances that led to the partial reconstruction were unique to Fort Union, there are lessons in its story for both proponents and opponents of historical reconstruction. Advocates of reconstruction should not underestimate the importance of a few persistent amateurs in perpetuating interest at Fort Union. At the same time, they should also note that the history buffs were unable to achieve the reconstruction by themselves. The Fort Union reconstruction effort demanded

Fig. 20. Aerial view of Fort Union NHS. Courtesy, Orville Loomer.

more planning, more expertise, and far more money than these amateurs could have ever hoped to marshal. Elected officials had to be courted assiduously to overcome the resistance of distant bureaucracies.

Furthermore, although supporters of the Fort Union reconstruction presented their project to the community as a potential stimulant for the local economy, they understood that those motivated by personal and even regional profit were at best erratic allies. The most effective champions of the reconstruction proved to be respected members of the community in need of a cause beyond themselves. Even Barry Mackintosh, a philosophical opponent of most reconstructions, has argued that the challenge of recreating nonexistent buildings perhaps impels reconstructionists as much as any economic motive: "People like doing it, and they like the results. It's fun!"[2]

Finally, advocates of the Fort Union reconstruction articulated why their structure was important enough to rebuild and phrased the argument in a way that resonated with their contemporaries. If the National Park System was oversupplied with any sort of historic site, it was glutted with forts. Yet Mark Andrews and others argued that Fort Union was unique because there the "white settler and the Native American worked side by side, traded in peace, and enjoyed each other's heritage."[3]

The reasons why reconstruction opponents failed to prevent the Fort Union reconstruction are also noteworthy. In part, their lack of success at the confluence stemmed from the inability of the National Park Service to speak with a single voice. The NPS *Management Policies* of 1975 virtually prohibited historical reconstructions, but Washington opponents of the Fort Union project could not enforce either their will or their rules on local and regional officials who supported rebuilding Fort Union. The Park Service career of Paul Hedren was advanced rather than retarded by his decision to back—and at times virtually lead—the pro-reconstruction forces.[4] The Fort Union reconstruction nicely illustrates Dwight Rettie's contention that the National Park Service, despite its uniforms, is "a remarkably undisciplined" organization allowing "uncommon leeway for policy and management variations. . . . Failed orders, ignored guidelines, and even overt insubordination seldom raise more than eyebrows."[5]

Another failure of the anti-reconstructionists was their inability to present their position effectively to area residents and the North Dakota congressional delegation. During the debate over the possible reconstruction of Fort Smith, Arkansas, the Park Service hired a University of Arkansas historian who determined that documentation for a proper reconstruction did not exist. Robert Utley, assistant director for park historic preservation, then took the historian's findings to the Arkansas congressional delegation and with some difficulty persuaded the politicians to support preservation of Fort Smith's ruins against the wishes of their constituents. Utley also attended a public meeting in the town of Fort Smith, where he denounced the proposed reconstruction as "a phony fort, a fraud, an untruth." At the time, the powerful John McClellan of Arkansas was chairman of the Senate Appropriations Committee; nevertheless, support for the reconstruction waned.[6]

Nothing similar was attempted by preservationists at the confluence. In the earlier stages of the Fort Union debate the Park Service might have offered North Dakotans a first-class visitor center with a complete range of contemporary gadgetry in exchange for the preservation of the ruins. That it did not may have been the result of a bureaucratic failure of imagination or simply the agency's underestimation of local frustration and the political clout of the North Dakota congressional delegation. Certainly no preservationists appeared in Williston to debate the merits of the proposal with the Friends of Fort Union. Ignoring opposition and postponing development had worked for Park Service officials elsewhere, but these tactics proved ineffective at the confluence.

Anti-reconstructionists also faced at least two important North Dakota politicians who had demonstrated genuine interest in the history of the site. Although the concern of Senators Andrews and Burdick was not on the same order as that of the two members of Congress who had forced the rebuilding of Forts Caroline and Vancouver after writing books about them, it was real enough for the North Dakotans to view skeptically the professional expertise claimed by preservationists. Anti-reconstructionists should have been especially wary of congressmen with an interest in history.

Two further lessons may be drawn from the reconstruction process itself. First, the strained relationship between archaeologists from the Midwest Archeological Center and the Friends of Fort Union stood in striking contrast to the enthusiastic cooperation achieved by the historic architects. Of course, many difficulties the archaeologists faced and many advantages the architects enjoyed were inherent in the situation and could not have been altered by a change in personalities. Nevertheless, it is interesting to speculate about what might have happened if the fine archaeologists who directed the Fort Union excavation had been less diffident about selling their dig to the local activists—or if the historical architects had made less of an effort to engage the interest of the community.[7]

Finally, one of the most unusual and successful features of the Fort Union reconstruction has been largely ignored, perhaps because it was unintended and a source of frustration to nearly everyone involved. At Fort Union the local community was allowed significant superintendence of the project because of its financial contribution. Holding public meetings to solicit advice was one thing. Allowing the community to become, in effect, a watchdog of an NPS development was another. At nearly every stage of the reconstruction lawyer/entrepreneur Marv Kaiser complained about the sluggishness, expense, and priorities of the Fort Union project, annoying any number of Park Service employees and saving the taxpayers thousands of dollars. Future Park Service projects might also be strengthened by requiring a similar financial contribution from the local community and a de facto oversight that would permit local leaders to ask pointed questions about the Park Service's procedures on a regular basis. Without doubt, it would be a professional's nightmare.

But just as history is too important to leave to historians, archaeology is too important to leave to archaeologists, and cultural resource management is too important to leave to cultural resource managers. In a democratic society the National Park Service should not be allowed fiat authority to decide how historic sites can be developed. The "public good" is not necessarily what a government agency decides is suitable for those who pay its salaries. Conflicts between lay and professional interest groups should continue to be decided by Congress on an ad hoc basis with little concern for philosophic consistency.

It is impossible to determine empirically if the Fort Union reconstruction achieved the success predicted for it by its supporters in the mid-1980s. Once the project was complete, both the Park Service and the community lost interest in determining such questions as whether the reconstruction was a better educational tool than some other form of interpretation or whether the reconstruction really did stimulate the local economy more than another form of park development might have done.

Nevertheless, the reconstruction at Fort Union Trading Post NHS may be considered a success on more subjective grounds. The reconstruction's $4.5 million cost was remarkably low and probably on a par with what would have been paid for an elaborate visitor center and the exhibition of the site's archaeological ruins. Furthermore, the reconstruction has been popular with visitors and will likely continue to help the public visualize the historic fort long after the electronic wizardry accompanying the ghosted house of Benjamin Franklin has become embarrassingly passé.[8]

Author Ian Frazier, who viewed the undeveloped park during the early 1980s, said that he liked the park better before the reconstruction—until he saw it. "Now I see I was wrong," he said. "I like this better." Likewise, Chief Historian Edwin Bearss, a critic of some earlier Park Service reconstructions, described the new Fort Union as "in a class by itself, a masterpiece . . . a world-class educational site." Even longtime reconstruction opponent Robert Utley declared that "without yielding on principle," he believed the reconstructed Fort Union had given him a "graphic feel" for the historic fort and "an exceptional interpretive experience."[9] Opponents of historical reconstructions may wish to keep their distance from the confluence of the Missouri and the Yellowstone. Especially viewed from outside the palisades and at dawn and dusk, the new Fort Union weakens one's resistance to the romance of the recreated past.

APPENDIX A   The "Old Tunnel"

SECRET TUNNELS, real and imaginary, have long fascinated tourists at historic sites. At the end of the nineteenth century those who visited Washington's headquarters at Valley Forge were shown into a "dismal subterranean chamber" and told of a tradition that a secret passage once led from it to the Schuylkill River, providing the general with a means of escape. In fact, the basement room was probably an early-nineteenth-century root cellar.[1]

About the same time, old-timers began to tell tales of a tunnel at Fort Union that had been used "for securing water during periods of Indian raids." Beginning in 1917 lawyer and antiquarian Charles Kessler, a resident of Helena, Montana (and later Los Angeles), wrote several letters to Mondak resident W. A. Shoup concerning the condition of the Fort Union ruins and the alleged tunnel. Shoup, proprietor of the Rex Saloon (aka the Rex Buffet), replied that he had made a "careful and minute search" for the tunnel and "found absolutely nothing that would indicate it at all." The tunnel, he wrote, was a "myth."[2]

Unfortunately, Kessler was also corresponding with Joseph Culbertson, a former Indian scout and son of Natawistacha and Alexander Culbertson, the successor of Kenneth McKenzie as Fort Union bourgeois. Joseph Culbertson was a believer in the Fort Union tunnel. In 1919 he claimed that it had been recently discovered by plowing, although he allowed "if one didn't know there had been a tunnel there, he could never tell the difference." Culbertson drew a map that showed the tunnel exiting in a southwesterly direction from the northwest corner of the fort—the ice house depression—and ending in a ravine that ran down to the Missouri.[3]

When Ralph Budd asked Kessler for information about Fort Union for his Upper Missouri Historical Expedition, Kessler passed on Culbertson's story. Budd, in turn, gave it to the writer of his Fort Union brochure, Frank Harper. Because the brochure was distributed free by the Great Northern railroad, the tunnel story gained wide circulation.[4]

No evidence of a tunnel was discovered during the archaeological excavations at Fort Union. In any case, it would have made little sense for men seeking an emergency supply of water to have run a shaft from the corner of the fort farthest from the river. What Culbertson mistook for a tunnel was almost certainly a gutter built not to collect water but to drain it away. Archaeologists rediscovered it during the 1980s. Because it was a historic feature and a drain was needed in the low northwest corner anyway, the historical architect incorporated it into the design, and it was rebuilt. Former superintendent Paul Hedren quipped that even if the gutter was just big enough to "pass a cat . . . a drain culvert is a tunnel anyway, no?"[5]

APPENDIX B The Snowden Bridge

THE BURLINGTON Northern Railroad bridge over the Missouri River connecting Roosevelt and Richland Counties, Montana, is known locally as the Snowden or Nohly Bridge.[1] Designed by the Kansas City firm of Waddell and Harrington, it was built in 1913 for the Great Northern Railway. At the turn of the twentieth century John Alexander Low Waddell (1854–1938) was perhaps the most prominent designer of railroad bridges in the United States. He invented and successfully introduced a high-clearance, vertical-lift bridge that was especially useful for railroad crossings over waterways where navigational clearance was necessary. Waddell based his design for the Snowden Bridge and its companion, the Fairview Bridge across the Yellowstone River, on the South Halsted Street Bridge in Chicago (1893), the first of his many structures of this type. When completed, the Snowden Bridge was the longest (1,159 feet) vertical-lift bridge in the world and had the second-largest clear opening (296 feet) of all movable bridges.[2]

The War Department considered the Missouri navigable and so required a movable span, but few large steamboats ventured that far up river after the turn of the century, and the bridge was rarely raised. A kerosene engine in the lift house above the movable span could lift it 43 feet in about thirty minutes, and a capstan also allowed it to be raised by hand. The bridge design permitted its steel towers and the 350-ton concrete counterweights they supported to be moved to other spans when the Missouri's navigational channel shifted, but the towers were never actually relocated. The vertical lift was last raised in 1935, and the lift machinery was removed in 1943.[3]

In preparation for the 1925 Upper Missouri Historical Expedition, Great Northern president Ralph Budd had a timber approach ramp and a plank roadbed built for vehicular and foot traffic. In 1927 the toll rates were 15 cents for horses and cattle, 25 cents for pedestrians, 50 cents for a car and driver, and 15 cents for additional male passengers over fifteen. Women and children were free, and male passengers were sometimes smuggled over in car trunks. The bridge was operated by tollmen until 1955, when an automatic signal system was installed and the fees were ended. By local custom, the signals were ignored, and the first person on the bridge had the right of way.[4]

Although a long bridge that allowed only one-way traffic and was shared with railroad trains should have been spectacularly hazardous, very few accidents occurred on the Snowden Bridge. A 1981 study attributed its good safety record to the fact that it was "so dangerous that it [was] safe." That is, drivers were extraordinarily cautious when crossing.[5]

Nevertheless, by the 1970s the roadbed and the approach roads to the bridge were obviously deteriorating. Holes appeared in the plank deck, and spikes protruded from the boards. Guard rails were too weak to prevent vehicles from plunging into the river in the event of an accident. Approach roads were rutted and washboarded from use by heavy farm and oil industry trucks, and since the approaches were much lower than the structure itself, there was zero visibility until cars were actually on the bridge.[6]

In June 1977 the Burlington Northern—undoubtedly contemplating its legal liability—publicized its intent to exclude vehicles from the Snowden Bridge. Because it provided the only crossing of the Missouri River for forty miles and because it was economically important to both farmers and the oil industry, the span was not closed to motor traffic until 1985, when the so-called MonDak Bridge was completed.[7]

The Snowden Bridge may have been the last bridge in the United States to accommodate rail and vehicular traffic on the same roadbed, and in 1977 it was nominated for the National Register of Historic Places by the Montana State Historic Preservation Review Board. The Burlington Northern Railroad objected to the nomination, which prevented its listing. Nevertheless, in 1982 the keeper of the National Register deemed it eligible for the register and thereby provided the Snowden Bridge with the same status as if it had been listed.[8]

ABBREVIATIONS

FOUS	Fort Union Trading Post National Historic Site
GN	Great Northern Railway Company
MWAC	Midwest Archeological Center, Lincoln, Nebraska
NHS	National Historic Site
RMR	Rocky Mountain Region
SHPO	State Historic Preservation Officer(s)
SHSND	State Historical Society of North Dakota, Bismarck
THRO	Theodore Roosevelt National Park
WASO	National Park Service, Washington DC office

NOTES

1. Historical Reconstructions

1. Charles B. Hosmer Jr., *Presence of the Past: A History of the Preservation Movement in the United States before Williamsburg* (New York: G. P. Putnam's Sons, 1965), 126–27, 146, 91–93; http://cal-parks.ca.gov/districts/goldrush/sfshp.htm [March 2000].

2. The reconstructed Hancock house was based on measured drawings made before destruction of the original structure—perhaps the first such drawings made of an old building in the history of the United States. The reconstruction once served as the headquarters of the New York State Historical Association. Hosmer, *Presence of the Past*, 40, 277.

3. Hosmer, *Presence of the Past*, 147–52. In 1963 the Theodore Roosevelt Association donated the site to the National Park Service. In 1919 the Illinois legislature charged its Department of Public Works with the responsibility of completing "a restoration of, as far as possible," all the buildings in Abraham Lincoln's New Salem; but the work did not begin until 1932. Hosmer, *Presence of the Past*, 147; see also Benjamin P. Thomas, *Lincoln's New Salem* (New York: Alfred A. Knopf, 1954), 154–58. How entrepreneurial ingenuity created a birthplace for Lincoln thirty years after his death is a tale amusingly retold in James W. Loewen, *Lies across America: What Our Historic Sites Get Wrong* (New York: New Press, 1999), 166–69. The birthplace cabin is more amiable fraud than reconstruction.

4. *New York Times*, 1 May 1923, 23; Hosmer, *Presence of the Past*, 150–51.

5. Charles B. Hosmer Jr., *Preservation Comes of Age: From Williamsburg to the National Trust, 1926–1949*, 2 vols. (Charlottesville: University Press of Virginia, 1981), 1:71; Carroll Van West, "Reconsidering Western Historic Sites," *North Dakota History* 62 (winter 1995): 6–7; Daniel J. Boorstin, "An American Style in Historical Monuments," in *Hidden History* (New York: Harper & Row, 1987), 153–57; William J. Murtagh, *Keeping Time: The History and Theory of Preservation in America* (New York: Ster-

ling Publishing Co., 1988), 3; Dwight T. Pitcaithley, "Pious Frauds: Federal Reconstruction Efforts during the 1930s," unpublished ms. in possession of author, 1989, 2; Shannon Ricketts, "Raising the Dead—Reconstruction within the Canadian Parks Service," CRM 15, no. 5 (1992): 15; Terry Maclean, *Louisbourg Heritage: From Ruins to Reconstruction* (Sydney, Nova Scotia: University College of Cape Breton Press, 1995), 83; quotation from Gordon Bennett, "Evoking the Past or Provoking the Gods? Some Observations on Period Reconstructions," CRM 15, no. 5 (1992): 21.

6. Barry Mackintosh, "Reconstruction: Controversy on Both Sides of the Border," CRM 15, no. 5 (1992): 13.

7. Mackintosh, "To Reconstruct or Not to Reconstruct: An Overview of NPS Policy and Practice," CRM 13, no. 1 (1990): 5; Pitcaithley, "Pious Frauds," 7. The Washington birthplace story is told in depressing detail by Hosmer, *Preservation Comes of Age*, 1:478–93. The Park Service obtained handmade bricks for the reconstruction but only by borrowing craftsmen from Colonial Williamsburg.

8. Mackintosh, "To Reconstruct or Not to Reconstruct," 5.

9. Mackintosh, "To Reconstruct or Not to Reconstruct," 6; Hosmer, *Preservation Comes of Age*, 1:620–26, 2:733–35 (quotation from 2:735).

10. The non–fort reconstruction was the Graff House, where Thomas Jefferson drafted the Declaration of Independence. Constance M. Greiff, *Independence: The Creation of a National Park* (Philadelphia: University of Pennsylvania Press, 1987), 263–64. Again, opposition within the Park Service was overwhelmed by political support, in this case generated by the private Independence Hall Association.

11. John F. Luzader, Louis Torres, and Orville W. Carroll, *Fort Stanwix* (Washington DC: GPO, 1976), v–vi; Gary W. Warshefski, Superintendent, to author, 29 September 1997. Fort Stanwix had the advantage of a very early congressional authorization (1935) and the support of the powerful senator Jacob Javits (D-NY) and Congressman Alexander Pirnie (R-NY), a politician "who answered his mail." Nevertheless, Fort Stanwix is something of an anomaly compared with other reconstructed forts. For instance, no politician seemed especially interested in its history, and the reconstruction was uniquely aided by the partial demolition of downtown Rome—including some historic structures—underwritten by the Housing and Home Finance Agency. "Alexander Pirnie," *Daily Sentinel* (Rome NY), 15 June 1982, 4; see also Michael James Kelleher, "Making History: Reconstructing Historic Structures in the National Park System," M.S. thesis, University of Pennsylvania, 1998, 45–56.

12. Mackintosh, "To Reconstruct or Not to Reconstruct," 6; Richard W. Sellars and Melody Webb, *An Interview with Robert M. Utley on the History of Historic Preservation in the National Park Service, 1947–1980* (Santa Fe: Southwest Cultural Resources Center, 1988), 33; telephone conversation with David Hansen, Curator, Fort Vancouver NHS, 4 September 1997; Jane T. Merritt, *The Administrative History of Fort Vancouver National Historic Site* (Seattle: National Park Service, Pacific Northwest

Region, 1993); *Fort Vancouver* (Washington DC: National Park Service, 1981), 125; Sarah Stage, "Hansen," *Encyclopedia of World Biography*, 14 (1987).

13. Barry Mackintosh, "Fort Scott National Historic Site," unpublished ms., National Register, History, and Education, WASO (second quotation); Sellars and Webb, *Interview with Utley*, 47; John Jacobs, *A Rage for Justice: The Passion and Politics of Phillip Burton* (Berkeley: University of California Press, 1995), 355 (first quotation); Leo E. Oliva, *Fort Scott: Courage and Conflict on the Border* (Topeka: Kansas State Historical Society, 1984), 81.

14. *Laudonniere and Fort Caroline: History and Documents* (Gainesville: University of Florida Press, 1964). Bennett, a conservative Democrat and World War II hero noted for his "straight arrow" ethical code, helped create the House Ethics Committee and wrote the legislation that made "In God We Trust" the national motto.

15. Mackintosh, "To Reconstruct or Not to Reconstruct," 6 (first quotation); Sellars and Webb, *Interview with Utley*, 54; Paul Ghiotto to author, 26 August 1997 (second quotation).

16. Merrill J. Mattes, "From Ruin to Reconstruction, 1920–1976," *Colorado Magazine* 54 (1977): 57–101.

17. Interview of Paul Hedren, 6 August 1996; Rick Cronenberger to author, 28 January 1998; see also remarks of John Lancaster at NPS Open Meeting, 12 April 1978, audiotape, Innis Papers; "Drive to Rebuild Historic Fort Union Heats Up," *Sidney Herald*, 15 July 1994; Sellars and Webb, *Interview with Utley*, 62; telephone conversation with Don Hill, Superintendent, Bent's Old Fort NHS, 10 September 1997.

18. Mackintosh, "To Reconstruct or Not to Reconstruct," 7; Carla Kelly, "Robert Utley: Carrying History to the People," M.A. thesis, Northeast Louisiana University, 1992.

19. Mackintosh, "To Reconstruct or Not to Reconstruct," 7; Utley to author, 14 July 1996.

20. Mackintosh, "The Case against Reconstruction," CRM 15, no. 1 (1992): 17; Sellars and Webb, *Interview with Utley*, 66.

21. Ricketts, "Raising the Dead," 18–19; Barry Mackintosh, "The NPS Experience with Reconstruction," in *Proceedings of the Canadian Parks Service Reconstruction Workshop: Hull, Quebec, 11–13 March 1992* (Ottawa: National Historic Sites, Parks Service, Environment Canada, 1993), 35.

22. Hosmer, *Preservation Comes of Age*, 1:482 (quotation); Kay Weeks, "Are We Losing Authenticity to Recover Appearances?" CRM 17, no. 5 (1994): 26; Richard Sellars and Dwight Pitcaithley, "Reconstructions: Expensive, Life-Size Toys?" CRM 2, no. 4 (1979): 6; Paul R. Huey, Letter to Editor, CRM 13, no. 1 (1990): 2; interview of Barry Mackintosh, 20 May 1996.

23. Mackintosh, "Case against Reconstruction," 18; Huey, Letter to Editor; Sellars and Pitcaithley, "Reconstructions," 6–7.

24. Mackintosh, "Case against Reconstruction," 17; Huey, Letter to Editor; V. Aubrey Neasham quoted in Hosmer, *Preservation Comes of Age*, 2:953; Dwight T. Pitcaithley, "Re-Creating the Past," CRM 17, no. 5 (1994): 28; Northrop Frye quoted in Bennett, "Evoking the Past," 21.

25. Good quoted in Mackintosh, "To Reconstruct or Not to Reconstruct," 6; Whitehill, "The Right of Cities to Be Beautiful," in *With Heritage So Rich* (New York: Random House, 1966), 53; Bennett, "Evoking the Past," 22; Huey, Letter to Editor; Ada Louise Huxtable, "Inventing American Reality," *New York Review of Books* 30 (3 December 1992): 25.

26. David Lowenthal, *The Past Is a Foreign Country* (Cambridge: Cambridge University Press, 1985), 280. Paradoxically, the American public is also "obsessed with original fabric" (Sellars and Webb, *Interview with Utley*, 67). Interpreters at virtually any historic house in North America will testify to visitors' continual inquiries about what is "original."

27. Robert M. Thorne and Melissa H. Reams, "Preservation Is a Use: Archaeological Site Stabilization and Protection as Primary Means of Reducing Resources Damage or Destruction," *Public Historian* 13 (summer 1991): 142. Site burial may cause increased compression, an improved habitat for microorganisms and burrowing mammals, and changes in the freeze/thaw cycle, level of groundwater, pH characteristics, and presence or absence of air. Ivor Noël Hume ironically records his satisfaction at having deliberately left several archaeological sites unexcavated as "a gift to archaeologists yet unborn"—only to have one of them obliterated by clear-cut logging just eleven years later. Hume, *Martin's Hundred*, rev. ed. (Charlottesville: University Press of Virginia, 1991), 361–62.

28. Liping Zhu, *Fort Union National Monument: An Administrative History* (Santa Fe: Southwest Cultural Resources Center, 1992), 37, 39, 41, 45. Application of silicone to the adobe was thought to protect the ruins but actually weakened them by trapping moisture inside the structures. The white silicone also changed the appearance of the ruins.

29. John Robbins, *Historic Structures Report: Ruins Stabilization, Architectural Data, Fort Bowie National Historic Site, Cochise County, Arizona* (Denver: Denver Service Center, National Park Service, 1983), 8, 51; see also Robert Hartzler, "Holding Down the Forts: The Army, Adobe, and Preservation," CRM 22, no. 6 (1999): 55–58. Incompatibility of the materials hastened erosion of historic adobe and stone ruins, and in the late 1970s the nonhistoric materials were removed—with far more care and documentation than when they had been applied. A special irony of the Fort Bowie case is that its interpretive theme was supposed to be "historical abandonment," that is, the ruins were to be preserved as ruins. The application of nonhistoric materials to original fabric not only accelerated the fabric's deterioration; it prevented the site from looking abandoned.

30. An appreciative article in the *Chronicle of Higher Education* 40 (16 February

1994): A6, said that the chapel looked "like an archaeological ruin." Perhaps the most sympathetic perspective on the stark remains is that of Curator Vivien Rose, who said that in "the evening, when the Chapel is lit, there is a great light that shines out from it. To my eye, it is stirring and inspirational, perhaps because it is not grand architecture." Vivien Rose to author, 10 September 1997.

31. Mackintosh, "NPS Experience with Reconstruction," 34; Sellars and Webb, *Interview with Utley*, 24, 65; Rodd L. Wheaton, "Considering Reconstruction as an Educational Tool," CRM 15, no. 1 (1992): 18.

32. Wheaton, "Reconstruction as an Educational Tool," 16; cf. Billy Garrett, "Clarifying Stories for Public Education," CRM 17, no. 5 (1994): 27–28; Boorstin, "American Style," 154–55; Cindy S. Aron, "The Education-Entertainment Continuum: A Historical Perspective," AHA *Perspectives* (March 1995): 5–6.

33. Sellars and Webb, *Interview with Utley*, 56; Pitcaithley, "Re-Creating the Past," 28; Bennett, "Evoking the Past," 22. As Daniel Boorstin has noted, latent within every professional creed is the "article of faith" that "the Profession really exists for the sake of the professionals." "The Amateur Spirit and Its Enemies," in *Hidden History*, 222–23.

34. David Lowenthal, *Possessed by the Past: The Heritage Crusade and the Spirit of History* (New York: Free Press, 1996), 102; David Hackett Fischer, "Hubris But No History," review of the film *The Patriot*, *New York Times*, 1 July 2000, A13.

35. C. V. Wedgwood, *The Sense of the Past* (New York: Collier, 1967), 24–25; Lowenthal, *Possessed by the Past*, 114.

2. Historic Fort Union

1. Elwyn B. Robinson, *History of North Dakota* (Lincoln: University of Nebraska Press, 1966), 86; Elbert B. Smith, *Magnificent Missourian: The Life of Thomas Hart Benton* (Philadelphia: J. B. Lippincott, 1958), 80–82.

2. Ray Allen Billington, *Westward Expansion: A History of the American Frontier* (New York: Macmillan, 1967), 459–62; Erwin N. Thompson, *Fort Union Trading Post: Fur Trade Empire on the Upper Missouri* (Williston ND: Fort Union Association, 1994), 1–7.

3. *Dictionary of American Biography*, 12:94, s.v. "Kenneth Mackenzie"; Thompson, *Fort Union Trading Post*, 4, 34.

4. The date of Fort Union's construction is a matter of debate: see Thompson, *Fort Union Trading Post*, 10–11; Barton H. Barbour, *Fort Union and the Upper Missouri Fur Trade* (Norman: University of Oklahoma Press, 2001), 39–43; and William J. Hunt Jr., "'At the Yellowstone . . . to Build a Fort': Fort Union Trading Post, 1828–1833," in *Fort Union Fur Trade Symposium Proceedings, September 13–15, 1990* (Williston ND: Friends of Fort Union Trading Post, 1994), 7–9. I have followed Hunt.

5. Hiram Martin Chittenden, *The American Fur Trade of the Far West*, 2 vols. (New York: Barnes & Noble, 1935), 2:933–34.

6. Thompson, *Fort Union Trading Post*, 12. Grant Marsh, who spent most of his life as a steamboat captain on the Missouri, said that Fort Union's gravel bank was the only one he knew of on the river. W. A. Shoup to Charles Kessler, 31 December 1917, Kessler Papers, William Andrews Clark Memorial Library, UCLA.

7. Hunt, "At the Yellowstone," 15.

8. Chittenden, *American Fur Trade*, 1:385, 2:934. The fort remained a parallelogram rather than a rectangle, but the angle of deviation was small.

9. Hunt, "At the Yellowstone," 17–19.

10. Henry Markowitz, ed., *American Indians* (Pasadena: Salem Press, 1995), 1:78.

11. Chittenden, *American Fur Trade*, 1:336; Harry Sinclair Drago, *The Steamboaters* (New York: Dodd, Mead, 1967), 123–25.

12. Drago, *Steamboaters*, 127; Donald Jackson, *Voyages of the Steamboat Yellow Stone* (Norman: University of Oklahoma Press, 1985); George Catlin, *Letters and Notes on the Manners, Customs, and Condition of the North American Indians*, 2 vols. (London: Tosswill & Myers, 1841), 1:20–21.

13. *Journal of Rudolph Friderich Kurz*, Smithsonian Institution, Bureau of American Ethnology, Bulletin 115 (Washington DC: Government Printing Office, 1937), 234; Ben Innis, *Sagas of the Smoky-Water* (Williston ND: Centennial Press, 1985), 101–3; David J. Wishart, *The Fur Trade of the American West, 1807–1840: A Geographical Synthesis* (Lincoln: University of Nebraska Press, 1979), 82; Steven Leroy DeVore, *Beads of the Bison Robe Trade: The Fort Union Trading Collection* (Williston ND: Friends of Fort Union Trading Post, 1992), 53–57.

14. Leonard Lee Rue III, *The World of the Beaver* (Philadelphia: J. B. Lippincott, 1964), 136; Paul Chrisler Phillips, *The Fur Trade*, 2 vols. (Norman: University of Oklahoma Press, 1961), 2:466–67.

15. Robinson, *History of North Dakota*, 94; Phillips, *Fur Trade*, 2:403; Innis, *Sagas*, 101. Indians used buffalo skins for tepees, parfleches, and containers, but whites did not use bison hide for commercial leather until 1871, after the destruction of Fort Union. David A. Dary, *The Buffalo Book: The Full Saga of the American Animal* (Chicago: Swallow Press, 1974), 92–95; Billington, *Westward Expansion*, 670; see also Innis, *Sagas*, 101.

16. Thompson, *Fort Union Trading Post*, 16–17, 43, 51, 59; Charles Larpenteur, *Forty Years a Fur Trader on the Upper Missouri* (Lincoln: University of Nebraska Press, 1989), 67–70.

17. Larpenteur, *Forty Years*, 81. Nine Deschamps were killed without any legal consequence. See Edwin Thompson Denig, *Five Indian Tribes of the Upper Missouri* (Norman: University of Oklahoma, 1961), 178–79.

18. Catlin, *North American Indians*, 1:27; Thompson, *Fort Union Trading Post*, 53–54, 58 (quotation), 60.

19. Kurz, *Journal*, 124, 199–200.

20. Thompson, *Fort Union Trading Post*, 24–25; Larpenteur, *Forty Years*, 85.

21. For examples of violence at Fort Union, see Thompson, *Fort Union Trading Post*, 79; Larpenteur, *Forty Years*, 80–84, 134–35, 145–46. David T. Courtwright, *Violent Land: Single Men and Social Disorder from the Frontier to the Inner City* (Cambridge: Harvard University Press, 1996), 32–34.

22. Denig, *Five Indian Tribes*, 157–58, 54, 116–17, 132, 148, 77. The Gauche escaped, having earlier survived the disease.

23. Larpenteur, *Forty Years*, 109–12 (quotations from 109–10); Denig, *Five Indian Tribes*, 71–73; Chittenden, *American Fur Trade*, 2:619; Clyde D. Dollar, "The High Plains Smallpox Epidemic of 1837–38," *Western Historical Quarterly* 8 (1977): 15–38; Arno Karlen, *Man and Microbes* (New York: G. P. Putnam's Sons, 1995), 105. The mechanism for the spread of the disease from the *St. Peter* to the tribes of the upper Missouri is controverted. Michael K. Trimble, *An Ethnohistorical Interpretation of the Spread of Smallpox in the Northern Plains Utilizing Concepts of Disease Ecology* (Lincoln NE: J & L Reprint Co., 1986), provides four possible scenarios for transmission of the virus at Fort Clark, which proved so deadly that the introduction of smallpox at Fort Union may have been superfluous. Fort Union had the better chroniclers in Larpenteur and Denig and thereby probably achieved more notoriety than it deserved.

24. Chittenden, *American Fur Trade*, 2:612–19, makes the case against the company; Bernard DeVoto, *Across the Wide Missouri* (New York: Houghton Mifflin, 1957), argues that Chittenden's charges are anachronistic; see also Dollar, "High Plains Smallpox Epidemic," 15–16. Alfred W. Crosby, *Ecological Imperialism: The Biological Expansion of Europe, 900–1900* (Cambridge: Cambridge University Press, 1986), 197 (quotation).

25. Chittenden, *American Fur Trade*, 1:23–31; U.S. Statutes at Large, 4:729–35; Robinson, *History of North Dakota*, 95; Wishart, *Fur Trade*, 69–71.

26. Chittenden, *American Fur Trade*, 1:363; Thompson, *Fort Union Trading Post*, 31 (quotation). Ironically, Cass was a staunch opponent of drink. At a treaty signing during his earlier years he had poured on the ground the alcohol that was to have celebrated the agreement.

27. Chittenden, *American Fur Trade*, 1:26–27; Larpenteur, *Forty Years*, 162–65; Kurz, *Journal*, 177; Leslie V. Tischauser, "Alcoholism," in *American Indians*, ed. Harvey Markowitz (Pasadena: Salem Press, 1995), 19–20; see also Peter C. Mancall, *Deadly Medicine: Indians and Alcohol in Early America* (Ithaca: Cornell University Press, 1995); William E. Unrau, *White Man's Wicked Water: The Alcohol Trade and Prohibition in Indian Country, 1802–1892* (Lawrence: University Press of Kansas, 1996); Ian Frazier, *Great Plains* (New York: Farrar, Straus, Giroux, 1989), 23.

28. Innis, *Sagas*, 115–17. The description originally appeared in Maria Audubon, *Audubon and His Journals* (1897).

29. Chittenden, *American Fur Trade*, 1:379, 383; John E. Sunder, *The Fur Trade on the Upper Missouri, 1840–1860* (Norman: University of Oklahoma Press, 1965), 52, 156–57, 177, 202.

30. Mike Foster, *Strange Genius: The Life of Ferdinand Vandeveer Hayden* (Niwot CO: Roberts Rinehart, 1994), 69, 132, 351.

31. C. A. Armstrong, "Ground Water Resources at Fort Union Trading Post National Historic Site, North Dakota–Montana," U.S. Geological Survey, 1969 [Fort Union Trading Post NHS Library]; Denig, *Five Indian Tribes*, 65. The Fort Union Formation has since been subdivided into the Fort Union Group of formations. John P. Bluemle, "Guide to the Geology of Northwestern North Dakota," North Dakota Geological Survey, 1980.

32. Armstrong, "Ground Water," 4; Thompson, *Fort Union Trading Post*, 47.

33. F. V. Hayden, *Sun Pictures of Rocky Mountain Scenery* (New York: J. Bien, 1870), 40; Denig, *Five Indian Tribes*, 49.

34. Reuben Gold Thwaites, ed., *Original Journals of the Lewis and Clark Expedition, 1804–1806* (New York: Dodd, Mead, 1904–5), 5:237, 323; Thompson, *Fort Union Trading Post*, 40; Denig in Innis, *Sagas*, 116.

35. Kurz, *Journal*, 168; Thompson, *Fort Union Trading Post*, 23; Denig in Innis, *Sagas*, 118.

36. Kurz, *Journal*, 168; Larpenteur, *Forty Years*, 163; Denig, *Five Indian Tribes*, 67; Richard Wood, ed., *Weather of U.S. Cities* (New York: Gale Research, 1995), 716. Monthly precipitation between November and February averages only a half-inch per month.

37. Wood, *Weather*, 716; Denig, *Five Indian Tribes*, 68.

38. Thompson, *Fort Union Trading Post*, 79–80; Denig, *Five Indian Tribes*, 36–39.

39. Drago, *Steamboaters*, 158.

40. Henry A. Boller, *Among the Indians: Eight Years in the Far West, 1858–1866* (Philadelphia: T. Ellwood Zell, 1868), 371.

41. Robinson, *History of North Dakota*, 99; Sunder, *Fur Trade*, 252.

42. Barbour, *Fort Union*, 216.

43. Sunder, *Fur Trade*, 220, 235; Barbour, *Fort Union*, 217–21.

44. Barbour, *Fort Union*, 227; Thompson, *Fort Union Trading Post*, 84, 90–91.

45. Larpenteur Journal, vol. 3, Larpenteur Papers, Minnesota Historical Society.

3. The Neighboring Ruin

1. Unless otherwise noted, information in this section is derived from Robert M. Utley, "The Military Frontier on the Northern Plains, 1850–1900," and Ronald Phil Warner, "A History of Fort Buford, 1866–1895," in *Fort Buford and the Military Fron-*

tier on the Northern Plains, 1850–1900, ed. Larry Remele (Bismarck: State Historical Society of North Dakota, 1987), and Ben Innis, *Sagas of the Smoky-Water* (Williston ND: Centennial Press, 1985).

2. Robert M. Utley, *The Lance and the Shield: The Life and Times of Sitting Bull* (New York: Random House, 1993), 71.

3. David Hilger, "Reminiscences of Fort Union, Dakota Territory, in 1867," State Historical Society of North Dakota.

4. Paul L. Hedren, "Sitting Bull's Surrender at Fort Buford: An Episode in American History," *North Dakota History* 62 (fall 1995): 2–15.

5. Warner, "History of Fort Buford," 55; *Statutes at Large*, 31, § 484, 56th Cong., 1st. sess., 19 May 1900; Ralph W. Hidy et al., *The Great Northern Railway: A History* (Boston: Harvard Business School Press, 1988), 58–60; Albro Martin, *James J. Hill and the Opening of the Northwest* (New York: Oxford University Press, 1976), 346–47.

6. James Stuart, "Adventure on the Upper Missouri," *Contributions to the Historical Society of Montana* 1 (1876): 80–89; Dan L. Thrapp, *Encyclopedia of Frontier Biography* (Glendale CA: Arthur H. Clark Co., 1988), 3:1380–82.

7. Washington Matthews, Post Surgeon, Fort Buford, Records of the Adjutant General's Office, Record Group 94, National Archives; Luther S. Kelly, *"Yellowstone Kelly": The Memoirs of Luther S. Kelly* (New Haven: Yale University Press, 1926), 53.

8. John S. Gray, "Last Rites for Lonesome Charley Reynolds," *Montana: The Magazine of Western History* 13 (summer 1963): 47, 49; *The Field Diary of Lt. Edward Settler Godfrey* . . . (Portland OR: Champoeg Press, 1957), 53 (18 September 1876). The following year a future army chief of staff noted the remains of the former "emporium of the Northwest, now destroyed." Hugh Lenox Scott, *Some Memories of a Soldier* (New York: Century Co., 1928), 83.

9. Gray, "Last Rites," 47. It is also possible that the vegetables had been grown by soldiers at Fort Buford. In October 1875 a fifty-man fatigue detail built a dam in Garden Coulee "for purposes of irrigation." Washington Matthews, Post Surgeon, Fort Buford, Records of the Adjutant General's Office, National Archives.

10. James P. Kimball, "Descriptions of Military Posts: Fort Buford, Dakota Territory" (1870), in Innis, *Sagas*, 25 (quotations); Steven Leroy DeVore and William J. Hunt Jr., *Fort Union Trading Post National Historic Site (32WI17): Material Cultural Reports, Part X: Native American Burials and Artifacts* (Lincoln NE: Midwest Archeological Center, National Park Service, 1994), 23–25, 30.

11. Unless otherwise indicated, information about Crow-Flies-High village is taken from Gregory L. Fox, *A Late Nineteenth Century Village of a Band of Dissident Hidatsa: The Garden Coulee Site (32WI18)* (Lincoln NE: J & R Reprint Co., 1988). The work includes fourteen contemporary documents about the Crow-Flies-High band.

12. Carl G. Flagstad, "Old Diary Outlines Indian Band's Exile," *Minot (ND) Daily News*, 16 August 1987, B4. Crow Flies High was also known as Crow Fly, Crow Flies,

Crow That Flies High, Crow Fly High, Raven Ascending, and Heart. Fox, *Garden Coulee Site*, 10.

13. Fox, *Garden Coulee Site*, 10–13; Flagstad, "Old Diary."

14. Fox, *Garden Coulee Site*, 13–14, 15, 16, 38, 41, 64, 66–67, 90.

15. Flagstad, "Old Diary"; Fox, *Garden Coulee Site*, 14, 16.

16. Fox, *Garden Coulee Site*, 44–50.

17. DeVore and Hunt, *Burials and Artifacts*, 17–22.

18. For instance, N. J. Collette to Ralph Budd, 25 June 1925, Great Northern Files (11619), Minnesota Historical Society; "Robert C. Matthews," in "Biographical Sketches of North Dakota Pioneers," ed. Orin G. Libby, in *Collections of the State Historical Society* 7 (1925): 99.

19. Fox, *Garden Coulee Site*, 16, 18; J. N. G. Whistler to the Assistant Adjutant General, 20 September 1884; deposition of Crow Flies High before Indian agent Abram J. Gifford and interpreter Joseph Packineau, 28 June 1886, in Fox, *Garden Coulee Site*, 114, 119; Innis, *Sagas*, 324, 326.

20. Joseph Culbertson Sr., "Joseph Culbertson, the Boy Scout," mimeograph (1957), 30, in Fort Union Trading Post NHS Library; *Washburn (ND) Leader*, 31 March 1894, 1. Crow Flies High died of pneumonia on the Fort Berthold reservation in 1900.

21. Innis, *Sagas*, 242–45.

22. Ray Allen Billington, *Westward Expansion: A History of the American Frontier* (New York: Macmillan, 1967), 716.

23. Bruce Nelson, *Land of the Dacotahs* (Minneapolis: University of Minnesota Press, 1946), 244–45.

24. Innis, *Sagas*, 424; Ian Frazier, *Great Plains* (New York: Farrar, Straus, Giroux, 1989), 21–22. Williston might have done worse for a namesake. D. Willis James (1832–1907) was a genuinely good man of impeccable character, a secret philanthropist, who Charles Parkhurst said loved everything in the universe "from God down to the newsboy." He was also one of the few men who could stand up to James J. Hill. *Dictionary of American Biography*, 9:573–74, s.v. "Daniel Willis James"; Martin, *James J. Hill*, 321–22.

25. J. G. Houston, "Buford—Just Another Ghost Town," and Marlene Eide, "Buford," in Williams County Historical Society, *The Wonder of Williams County, North Dakota*, 2 vols. (n.p.: Williams County Historical Society, 1975), 1:433–35.

26. Alice M. Sweetman, "Mondak: Planned City of Hope Astride Montana–Dakota Border," *Montana* 15 (autumn 1965): 12–13; T. R. Forbes, "Mondak and Its History," *Yellowstone News*, 7 September 1912; interview of Ralph Chase, 25 June 1996.

27. Sweetman, "Mondak," 12–16; Historical Research Associates, "Testing and Evaluation of Cultural Resource Site 24RV102, The Mondak Townsite, Roosevelt County, Montana" (1982) [Fort Union Trading Post NHS Library], 33–37.

28. R. S. Nutt, "Montana Centennial News," June 1963, typescript in Park History Files, National Register, History, and Education, WASO; "Life History of Mrs. Bertha (Josephsen) Anderson," edited typescript in Fort Union Trading Post NHS Library, ms. at Mon–Dak Heritage Center, Sidney MT.

29. "Java," in *Courage Enough: Mon-Dak Family Histories* (Sidney MT: Mondak Historical and Arts Society, 1975), 349–50; Bill Shemorry, *More Lost Tales of Old Dakota* (Williston ND: privately published, 1988), 327. The Java post office opened in 1907 (*Yellowstone News*, 27 July 1907). The Missouri has encroached on the town site, and today there are no visible remnants of Java.

30. Chase interview; Ralph Chase, "Mondak," in *Courage Enough*, 355; John O. Lancaster to Alice Fryslie, 10 February 1977, H22 (FOUS), THRO; "Java," 350. On the Snowden Bridge, see appendix B.

31. Leonard Lund, "Only Three 'Skeletons' of Lusty Past Remain at Mondak," *Minot Daily News*, 2 December 1972; Chase, "Mondak," 355; Chase interview.

32. Sweetman, "Mondak," 16; "Testing and Evaluation of Cultural Resource Site 24RVI02," 36, 41. One former resident remembered that "the prostitutes were 'good girls' and made an effort not to be intrusive by dress or manner during their visits to town" (43). The archeological remains of the bawdy houses are also located within FOUS boundaries. Ralph Chase, "Mondak Celebration of 1925: A Paper Boy's Last Walk," August 1997, typescript in possession of author.

33. Sweetman, "Mondak," 16; Otto Seel quoted in "Testing and Evaluation of Cultural Resource Site 24RVI02," 41.

34. *Yellowstone News*, 10 February 1906; see also 5 March 1910, 30 November 1912, 13 September 1913, 17 April 1915, 6 November 1915; and "Willard and Nellie Saxton," in *Courage Enough*, 457.

35. *Yellowstone News*, 12 April 1913; Sweetman, "Mondak," 23–24.

36. *Yellowstone News*, 13 January 1913, 14 December 1912, 6 September 1913, 24 October 1914; Lund, "Only Three 'Skeletons.'" The railroad crossing was a very dangerous one as well. *Fairview (MT) News*, 13 March 1924.

37. *Yellowstone News*, 4 February 1905; Chase interview; Sweetman, "Mondak," 16; "Java," 349.

38. *Yellowstone News*, 16 November 1912; Sweetman, "Mondak," 18; see also Robert W. Lind, *Brother Van: Montana Pioneer Circuit Rider* (Helena MT: Falcon Press, 1992); *Yellowstone News*, 7 September 1912.

39. John F. Neihardt, *The River and I* (Lincoln: University of Nebraska Press, 1968), 258–59, 271.

40. W. A. Shoup to Charles Kessler, 19 March 1918, Kessler Papers, William Andrews Clark Memorial Library, UCLA.

41. Kate Hammond Fogarty, "A Visit to Old Fort Union," undated typescript, Kate Hammond Fogarty Papers, Montana Historical Society.

42. Fogarty, "Visit"; W. A. Shoup to Charles Kessler, 31 December 1917.

43. *Yellowstone News*, 6 January 1912; Shemorry, *More Lost Tales*, 324–25.

44. Fred Smith, "Remembering a Forgotten Place," *Bismarck Tribune*, 15 June 1986, 1C; Chase interview.

45. *Yellowstone News*, 21 June 1919.

46. *Yellowstone News*, 20 May 1905.

47. Chase interview; Michael P. Malone and Richard B. Roeder, *Montana: A History of Two Centuries* (Seattle: University of Washington Press, 1976), 204.

48. "Testing and Evaluation of Cultural Resource Site 24RVI02," 43–44; Sweetman, "Mondak," 22, 27. In 1913 North Dakotans owned 13,075 automobiles; in 1920, 92,000. Elywn B. Robinson, *History of North Dakota* (Lincoln: University of Nebraska Press, 1966), 379.

49. *Yellowstone News*, 8 July 1916, 23 December 1916, 3 March 1917, 7 July 1917, 30 March 1918; Chase interview; "Testing and Evaluation of Cultural Resource Site 24RVI02," 37.

50. Malone and Roeder, *Montana*, 190–91. The profit to the promoters came from organizing, for a fee, the necessary petition signings and elections necessary to break up the old counties. Of course, the multiplication of county governments cost the taxpayers dearly in bad times. Sweetman, "Mondak," 26; "Fort Union Loses Stockyard," *Circle (MT) Banner*, 15 November 1929.

51. *Circle Banner*, 15 November 1929; Leonard Lund, "Only Three 'Skeletons'"; Chase, "Mondak," 356; *Fairview News*, 12 March 1925, 23 April 1925.

52. *Williston Herald*, 4 October 1928, 1. The local legend that sparks from Sousa's train started the fire is not confirmed by contemporary newspapers. But the *Herald* reported that another fire, which began about the same time in Trenton, fifteen miles east of Mondak, was started by the special train.

In 1929 the Great Northern removed the stockyards from Mondak to Buford. The school closed in the 1930s and was dismantled after World War II for its brick and maple. *Circle Banner*, 15 November 1929; Leonard Lund, "Only Three 'Skeletons."

4. Ralph Budd

1. Richard C. Overton, *Perkins/Budd: Railway Statesmen of the Burlington* (Westport CT: Greenwood Press, 1982), 91; Overton, "Ralph Budd," *Dictionary of American Biography*, Supplement 7, 89.

2. Overton, "Ralph Budd"; Albro Martin, *Railroads Triumphant: The Growth, Rejection, and Rebirth of a Vital American Force* (New York: Oxford Press, 1992), 299–300; Michael P. Malone, *James J. Hill: Empire Builder of the Northwest* (Norman: Univer-

sity of Oklahoma Press, 1996), 266; Albro Martin, "Ralph Budd," in *Railroads in the Age of Regulation, 1900–1980,* ed. Keith L. Bryant Jr. (New York: Facts on File, 1988), 56–60. See also the appreciative treatment of Budd and his historical expeditions in Michael Kammen, *In the Past Lane: Historical Perspectives on American Culture* (New York: Oxford University Press, 1997), 132–39.

3. Overton, *Perkins/Budd,* 92–93; *Current Biography,* 1940, 121, s.v. "Ralph Budd"; *New York Times,* 3 February 1962, 21.

4. *Current Biography,* 1940, 121; Overton, *Perkins/Budd,* 93; W. B. Overson to Ralph Budd, 29 May 1925, Great Northern President Subject Files (11337), Minnesota Historical Society. (Original file numbers are cited because they were often penciled on the documents.)

5. Elwyn B. Robinson, *History of North Dakota* (Lincoln: University of Nebraska Press, 1966), 241; Ralph W. Hidy et al., *The Great Northern Railway: A History* (Boston: Harvard Business School Press, 1988), 99–103. In "dry farming" farmers were supposed to bring moisture to the surface by deep plowing and then work the soil to maintain a dust mulch that would prevent evaporation. Malone, *James J. Hill,* 236.

6. Malone, *James J. Hill,* 200 (quotation), 327–70; Budd, "Transportation in North Dakota—Past and Present" (1928), in *Perkins/Budd,* 97; Martin, *Railroads Triumphant,* 350, 299–300.

7. Albro Martin, "Louis W. Hill, Sr.," in Bryant, *Railroads,* 200; Dorothy M. Johnson, "Carefree Youth and Dudes in Glacier," *Montana* 25 (summer 1975): 48–49; Roberta Carkeek Cheney, "Montana Place Names," *Montana* 20 (winter 1970): 50–51; Hidy et al., *Great Northern Railway,* 182: "Thus, for instance, Kilroy became Spotted Robe, Lubec became Rising Wolf, Cadmus was changed to Gunsight, and Egan to Grizzly."

8. Overton, *Perkins/Budd,* 91; Budd to M. L. Wilson, 8 December 1924; "G.N. Ry Co. Restoration of Palisade & Bastions of American Fur Cos Fort Union ND at Junction of Yellowstone and Missouri Rivers," 4 October 1924, GN Files (11337).

9. W. R. Ballord to A. H. Hogeland, 8 November 1924; Thomas D. McMahon to A. H. Hogeland, 5 November 1924; A. H. Hogeland to Ralph Budd, 6 November 1924, GN Files (11337).

10. Budd to A. H. Hogeland, 13 November 1924; Hogeland to Budd, 28 November 1924, GN Files (11337). Commemorative cairns were popular at the time. Louisbourg received four from the Canadian government in 1926. Terry Maclean, *Louisbourg Heritage: From Ruins to Reconstruction* (Sydney, Nova Scotia: University College of Cape Breton Press, 1995), 16.

11. Robinson, *History of North Dakota,* 374.

12. *National Cyclopedia of American Biography,* 55:146–47; Hidy et al., *Great Northern Railway,* 190–91; M. L. Wilson to Budd, 28 January 1925, GN Files (11337). Milburn Lincoln Wilson (1885–1969) was undersecretary of agriculture, 1937–40, and director of the Federal Extension Service, 1940–53.

13. F. A. Weinrich to Wilson, 13 November 1924; Budd to L. C. Gilman (telegram), 28 May 1925; Gilman to Budd, 21 May 1925, GN Files (11337).

14. Weinrich to Wilson, 26 December 1924, GN Files (11337); Robert P. Wilkins, "Orin Grant Libby," *Dictionary of American Biography*, Supplement 5, 429–30; George F. Shafer, "Dr. Orin Grant Libby," *North Dakota History* 12 (July 1945): 107–10.

15. Robinson, *History of North Dakota*, 509–10; *Williston Herald*, 16 July 1925, 10; see also Budd to Wilson, 15 December 1924, and Wilson to Budd, 26 December 1924, GN Files (11337). On Willard Bella Overson (1872–1951), see Clement Augustus Lounsberry, *North Dakota: History and People* (Chicago: S. J. Clark, 1917), 3:30–33, and obituary, *Williston Herald*, 19 March 1951, 1.

16. Budd to Wilson, 18 December 1924; Wilson to Budd, 26 December 1924, GN Files (11337).

17. Wilson to Budd, 4 December 1924; Wilson to Budd, 28 January 1925, GN Files (11337).

18. Overson to Budd, 14 February 1925; L. C. Gilman to Budd (telegram), 17 May 1925; Gilman to Budd, 21 May 1925; Gilman to Budd, 28 May 1925; Budd to James T. Maher, 27 June 1925, GN Files (11337).

19. Budd to Wilson, 8 December 1934, GN Files (11337); William J. Murtagh, *Keeping Time: The History and Theory of Preservation in America* (New York: Sterling Publishing Co., 1988), 30, 37–38; Charles B. Hosmer Jr., *Preservation Comes of Age: From Williamsburg to the National Trust, 1926–1949*, 2 vols. (Charlottesville: University Press of Virginia, 1981), 1:18, 175; James M. Lindgren, "'A New Professionalism' and Conflicting Concepts of Material Culture in the Late Nineteenth and Early Twentieth Centuries," *Public Historian* 18 (spring 1996): 41–60; Patricia West, *Domesticating History: The Political Origins of America's House Museums* (Washington DC: Smithsonian Institution Press, 1999), 101–3.

20. Hosmer, *Preservation*, 1:471–72.

21. Budd to M. L. Wilson, 8 December 1924; W. P. Kenney to Budd, 31 January 1925, GN Files (11337). Kenney complained that there "seemed to be a general lack of knowledge that there ever was a Fort Union and, of course, that is to be expected."

22. *New York Times*, 22 January 1925, 19; Hosmer, *Preservation*, 1:473.

23. Hidy et al., *Great Northern Railway*, 181–82; *Fairview (MT) News*, 22 May 1924.

24. Speech of Ralph Budd at Two Medicine Lake, 20 July 1925, typescript; T. A. Black to Budd, 20 August 1925; see also Clara S. Paine to Budd, 3 July 1925, GN Files (11619).

25. The best summary of the expedition is the contemporary report by the distinguished American historian and University of Minnesota professor Solon J. Buck, "The Upper Missouri Historical Expedition," *Mississippi Valley Historical Review* 12 (December 1925): 385–91. Edmond L. DeLestry, "Perpetuating Historic Events,"

Western Magazine 26 (August 1925): 3–5; "Memorandum," in GN Files (11619), folder 6; Budd to W. P. Kenney, 3 May 1926 (11620); "Hugh Lenox Scott," *Dictionary of American Biography,* Supplement 1, 651–52.

26. See Budd to C. O. Jenks, 9 July 1925, and other correspondence in GN Files (11619, folder 8).

27. Budd to Grace Flandreau, 2 June 1925, GN Files (11337); Buck, "Upper Missouri Historical Expedition," 386.

28. Cheney, "Montana Place Names," 50; Douglas A. Wick, *North Dakota Place Names* (Bismarck: Hedemarken Collectibles, 1988); C. O. Jenks to Budd, 20 February 1925, GN Files (11437); "Circular," 25 February 1925, GN Files (11337); "Circular," 9 May 1925, GN Files (11619); *Minneapolis Tribune,* 2 August 1925. Mondak's name change was effective 1 March 1925. Budd originally intended to rename Felsen "Thompson," but there already was a Thompson, North Dakota. *Minot Daily News,* 17 July 1925, 1. The potency of the railroad as an ultimate arbiter of place names is demonstrated by a request from Orin Libby to Budd that the town of Dogden be renamed "Stevens" in honor of a former governor—largely to prevent the residents from calling the place "Butte." Libby to Budd, 30 November 1926, GN Files (11620). None of the renamed hamlets has survived as more than a geographical expression.

29. Buck, "Upper Missouri Historical Expedition," 387–88; DeLestry, "Perpetuating Historic Events," 3–4. The Thompson Monument is located on a gravel road east of Velva and, as a tourist booklet notes, is "somewhat difficult to find."

30. Buck, "Upper Missouri Historical Expedition," 388–90. Stevens had explored the Marias Pass and noted its suitability as a railroad route.

31. Bernard Lewis, *History: Remembered, Recovered, Invented* (Princeton: Princeton University Press, 1975); Buck, "Upper Missouri Historical Expedition," 386; Upper Missouri Historical Expedition invitation in FOUS museum storage.

32. *Fairview News,* 28 May 1925; *Williston Herald,* 16 July 1925, 10; Overson to Budd, 14 July 1925, GN Files (11619).

33. C. O. Jenks to Budd, 1 June 1925; Budd to Jenks, 4 June 1925, GN Files (11337).

34. James T. Maher to Budd, 5 May 1925; Budd to J. A. Lengby, 6 May 1925 (telegram); Budd to Maher, 6 May 1925; Lengby to Budd, 6 May 1925 (telegram); C. O. Jenks to J. H. O'Neill, 6 May 1925 (telegram); Budd to Jenks, 11 May 1925, GN Files (11337).

35. Overson to Budd, 3 June 1925; Weinrich to Budd, 16 July 1925 (telegram); Budd to Weinrich, 16 July 1925 (telegram), GN Files (11619).

36. W. R. Mills to Budd, 1 May 1925; Weinrich to Mills, 16 September 1925; Mills to Budd, 21 September 1925; Budd to Weinrich, 22 September 1925; Overson to Budd, 24 July 1925, GN Files (11619); *Minneapolis Tribune,* 2 August 1925.

37. Jim Miculka, "Snowden Bridge," leaflet published by the Theodore Roosevelt Na-

ture and History Association (1980), FOUS; *Williston Herald*, 23 July 1925, 1; *Fairview News*, 16 July 1925, 23 July 1925; Weinrich to Budd, 2 August 1925, GN Files (11337). On the Snowden Bridge, see appendix B.

38. *Sidney Herald*, 24 July 1925, 1; *Williston Herald*, 16 July 1925, 23 July 1925.

39. Buck, "Upper Missouri Historical Expedition," 388; *Minneapolis Tribune*, 2 August 1925; Harold E. Keyes to Ben Innis, 12 February 1977, Ben Innis Papers, FOUS; Alice M. Sweetman, "Mondak: Planned City of Hope Astride Montana–Dakota Border," *Montana* 15 (autumn 1965): 27. For instance, during the same month, Vice President Charles Dawes was adopted by the Sioux as "White Father No. 2."

40. *Sidney Herald*, 24 July 1925; *Fairview News*, 23 July 1925; *Minneapolis Tribune*, 2 August 1925.

41. Budd to B. E. Burr, 23 July 1925, GN Files (11337); *Williston Herald*, 23 July 1925, 3; "The Upper Missouri Historical Expedition and Its Significance," *Williston Herald*, 16 July 1925, 6.

42. Budd to John Oliver, 25 July 1925; Budd to Louis Hill, 23 July 1925, GN Files (11619).

43. Buck, "Upper Missouri Historical Expedition," 390; GN Files, Advertising/Publicity Department, "Upper Missouri Historical Expedition," microfilm roll 7, volume 10, Minnesota Historical Society; *Cincinnati Times-Star*, 24 August 1925.
Media coverage of the Scopes trial was "unprecedented," and the event was front-page news across the United States for two weeks. A sociologist who investigated press coverage found "no periodical of any sort," including agricultural and trade journals, that ignored the trial. Edward J. Larson, *Summer for the Gods: The Scopes Trial and America's Continuing Debate over Science and Religion* (New York: Basic Books, 1997), 202–3.

44. Even the official history of the Great Northern says that the Indian ceremonies occurred at Williston (Hidy et al., *Great Northern Railway*, 182). The *New York Times* covered the expedition with a two-paragraph article about the Stevens statue on 23 July 1925 (20) and six photographs published on 2 August in its "Rotogravure Picture Section." The seriousness of national newspaper reporting may be judged by one photo, on the first page of the section, that featured a large Blackfoot woman who had taken second prize in the "tom tom shimmying event." Later that month the Great Northern released a picture of the winner, a four-hundred-pound Assiniboine. The release called her "Big Bertha" and reported that she was "so ponderous" that when she danced "the seismographs register[ed] a real prairie quake." Press release, 11 August 1925, GN Files (11337).

45. Libby to Budd, 10 March 1926; Budd to Libby, 18 March 1926, GN Files (11337).

46. Overson to Budd, 6 May 1926, GN Files (11620); *Fairview News*, 8, 15, 22 July 1926; *Williston Herald*, 10 June 1925, 22 July 1926. Budd dedicated three more monuments and changed the name of at least one town on this trip. "Ralph Budd" folder,

Charles H. Carey Papers, Oregon Historical Society. One guest on the 1927 expedition was the distinguished historian Samuel Eliot Morison, who wished that "there was some provision for forcibly dragging all American historians around the country like this at least once in five years." Morison to Albert Beveridge, 30 July 1926, in Gregory M. Pfitzer, *Samuel Eliot Morison's Historical World* (Boston: Northeastern University Press, 1991), 100. The trip cemented a friendship between Morison and Budd, and Budd served as the toastmaster when Morison was elected president of the American Historical Association in 1950 (201).

47. Hidy et al., *Great Northern Railway*, 166–69, 191–95, 198–99; Overton, "Ralph Budd," *Dictionary of American Biography*, Supplement 7, 90.

48. Maher to Budd, 25 November 1927; Budd to Maher, 2 December 1927, GN Files (11437); H. R. M. Zahl to Russell Reid, 10 January 1941, Park Files (BU–C–27), SHSND; F. J. Gavin to J. A. Tauer, 12 July 1949, GN Files (11619).

49. Frank B. Harper, "Fort Union and Its Neighbors: A Chronological Record of Events," pamphlet published by the Great Northern Railway, 1925, FOUS Library. For the origin and possible explanation of the tunnel legend, see appendix A.

50. John Bodnar, *Remaking America: Public Memory, Commemoration, and Patriotism in the Twentieth Century* (Princeton: Princeton University Press, 1992), 123–25.

5. Depression Years

1. Elwyn B. Robinson, *History of North Dakota* (Lincoln: University of Nebraska Press, 1966), 398–402; Michael Malone and Richard B. Roeder, *Montana: A History of Two Centuries* (Seattle: University of Washington Press, 1976), 226–27; Robert P. Wilkins and Wynona Huchette Wilkins, *North Dakota: A Bicentennial History* (New York: W. W. Norton, 1977), 101–3.

2. Ray H. Mattison, "The State Historical Society of North Dakota: A Brief History," *North Dakota History* 34 (fall 1967): 309–10.

3. *Popular Science Monthly* 118 (May 1931): 91–92, and (June 1931): 92–93; Odie B. Faulk, "Clarence Edward Mulford," *Dictionary of American Biography*, Supplement 6, 466–67; "Clarence Edward Mulford," in *Twentieth Century Authors*, ed. Stanley J. Kunitz and Howard Haycraft (New York: H. W. Wilson Co., 1942). Mulford (1883–1956) called the Hollywood version of Cassidy "an absolutely ludicrous character."

4. "The fort was begun in 1829, completed in 1833, and sold to the U.S. Government in 1869; then it was torn down and its materials hauled off for the erection of Fort Benton." *Popular Science Monthly* 118 (May 1931): 92. Nevertheless, Mulford located the fort well where archaeologists discovered it in the 1980s despite the lack of any extant reference in written sources. It is possible, therefore, that Mulford had some additional information about the fort that has since been lost. Conversation with Thomas Thiessen, 9 June 1998.

5. Edward A. Hummel, "Memorandum Re Fort Union Diorama," 2 April 1938, Park

History Files, National Register, History, and Education, National Park Service, Washington DC; Russell Reid to *Popular Science Monthly*, 4 January 1934, Superintendents Correspondence, series 203, box 5, SHSND; *Williston Herald*, 20 February 1941.

6. Kenneth E. Hendrickson Jr., "Relief for Youth: The Civilian Conservation Corps and the National Youth Administration in North Dakota," *North Dakota History* 48 (fall 1981): 17–27; Jo Ann Winistorfer, "The Civilian Conservation Corps: The Legacy Lives On," *ND REC/RTC Magazine* (November 1990): 36–40. Officially, the CCC was the ECW—Emergency Conservation Work—until 1937, when the name was changed to follow the popular designation. The exact number of CCC camps in North Dakota is difficult to determine because some were summer operations whose enrollees returned to the Bismarck area in the winter. In 1935 there were nineteen camps in North Dakota, less than 1 percent of the 2,110 camps nationwide. For practical purposes, Congress abolished the agency by voting $8 million for its liquidation in June 1942. By this time, enrollees in the one remaining North Dakota camp "were clamoring for an early discharge." John A. Salmond, *The Civilian Conservation Corps, 1933–1942: A New Deal Case Study* (Durham NC: Duke University Press, 1967), 217; Hendrickson, "Relief for Youth," 26.

7. Charles B. Hosmer Jr., *Preservation Comes of Age: From Williamsburg to the National Trust, 1926–1949*, 2 vols. (Charlottesville: University Press of Virginia, 1981), 1:529–33; John C. Paige, *The Civilian Conservation Corps and the National Park Service, 1933–1942* (Washington DC: National Park Service, 1985), 110–16; Salmond, *Civilian Conservation Corps*, 126–27.

8. Robinson, *History of North Dakota*, 510; Robert Cory, "Russell Reid: A Friend's Recollection," *North Dakota History* 34 (fall 1967): 283–94; Hendrickson, "Relief for Youth," 18; Russell Reid, "The North Dakota State Park System," *North Dakota Historical Quarterly* 8 (October 1940): 67.

9. *Williams County Farmers Press*, 23 August 1934, 1; *Williston Herald*, 24 August 1934, 10; R. S. Nutt to W. P. Kenney, 17 September 1934, Great Northern Railway Co., Files of the President (14684), Minnesota Historical Society.

10. Nutt to Kenney, 17 September 1934; Kenney to Nutt (telegram), 19 September 1934; Nutt to Robert Stechner, 20 September 1934; Nutt to Kenney, 22 September 1934; Kenney to H. H. Brown, 28 September 1934, GN Files (14684); *Sidney MT Herald*, 30 August 1928. Nutt's enthusiastic, if dubious, promotional letter to Stechner, the director of Unemployment Relief in Washington, promised abundant timber resources along the Missouri and Yellowstone Rivers and the possibility of hiring unemployed men throughout the winter months.

11. Interview of Edward A. Hummel, 5 January 1971, Oral History Project, National Park Service, Harpers Ferry Center Library, 32–33.

12. B. F. Tillotson, Assistant Attorney General, to Russell Reid, 17 May 1938, "Fort Union" File, SHSND.

13. Clinker, or "scoria," formed by the burning of clays above lignite beds, was also used to surface a few gravel roads, especially in the southwestern part of the state.

14. A. G. Leonard, "Gravel Deposits of North Dakota Suitable for Road Surfacing and Construction Work," *Quarterly Journal of the University of North Dakota* 14 (1923–24): 383–93; interview with Ralph Chase, 25 June 1996. Large pebbles do not work down into the clay of the grade and therefore make for a rougher road.

Rick Cronenberger, the project manager for the Fort Union reconstruction, discovered that gravel underlay the entire site five feet below grade. Foundation bores conducted during the 1980s extended approximately twenty feet into this gravel without hitting bottom. Cronenberger believed the gravel was so stable that it could be cut vertically and "hold its shape for many years." Rick Cronenberger to author, 24 March 1997.

15. Weinrich to M. L. Wilson, 13 November 1924, GN Files (11337); Chase interview; Edward A. Hummel, "Special Report: Fort Union, North Dakota," March 1938, FOUS Library (NPS Cultural Resources Bibliography Number 000336); Dana Wright to Russell Reid, 4 September 1936, Park Files (BU-n-11), SHSND.

Sometime before the fall of 1924 M. L. Wilson acquired large glossy photographs of the Fort Union site, which he mailed to Ralph Budd. The photographs reveal no sign of gravel mining. Edward Hummel's 1937 photographs, however, show part of the exposed foundation of the southwest bastion. The Wilson photographs are in 133.K.12.7(B), GN records, Minnesota Historical Society.

16. Barry Mackintosh, *The Historic Sites Survey and National Historic Landmarks Program: A History* (Washington DC: National Park Service, 1985), 4–7.

17. Hosmer, *Preservation Comes of Age*, 2:941–44; Barry Mackintosh to author, 19 February 1997; C. P. Russell to Ned [Burns], 17 December 1935, Park History Files, National Register, History, and Education, WASO; Elizabeth C. Morison, "Fort Union: A Fur-Trading Post on the Upper Missouri," 16 December 1935, Harpers Ferry Center Library (NPS Cultural Resources Bibliography Number 000339). The diorama, showing a view from inside the fort out the main gate toward the Missouri, was still on display at the Interior Department more than sixty years later.

18. *Who Was Who* (Chicago: Marquis Who's Who, 1981), vol. 7; Hummel interview, 5–6, 32. Many young historians hired during the 1930s had studied at the University of Minnesota. Verne Chatelain, the NPS chief historian, had himself been a student there before being hired by NPS director Horace Albright. Chatelain had the chairman of the Minnesota history department compile a list of his best students, to whom the Park Service then offered jobs. Hosmer, *Preservation Comes of Age*, 1:533.

At almost the same time that Hummel was investigating Fort Union on the Missouri, his counterparts in the Southwest were researching Fort Union, New Mexico, an army post (1851–91) on the Santa Fe Trail. This Fort Union also passed through a period of neglect and near destruction before becoming Fort Union National Monument in 1956. Liping Zhu, *Fort Union National Monument: An Administrative History* (Santa Fe: Southwest Cultural Resources Center, 1992), 15.

19. Edward Hummel, Memorandum Re: Fort Union Diorama, 2 April 1938, Park History Files; Hummel to Charles W. Moore, 2 July 1936, GN Files (17705); Hummel, "Special Report," 32–35; Hummel interview, 9–10.

20. Hummel, "Special Report," 2–4; Hummel to Director, 9 March 1937, Park History Files; Reid to Lee, 17 March 1937, Park Files (BU-f-65), SHSND; Reid to Lee, 6 August 1937, Superintendents' Correspondence, series 208, box 37, SHSND.

21. Federal Writers' Project, *Montana* (New York: Viking Press, 1939), 223–24. Federal Writers' Project, *North Dakota* (Bismarck: State Historical Society, 1938), 258, correctly places the fort "a few hundred yards E. of the present Montana Line." Nevertheless, Fort Union is mentioned only in connection with Fort Buford, and no directions are provided for the traveler.

22. Hummel, "Special Report," 34. The "shelves" were perhaps blocks of stone from the foundation of the fort used as supports for plank shelving.

23. In April 1917 the Missouri moved back toward the north bank, its position during the historic era. The river hugs the Fort Union side in the 1924 Wilson photographs. By 1936 the site seemed out of danger from the Missouri, and by the summer of 1939 the river had returned to the south bank. *Yellowstone News*, 28 April 1917; Dana Wright to Russell Reid, 4 September 1936 and 29 August 1939, Park Files (BU-n-11, 16), SHSND.

24. A. H. Warren to Budd, 23 July 1925; Budd to Warren, 25 July 1925; Budd to Weinrich, 25 July 1925; Weinrich to Budd, 2 August 1925, GN Files (11337); Henry Morrow to "Pearl & Welland," December 1925, FOUS Archives (H1417XRC). I am indebted to Orville Loomer for suggesting that the piece of wood was intended as a post for a vice rather than for an anvil as was believed at the time. Williston High School used three feet of the post as an anvil block, and the rest was cut into souvenirs.

25. Reid to D. I. Todd, 9 July 1936, FOUS research files; Reid to Lee, 17 March 1937, Park Files (BU-f-65), SHSND; James B. Connolly, "Ft. Union a Precious Jewel in the Crown of America's Heritage," *Williston Plains Reporter*, 9 August 1972, 2.

26. Telephone conversation with Neva Hydle MacMaster, 3 March 1997. Nellie Salinda Johnson Hydle (1883–1972) was the daughter of U.S. senator Martin N. Johnson, co-valedictorian of the class of 1901 at the University of North Dakota, and a member of Phi Beta Kappa. After the death of her husband, Steward M. Hydle, in 1940 Mrs. Hydle succeeded to his office as city treasurer while continuing to manage his real estate and insurance business. Williams County Historical Society, *The Wonder of Williams: A History of Williams County, North Dakota*, 2 vols. (n.p.: Williams County Historical Society, 1976), 2:2256.

27. Russell Reid to Mrs. A. D. MacMaster, 12 April 1962, Neff Papers, box 2, SHSND; Hummel, "Special Report," 34; a copy of the deed is in the "Fort Union" file, SHSND.

A local newspaper announced state purchase of the site in *June* 1938. Presumably, a few more weeks were needed to iron out the details. *Circle (MT) Banner*, 24 June 1938.

28. Mattison, "State Historical Society," 310; Reid, "North Dakota State Park System," 64–65, 76.

29. Lee to Reid, 13 April 1939, Superintendents' Correspondence, series 203, box 37, SHSND.

30. Hummel to Arnold Goplen, 20 July 1937, Superintendents' Correspondence, series 203, box 25, SHSND.

31. *Circle Banner*, 24 June 1938.

32. *Williston Herald*, 20 February 1941; H. M. Zahl to Reid, 10 January 1941, Park Files (BU-C-27), SHSND; Reid to Zahl, 20 January 1941, Park Files (BU-C-28), SHSND.

33. Mattison, "State Historical Society," 313.

34. Utley to author, 10 August 1997.

6. State Ownership

1. Dana Wright to Russell Reid, 29 August 1939, Park Files (BU-n-16), SHSND; William Jefferson Hunt Jr., "Firearms and the Upper Missouri Fur Trade Frontier: Weapons and Related Materials from Fort Union Trading Post National Historic Site (23W117), North Dakota," Ph.D. diss., University of Pennsylvania, 1989, 67. The original document cited by Hunt, another letter from Wright to Reid, seems to have disappeared from the SHSND Library.

2. "State Park Committee Meeting," 9 May 1942, Park Files (BU-n-20), SHSND. The Fort Buford site came into the state park system in 1924, although much of the present state park property remained in private hands or had been acquired by the Federal Land Bank during the depression.

3. "Appropriation for North Dakota State Parks and Historic Sites for the Biennium Ending June 30, 1943," Park Files, SHSND.

4. State Park Committee Meeting, 14 July 1943, Park Files (BU-n-23), SHSND. Members of the local committee were Chris Arnt, J. H. Batty, Eugene Burdick, Nellie Hydle, J. B. Lyon, W. B. Overson, Harry E. Polk, E. B. Ulhman, and H. M. Zahl.

5. Reid to J. H. Batty, 17 September 1946, Park Files (BU-C-96), SHSND; Reid to F. A. Wenstrom, 24 September 1949 (BU-C-95); Reid to Harry E. Polk, 25 August 1954, Park Files (BU-e-92), SHSND.

6. Ray H. Mattison, "The State Historical Society of North Dakota: A Brief History," *North Dakota History* 34 (fall 1967): 314.

7. Reid to Edna La Moore Waldo, 9 August 1944, Park Files (BU-n-25), SHSND; Dana Wright, "Sites Owned by the Historical Society of North Dakota," 18 April 1955, Park Files (BU-n-27), SHSND.

8. "Tourists Flocking to Fort Union," *Williston Daily Herald*, 2 August 1987; interview of William J. Hunt, 9–10 July 1996; Yellowstone-Missouri Confluence Commission minutes, 4 April 1960, Park Files (BU-e-56), SHSND.

9. Report of Dana Wright, 4 August 1959, Park Files (BU-n-30), SHSND; interview of Dennis Borud, 28 June 1996.

10. Report of Dana Wright, 4 August 1959, Park Files (BU-n-30), SHSND; Gregory L. Fox, *A Late Nineteenth Century Village of a Band of Dissident Hidatsa: The Garden Coulee Site (32W118)* (Lincoln NE: J & R Reprint Co., 1988), 44.

11. Interview of Orville Loomer, 2 July 1996; minutes of the Yellowstone-Missouri Confluence Commission meeting, 11 February 1961, Park Files (BU-e-43), SHSND; David L. Hieb to O'Neil Jones, 31 May 1963, Mon-Dak Heritage Center, Sidney MT.

12. James A. Glass, *The Beginnings of a New National Historic Preservation Program, 1957 to 1969* (Nashville: American Association for State and Local History, 1990), xiii–xiv, 3–4.

13. There were exceptions. Ben Innis, an influential supporter of the reconstruction, said that he had never heard of the confluence forts until an eighth-grade teacher in the 1930s mentioned that Audubon had visited Fort Union. *Fort Buford Post* [photocopied newsletter, Fort Buford Sixth Infantry Regiment Association] (November–December 1983), 4.

14. Conrad W. Leifur, *Our State North Dakota* (New York: American Book Co., 1953), 176–77. At least Leifur's treatment was an improvement over an earlier text, W. M. Wemett, *The Story of the Flickertail State* (Valley City ND: privately published, 1923), which in its four sentences about Fort Union made four historical errors. Erling Nicolai Rolfsrud, *The Story of North Dakota* (Alexandria MN: Lantern Books, 1963), 68–71. The connection between Fort Union and the smallpox epidemic of 1837 was ignored by all three of these books.

15. Elwyn B. Robinson, *History of North Dakota* (Lincoln: University of Nebraska Press, 1966), 458–61; David Harmon, *At the Open Margin: The NPS's Administration of Theodore Roosevelt National Park* (Medora ND: Theodore Roosevelt Nature and History Association, 1986), 68–69; "West Has Oil Boom—or Bust," *U.S. News & World Report*, 20 July 1951, 24–25; "Oil Opens New Frontiers," *U.S. News & World Report*, 30 May 1952, 19–21.

16. Robinson, *History of North Dakota*, 460–61, 604.

17. Williams County Historical Society, *The Wonder of Williams: A History of Williams County, North Dakota*, 2 vols. (n.p.: Williams County Historical Society, 1975), 1:427; Ben Innis, *Sagas of the Smoky-Water* (Williston ND: Centennial Press, 1985), 246; Edna La Moore Waldo to Russell Reid, 9 August 1944; Reid to Waldo, 29 August 1944, Park Files (BU-n-25), SHSND; Yellowstone-Missouri Confluence Commission meeting minutes, 11 February 1961, Park Files (BU-e-43), SHSND.

18. Waldo to Reid, 9 August 1944; Reid to Waldo, 29 August 1944, Park Files

(BU-n-25), SHSND; Virginia Russell, "The First Pioneers on the Buford-Trenton Project," in Williams County Historical Society, *Wonder of Williams*, 1:418–19; Reid to Harry Polk, 14 September 1954, Park Files (BU-C-93), SHSND. Today the field officer's quarters are recognized as an earlier commanding officer's residence, the place where Sitting Bull surrendered to Fort Buford's senior officer, Major David Hammett Brotherton, on 19 July 1881. Paul L. Hedren, "Sitting Bull's Surrender at Fort Buford: An Episode in American History," *North Dakota History* 62 (fall 1995): 3–15.

The building of the irrigation canal across Fort Buford demonstrates just how heavy-handedly the federal government could operate before the passage of the National Historic Preservation Act of 1966. In 1940–41 the Bureau of Reclamation simply dug the ditch near the Buford cemetery and, after the fact, requested the State Parks Committee to approve its right-of-way through state lands. Russell Reid made a special effort to warn the bureau away from Fort Union, "a valuable historic site which we intend to develop at some future date." Nevertheless, it is probable that the future national park escaped only because its land was not wanted for the project. Reid to Parley R. Neeley, Resident Engineer, Bureau of Reclamation, 20 July 1940, 21 March 1941, 26 July 1943, Park Files (BU-d-88, 91, 84), SHSND.

19. *Williston Herald*, 17 June 1966, 1; John B. Oakes, "Conservation: Highway Programs," *New York Times*, 30 November 1958, sec. 2, 41; Connolly to Oakes, 12 December 1958, GN Files (17705); Connolly to John Budd, 30 December 1958, Great Northern Railroad, Presidents' Files (17705), Minnesota Historical Society.

20. Ironically, Oakes's opinion piece dealt with "how far development and construction programs ought to go . . . when the very act of construction may endanger or destroy the scenic grandeur, the wilderness atmosphere or the tranquil spirit that created the values that were originally worth protecting." Connolly argued that the historic sites at the confluence were being "lost through underdevelopment" rather than overdevelopment. Oakes, "Conservation."

21. Connolly to Budd, 30 December 1958; Frank F. Jestrab to Senator William Langer, 31 December 1958 [includes list of copies sent], GN Files (17705). On the Greater North Dakota Association, see Robinson, *History of North Dakota*, 434.

22. Michael Wallace, "Reflections on the History of Historic Preservation," in Susan Porter Benson, Stephen Brier, and Roy Rosenzweig, eds., *Presenting the Past: Essays on History and the Public* (Philadelphia: Temple University Press, 1986), 175–76.

23. Robinson, *History of North Dakota*, 458; Harmon, *At the Open Margin*, table 11.1; Connolly to Budd, 30 December 1958, GN Files (17705). The anomalous designation *Theodore Roosevelt National Memorial Park* annoyed North Dakota tourism promoters and state politicians almost as soon as it was conferred on the new NPS unit in 1947. The name seemed to classify a natural park as a historical one, and (said the mayor of a neighboring community) it had "the connotation of a graveyard plaque." After four tries, Senator Quentin Burdick succeeded in removing the word *Memorial* from the park name through the same omnibus bill that authorized the reconstruc-

tion of Fort Union in 1978. David Harmon, *At the Open Margin: The NPS's Administration of Theodore Roosevelt National Park* (Medora ND: Theodore Roosevelt Nature and History Association, 1986), 49–57.

24. Steve Heyd, "Early Confluence Commission Provided Major Push," *Williston Herald*, 9 August 1989, 3; Connolly to Governor-Elect William L. Guy, 6 December 1960, Park Files (BU-e-46), SHSND. Other commission members in the early 1960s included Lyla Hoffine, an English teacher at Minot State Teachers College; Rev. Louis Pfaller of Assumption Abbey in Richardson; and Ben Innis of Williston, who was to become the most significant figure in the reconstruction battle of the following decade. The commission also named "advisers."

25. *Williston Herald*, 9 August 1989, 3; Yellowstone-Missouri-Fort Union Commission minutes, 11 February 1961 (BU-e-43), 17 December 1962 (BU-e-28), Commission to Members of the Budget Board, 6 November 1962, Park Files, SHSND.

26. LaVern C. Neff to Russell Reid, 8 September 1959, Park Files (BU-e-87), SHSND; Henry B. Syverud to Neff, 23 February 1961, box 2, Neff Papers, SHSND.

27. Yellowstone-Missouri-Fort Union Commission minutes, 11 February 1961 (BU-e-43), 17 December 1962 (BU-e-28); Connolly to O'Neil Jones, 5 August 1963, Mon-Dak Heritage Center, Sidney MT; Historical Research Files (HRF 0039), FOUS. For instance, the American Medical Association was to be asked to memorialize F. V. Hayden (who was a doctor by training) and the Wildlife Federation, the hunter Sir George Gore.

28. Connolly to Rev. Louis Pfaller, O.S.B., 26 April 1966; Connolly to Pfaller, 12 May 1966, Neff Papers, box 2. The Knights of Columbus marker was largely the work of Pfaller, a commission member. Since the Masons had already erected a marker at Fort Buford, there may have been extra incentive for their fraternal rivals to lay claim to Union. Just before Pfaller's installation of the three-by-five-foot enameled plaque set in granite, the respected ethnologist John C. Ewers warned Connolly of the danger posed by individualistic memorials. Ewers to Connolly, 1 March 1961, Park Files (BU-e-41), SHSND. The sign was demolished during Wellman's superintendency.

29. On Mission 66, see Richard West Sellars, *Preserving Nature in the National Parks: A History* (New Haven: Yale University Press, 1997), 180–91. Yellowstone-Missouri-Fort Union Commission minutes, 11 February 1961, Park Files (BU-e-43), SHSND; Barry Mackintosh, *The Historic Sites Survey and National Historic Landmarks Program: A History* (Washington DC: National Park Service, 1985), 32–33; Roy E. Appleman to Director, 5 March 1962; Connolly to Jackson E. Price, 19 April 1962, Park History Files, WASO.

30. Appleman to Connolly, 2 May 1962, Park History Files, WASO; *Current Biography*, 1963, 51–52.

31. Yellowstone-Missouri-Fort Union Commission minutes, 11 February 1961, Park Files (BU-e-43), SHSND; Burdick to Connolly, 8 May 1961, Park Files (BU-e-39), SHSND; Appleman to Wirth, 5 March 1962; memorandum of a telephone conver-

sation between Appleman and Howard Baker, 5 March 1962, Park History Files, WASO. The misunderstanding about the appropriation apparently arose from the belief that Fort Union archaeology could be conducted with money from the Missouri Basin salvage operation.

32. Mackintosh, *Historic Sites Survey*, 34; Ray H. Mattison, "Fort Union: Its Role in the Upper Missouri Fur Trade," *North Dakota History* 29 (January–April 1962): 181–208.

33. "A Proposed Fort Union Trading Post National Historic Site" (Omaha NE: National Park Service, Midwest Region, 1962), 7, 12.

34. "Proposed Fort Union Trading Post," 13–14.

35. Yellowstone-Missouri-Fort Union Commission minutes, 17 December 1962, Park Files (BU-e-28), SHSND; cover note by Appleman on the above minutes, 31 December 1962; handwritten note of J. W. Walker, attached to a letter from Robert M. Utley to the SHSND, 29 March 1965, Park History Files, WASO.

36. Warren D. Hotchkiss to Regional Director, Midwest Region, 2 July 1963, Ben Innis Papers, FOUS; Rep. Don L. Short to Rep. Thomas G. Morris, 25 July 1963, GN Files (17705); Burdick to John Budd, 4 November 1963, GN Files (17705). John M. Budd (1907–79) had little of his father's interest in history, but he maintained a considerable pride in his father's Historical Expeditions. W. Thomas White, "John M. Budd," in *Railroads in the Age of Regulation, 1900–1980*, ed. Keith L. Bryant Jr. (New York: Facts on File, 1988), 53–55.

37. "Hearing before the Subcommittee on Public Lands of the Committee on Interior and Insular Affairs, United States Senate, Eighty-Eighth Congress, First Session, on S. 187," 2 August 1963 (Washington DC: GPO, 1963), 5 (quotation).

38. "Hearing before the Subcommittee on Public Lands," 9, 14.

39. See Burdick constituent letter, June 1964, in GN Files (17705). Jamestown Festival Park, created for the 350th anniversary celebration in 1957, was renamed Jamestown Settlement in 1990. James B. Connolly, "Fort Union Aims at Tourist Attraction," *The Fargo Forum*, 26 June 1966, C-14; Burdick to Connolly, 1 July 1966, Neff Papers, box 2, SHSND.

40. Don L. Short to Neff, 25 September 1964, Neff Papers, box 2, SHSND; Short to Thomas G. Morris, 25 July 1963, GN Files (17705).

41. Connolly to "Commissioners, Advisers, Consultants," 23 February 1965, Ben Innis Papers (26–035), FOUS; O'Neil Jones to Sen. Mike Mansfield, 21 September 1965, Mon–Dak Heritage Center. A Great Northern official wrote proudly to Connolly that during his visit to the site in 1958 he had "carried away two artifacts—a pair of handmade nails, which I use for desk paper weights." C. W. Moore to Connolly, 22 February 1965, GN Files (17705).

42. Fritz Kessinger to Chief, Division of Legislation and Regulations, 21 June 1965, H1415 (FOUS), THRO; draft transcript of testimony before the Subcommittee on Na-

tional Parks and Recreation Areas, House Committee on Interior and Insular Affairs, 21 June 1965, in George Benjamin Hartzog Papers, box 99, folder 1242, Special Collections, Clemson University Libraries, Clemson SC.

43. John A. Carver to Wayne Aspinall, 23 March 1965, H1415 (FOUS), THRO.

44. Roy Appleman, "Review Comments, 'Master Plan Fort Union Trading Post National Historic Site,' 1966," 2–3, Research Files, FOUS.

45. Appleman, "Review Comments," 3–4.

46. Public Law 89–458, 89th Congress, H.R. 3957.

47. Connolly to Neff, 30 December 1966, Neff Papers, box 2, SHSND.

7. A New National Historic Site

1. Barry Mackintosh, *The National Historic Preservation Act and the National Park Service: A History* (Washington DC: National Park Service, 1986); James A. Glass, *The Beginnings of a New National Historic Preservation Program, 1957 to 1969* (Nashville: American Association for State and Local History, 1990), 17–20; William J. Murtagh, *Keeping Time: The History and Theory of Preservation in America* (New York: Sterling Publishing Co., 1988), 62–77; Ronald A. Foresta, *America's National Parks and Their Keepers* (Washington DC: Resources for the Future, 1984), 131 (quotation).

2. Ronald F. Lee, *Family Tree of the National Park System* (Philadelphia: Eastern National Park and Monument Association, 1972), 75.

3. "Master Plan of Fort Union Trading Post National Historic Site/North Dakota–Montana" (Washington DC: National Park Service, 1967); Fred C. Fagergren to Chief, Resource Planning, 10 June 1966, H1415 (FOUS), THRO; Howard Stagner to Quentin Burdick, 20 July 1966, H1415 (FOUS), THRO; R. Merrick Smith to Assistant Director, Cooperative Activities, 1 September 1966, D18 (attic), FOUS; Dwight F. Rettie, *Our National Park System: Caring for America's Greatest Natural and Historic Treasures* (Urbana: University of Illinois Press, 1995), 106.

4. Master Plan (1967), 4, 11, 12, 14, 20; R. Merrick Smith to Assistant Director, Cooperative Activities, 1 September 1966, D18 (attic), FOUS. The few idiosyncrasies of the plan may be attributed to the era of its composition and its authors' limited knowledge of local geography. For instance, the suggestion that restrooms be located in the northeast bastion ignored the difficulty of heating them when temperatures dropped to minus forty degrees. And although a display of period river craft at a Missouri River boat dock might have appropriately interpreted the theme of river transportation, the notion that many visitors would arrive by boat was, at best, imaginative and perhaps attributable to the planning team's appearance during spring flood.

5. Roy E. Appleman, "Review Comments, 'Master Plan Fort Union Trading Post National Historic Site,' 1966," Research Files, FOUS; marginal comments on Erwin Thompson to Appleton, 29 May 1968, Park History Files, WASO.

6. Thompson to Mattes, 2 January 1968, Thompson Papers, FOUS; Thompson to Ap-

pleman, 29 May 1968, Park History Files, WASO; Thompson to author, 8 July 1996. The Great Northern's flagpole, a landmark at the fort site for more than thirty-five years, rotted at its base and fell during the summer of 1963. Connolly to "Friends," 24 February 1961, Park Files (BU-e-40), SHSND; C. W. Moore to John Budd, 5 September 1963, GN Files (17705)

7. Thompson to Wilfred M. Husted, 18 June 1970, Park History Files, WASO. Appleton wrote "Yes" next to the quoted comments.

Former chief historian Robert Utley called Thompson "the best historical researcher DSC [the Denver Service Center] had" (Utley to author, 10 August 1997). The short historical section of Thompson's study served as the standard history of the fort for more than thirty years. Erwin N. Thompson, *Fort Union Trading Post: Fur Trade Empire on the Upper Missouri* (Williston ND: Fort Union Association, 1994).

8. James Connolly to [Confluence] Commissioners, 1 June 1967, Park History Files, National Register, History, and Education, NPS, WASO; *Williston Herald*, 9 August 1989, 3. The Yellowstone-Missouri-Fort Union Commission (the Confluence Commission) was reactivated by Governor George Sinner in August 1985.

9. Conrad Wirth to Legislative Counsel, Office of the Solicitor, 12 April 1963, H1415 (FOUS), THRO; Master Plan, 1967, 7; A. W. Gray to Chief, Division of Land and Water Rights, WASO, 8 August 1968, L1429 (FOUS), THRO.

10. Nordell to Bill Wellman, 9 January 1976, Research Files, FOUS; John O. Lancaster to Regional Director, Rocky Mountain Region, 23 April 1976, A36, THRO; interview of William Wellman, 22 July 1996; Warranty Deed, 31 July 1976, L1429 (FOUS), THRO; John Lancaster to Bill Wellman, undated [July 1976], L1425, THRO.

11. Arthur L. Sullivan to James B. Connolly, 1 August 1966, Neff Papers, box 2, State Historical Society.

12. Adrienne Anderson to John O. Lancaster, 29 August 1975, H2215 (FOUS), THRO; William J. Hunt Jr., *Fort Union Trading Post National Historic Site (32WI17): Material Culture Reports, Part I: A Critical Review of the Archeological Investigations* (Lincoln NE: Midwest Archeological Center, 1986).

13. Roy E. Appleman, "Review Comments, 'Master Plan Fort Union Trading Post National Historic Site,' 1966," 6, Research Files, FOUS.

14. Hunt, *Critical Review*; interview of William J. Hunt, 9–10 July 1996; Anderson to Lancaster, 29 August 1975, H2215 (FOUS), THRO.

15. Vergil E. Noble, "Historical Archeology and the Management of Cultural Resources," CRM 11 (October–December 1988): 2; Master Plan, 1967, 11; see also William Jefferson Hunt, "Firearms and the Upper Missouri Fur Trade Frontier: Weapons and Related Materials from Fort Union Trading Post National Historic Site (23WI17), North Dakota," Ph.D. diss., University of Pennsylvania, 1989, 70–71, 109.

16. Ivor Noël Hume, *Historical Archaeology* (New York: Alfred A. Knopf, 1968), 6, 14–20; Hunt interview; interview of Wilfred M. Husted, 26 July 1996; Jackson W.

Moore to author, 27 September 1996. Noël Hume does not mention screens or screening in his literate guidebook for amateurs.

17. Moore to author, 27 September 1996; Merrill J. Mattes, "From Ruin to Reconstruction, 1920–1976," *Colorado Magazine* 54 (1977): 82–86. The conflicts, professional and personal, among officials of the River Basin Surveys and the National Park Service are beyond the scope of this work; see Thomas D. Theissen, ed., "An Interview with Wilfred D. Logan, Career National Park Service Archeologist," unpublished manuscript (1992), Midwest Archeological Center, Lincoln NE.

18. Hunt, *Critical Review*, 11, 18–19; *The Forum of Fargo-Moorhead*, 28 July 1968; Moore to Wilfred D. Logan, 20 June 1968, L58 MWR (HA), THRO. The Missouri River Basin Survey, fundamentally a salvage operation, was notorious for its reporting backlog, and that agency's casual attitude toward reports may have influenced the reporting style at Fort Union. Thiessen, "Interview with Logan," 35–36.

19. The Midwest Archeological Center continued to perform salvage archaeology in Missouri Basin reservoirs until 1975, when it became a support office for the National Park Service. Moore to author, 27 September 1996; Husted to author, 18 July 1996; Husted interview.

20. Hunt, *Critical Review*, 20; Husted interview; Fort Union Archeological Project, Report No. 2, 27 June 1969, H24, THRO; Superintendent, THRO, to Regional Director, 2 May 1969, A2615, THRO.

21. Hunt, *Critical Review*, 19–32; Moore interview; Husted interview. By the middle of July there had been so much rain that when the chief archaeologist visited the site, the caretaker at Fort Buford had to tow the party through the mud. Fort Union Archeological Project, Report No. 4 and 5, 18 July 1969, H24, THRO.

22. Hunt, *Critical Review*, 32; Husted to Bonnie Butler, 21 April 1972, curatorial file, 24–14, FOUS.

23. Hunt, *Critical Review*, 32–42; *Williston Herald*, 11 July 1972. Gillio's dig lasted only a little over five weeks, from 18 July to 25 August 1972.

24. Hunt, *Critical Review*, 41–42; see also Anderson to Lancaster, 29 August 1975, and the heated retort of Moore to Chief Archaeologist, WASO, 24 September 1975, H2215 (FOUS), THRO.

25. Hunt, *Critical Review*, 43–44; John W. Weymouth, "A Magnetic Survey of the Fort Union Trading Post National Historic Site: Correlations with Three Seasons of Excavations," report submitted to the Midwest Archeological Center, January 1991, FOUS Library.

26. Hank Schoch to author, 26 July 1996; telephone conversation with Arthur L. Sullivan, 5 September 1996; interview with Sylvester Putnam, 23 July 1996; Husted to Chief, MWAC, 17 June 1970, curatorial file, 24–7, FOUS.

27. Moore and his crew lived in Williston. Husted and Gillio stayed at farmhouses a

few miles away. Moore interview; Husted interview; James B. Thompson to Director, Midwest Region, 2 July 1970, A2615, THRO.

28. Moore to Chief, Archeological Research, Omaha, 20 June 1968; Husted, "Field Notes," curatorial file, 24-104, FOUS; Staff Archeologist to Chief, MWAC, 13 August 1970, curatorial file, 24-17, FOUS.

29. John Mortenson to Moore, 11 May 1969, curatorial file, 24-138, FOUS; Harold O. Bullis to Arthur L. Sullivan, 8 August 1969, W46, THRO; Wilfred D. Logan to Bullis, 21 August 1969, L58, THRO; Steven Leroy DeVore and William J. Hunt Jr., *Fort Union Trading Post National Historic Site (32WI17): Material Culture Reports, Part X: Native American Burials and Artifacts* (Lincoln NE: MWAC, 1994), 13-14.

30. Husted, "Field Notes," 26 June 1970, curatorial file, 24-104; Husted to Director, MWAC, 27 June 1970, curatorial file, 24-7; Staff Archeologist to Chief, MWAC, 13 August 1970, curatorial file, 24-17, FOUS.

31. Putnam interview; interview of William Wellman, 22 July 1996; see also Wellman to Superintendent, THRO, 1 December 1975, A2615, THRO. (Both Putnam and Wellman began their tenures at Fort Union as "management assistants" but were eventually given the title "superintendent," even though they remained subordinate to the superintendent at Theodore Roosevelt.) Wellman noted that by this time there was not enough showing on the surface at Fort Union to attract pothunters, and they moved outside park boundaries to rifle Mondak.

32. Wellman interview; Connolly to John C. Ewers, 7 May 1971, Ben Innis Papers, 0-20, FOUS. Ewers, a Smithsonian ethnologist, provided sound advice in reply: If the archaeology wasn't going fast enough, "holler. Now that the site is established, it may depend a lot on regional interest to move the project along. Let your Senators and Congressmen know your interest." Ewers to Connolly, 19 May 1971.

33. *Williston Herald*, 6 July 1972; Putnam interview; *Williston Plains Reporter*, 9 August 1972. The model—the first *not* to be based on Mulford's *Popular Science* drawings—was conceived by William Burnison, a young social studies and shop teacher in 1964. The model was well executed for a junior high project, and it remains on display at the Mon–Dak Heritage Center, Sidney MT. *Sidney Herald*, 6 May 1964.

34. James B. Connolly, "Ft. Union a Precious Jewel in the Crown of America's Heritage," *Williston Plains Reporter*, 9 August 1972.

8. Winning Congressional Authorization

1. Thomas S. Kleppe to James B. Connolly, 29 April 1976, 26-016, Innis Papers, FOUS; interview of William Wellman, 22 July 1996; interview of Paul Hedren, 18 June 1996.

2. "Pedigree," in Innis Papers, FOUS; interview of Jane Innis, 26 June 1996; Richard E. Collin, "Introduction to Revised Edition," in Ben Innis, *Bloody Knife: Custer's Favorite Scout* (Bismarck ND: Smoky Water Press, 1994), xiii.

3. Innis Papers, File 180 (on the proposal to change the name of Williston to "Sitting Bull" in February 1965), FOUS; Collin, "Introduction," xiii; Wellman interview; interview of Dennis Borud, 28 June 1996; interview of Richard E. Collin and Andrea Winkjer Collin, 31 July 1996; Hedren interview, 18 June 1996; interview of Orville Loomer, 2 July 1966.

4. Andrea Winkjer, "'How to Talk Trapper' the Title of New Book by Sergeant-Major Innis," *Williston Prism*, December 1983; "They Dig for Union," *The Forum*, 28 July 1968; *Williston Plains Reporter*, 9 August 1972.

5. "Constitution & By-Laws, Fort Union, Fort Buford Council," 26–002; minutes, 8 October 1975, 8 March 1976, 26–003–4, Innis Papers, FOUS.

6. Dwight F. Rettie, *Our National Park System: Caring for America's Greatest Natural and Historic Treasures* (Urbana: University of Illinois Press, 1995), 106.

7. "Public Involvement Program, Environmental Assessment: Fort Union Trading Post NHS" [1975–76], D18 (attic), FOUS; audiotape, "Williston Kiwanis" [31 December 1975], Innis Papers, FOUS.

8. Utley to author, 10 August 1997; David Clary to Utley, 12 July 1974, Park History Files, National Register, History, and Education, WASO. Clary laid the problems of interpretation at the feet of the interpreters: "At one time, we had interpreters who accepted the challenge of a difficult job. I wonder where they are now." In a pointed communication to the director of the Rocky Mountain Region that year, Utley chose to emphasize the lack of congressional intent to reconstruct. Utley to Regional Director, 10 October 1974, Park History Files, WASO.

9. Utley to author, 10 August 1997; Arthur Sullivan to Regional Director, 29 May 1969, H1415, FOUS; Utley to Chief, Division of Legislation, 17 July 1974, Park History Files, WASO; Connolly to Innis, 21 May 1971, Innis Papers, FOUS. In a prophetic understatement THRO superintendent Sullivan warned his superiors that Innis was "not easily discouraged and no doubt will persist in his campaign for some time to come."

10. Innis to Diane Bervig, 1 October 1975; Innis to Mark Andrews, 11 May 1976; Innis to Elvis J. Stahr, 12 May 1976, Innis Papers; *Williston Herald*, 16 October 1975; John Lancaster to Regional Director, 26 November 1975, A2615, THRO. Kleppe's appointment was a much larger event in North Dakota than it would have been elsewhere. A North Dakota history written two years later called it "the greatest honor ever paid the State." Robert P. Wilkins and Wynona Huchette Wilkins, *North Dakota: A Bicentennial History* (New York: W. W. Norton, 1977), 186.

11. Innis to Richard Madson, 21 October 1975; Innis to Stahr, 12 May 1976; press release, 1 July 1976, Innis Papers.

12. Innis and Wellman seem to have developed a sincere respect for each other. In a letter to Connolly, Innis described Wellman as "most accommodating [and] easily the best Park Service representative we have had here." Innis to Connolly, 16 August 1976, Innis Papers.

13. Richard F. Fenno Jr., *When Incumbency Fails: The Senate Career of Mark Andrews* (Washington DC: Congressional Quarterly Press, 1992), 120.

14. *Current Biography, 1954*, 669–70; *New York Times*, 1 June 1983; Innis to Mark Andrews, 22 January 1977, Innis Papers: "Senator Young has done absolutely nothing to help us, although we have asked his aid repeatedly. He is in a position to do us a great deal of good." Young was powerful enough to have a Coast Guard signal beam station installed in a wheatfield near his hometown of LaMoure ND. Fenno, *When Incumbency Fails*, 126–27.

15. Elwyn B. Robinson, *History of North Dakota* (Lincoln: University of Nebraska Press, 1966), 508; "Quentin N. Burdick," in *Congressional Quarterly's Politics in America, 1992*, ed. Phil Duncan (Washington DC: Congressional Quarterly, 1991), 1125–27: "Burdick has long been one of the more absent-minded senators; usually this causes him no particular trouble. In 1983, though, he absent-mindedly inserted in the Congressional Record not only a statement on the issue of truck-weight regulations, but private instructions he had received on the subject from a lobbyist." Interview with Rick and Andrea Collin, 31 July 1996; Marvin Kaiser to author, 4 November 1997. Nevertheless, Kaiser recalled that at the dedication banquet in 1989 Burdick "gave the best speech of all the politicians."

16. Fenno, *When Incumbency Fails*, 1, 279; interview of Mark Andrews, 10 July 1996. Andrews served for seventeen years in the House of Representatives. For the first nine years (1963–72), he represented eastern North Dakota as one of two House members from the state. After reapportionment in 1971 Andrews became North Dakota's only representative. When Andrews was defeated for a second term in the Senate in 1986, Senator Bob Dole quipped that since Andrews was gone "some of us may get some of the money—especially Kansas." Fenno, *When Incumbency Fails*, 279.

17. Andrews to Innis, 27 January 1977, Innis Papers; Andrews interview.

18. *Williston Herald*, 8 January 1976; a summary of comments made at the NPS public meetings is located in research file 562, FOUS; John Lancaster to Regional Director, 2 March 1976, A2615, THRO. Burdick's bill (S. 3501) was introduced on 27 May; Andrews's bill, co-sponsored by Montana congressman John Melcher, was introduced a month later (Innis Papers).

19. Andrews to Secretary of the Interior Thomas Kleppe, 3 August 1976, Park History Files, WASO; Innis to "Toni, Gilda, Vernon," 21 May 1976, Innis Papers.

20. Robert Utley to author, 14 July 1996 and 10 August 1997.

21. Curtis Bohlen, Deputy Assistant Secretary of the Interior, to Henry M. Jackson, Chairman, Committee on Interior and Insular Affairs, 23 July 1976, Innis Papers.

22. Andrews to Kleppe, 3 August 1976, Park History Files, WASO; Lancaster to Regional Director, Rocky Mountain Region, 4 August 1976.

23. "Agenda" for Fort Union-Fort Buford Council meeting, 11 August 1976; Innis to

Connolly, 16 August 1976, Innis Papers. Innis's perception of what had happened in Washington was faulty. He even blamed Burdick for jumping "the gun by asking for the hearing too early."

24. Burdick to Innis, 14 October 1976, Innis Papers; Andrews to Kleppe, 3 August 1976, Park History Files, WASO; Kent Frizell, Acting Secretary of the Interior, to Andrews, 9 September 1976; Andrews to Innis, 10 September 1976, Innis Papers; Roy C. Slatkavitz, Chief, Division of Planning and Design, RMR, to Associate Regional Director, RMR, 8 September 1976, Park History Files, WASO.

25. Untitled list, September 1976 (26–051); "Union: Then–Now–Forever!" [slide show script], February 1977 (26–052), Innis Papers. Before appealing for support, Innis closed with the strained argument that historic sites at two other confluences —at Pittsburgh and St. Paul—had "vanished into urbanism. . . . Let's not let that happen here!" Of all the threats to the Fort Union site, "urbanism" was certainly one of the most remote.

26. S. 491 and H.R. 3471; Andrews to Innis, 27 January 1977; Andrews to Tony Clausen, 18 May 1977; Andrews to Innis, 23 May 1977; Innis to Andrews, 31 May 1977; Innis to Mary Mercer, 1 June 1977; "Radio/TV Spot Announcements," 1 June 1977, Innis Papers.

27. Andrews to Innis, 6 June 1977, Innis Papers; Richard W. Sellars and Melody Webb, *An Interview with Robert M. Utley on the History of Historic Preservation in the National Park Service, 1947–1980* (Santa Fe: Southwest Cultural Resources Center, 1988), 17, 62; Carla Kelly, "Robert Utley: Carrying History to the People," M.A. thesis, Northeast Louisiana University, 1992, 94–97; Gary Everhardt to Dick Curry, 24 June 1977, Park History Files, WASO. Everhardt had left the directorship a month before and was replaced in July by William J. Whalen.

28. "Statement of the Department of the Interior before the Park and Recreation Subcommittee, Senate Committee on Energy and Natural Resources, Concerning S. 491, June [28], 1977," (26–038) Innis Papers; see also Bob Herbst, Assistant Secretary of the Interior, to Senator Henry M. Jackson, Chairman, Committee on Energy and Natural Resources, 19 August 1977, H3015-86 (attic), FOUS; Andrews to John H. MacMaster, 6 December 1977, Innis Papers; *Williston Herald*, 23 July 1978; P.L. 95–625.

29. "Omnibus Parks Bill," *Congressional Quarterly Almanac* 34 (1978): 704–5. Phillip Burton (1926–83), a liberal Democrat from San Francisco who possessed vast political talents, was both respected and feared by his colleagues. Despite his mastery of the secret political deal, his abrasive personality probably resulted in his one-vote loss for House majority leader in 1976. Burton had no personal interest in parks natural or historic—he told a friend the closest he got to being outdoors was heading fifty yards into the forest to relieve himself—but he understood how he "could turn environmentalism into an elaborate system of chits." Mark Andrews could not remember what he traded with Burton for the inclusion of the North Dakota items in

the omnibus bill, but he said, "Burton never did anything for nothin'." John Jacobs, *A Rage for Justice: The Passion and Politics of Phillip Burton* (Berkeley: University of California Press, 1995), 351–79; *Newsweek*, 25 April 1983, 27; Andrews interview.

30. Burton I. Kaufman, *The Presidency of James Earl Carter, Jr.* (Lawrence: University Press of Kansas, 1993), 109–13.

31. P.L. 95–625, Sec. 309, 10 November 1978. The bill authorized $280,000 for the acquisition of lands and $4,416,000 for park development; see also Herbst to Jackson, 19 August 1977, H3015-86 (attic), FOUS; "Report to Accompany S. 3501," 26 September 1976, Report No. 94-1355, Innis Papers; Roy Appleman, "Review Comments, 'Master Plan Fort Union Trading Post National Historic Site,' 1966," Research Files, FOUS; interview of William Wellman, 22 July 1996. Presumably in return for the $8.5 million figure, Burdick allowed the Senate version to include a requirement that no funds could be spent for reconstruction "unless the Secretary of the Interior has determined, on the basis of historical documentation satisfactory to him, that such reconstruction can be accomplished with a minimum of conjecture." Andrews thought that language left too much to the discretion of the department and had the virtual carte blanche tamed in the final version. Andrews to John MacMaster, 6 December 1977, Innis Papers.

32. *Williston Herald*, 23 July 1978.

9. Reenergizing the Project

1. Interview of Tom Rolfstad, 16 July 1996; telephone conversation with Richard Collin, 17 July 1996.

2. Burton I. Kaufman, *The Presidency of James Earl Carter, Jr.* (Lawrence: University Press of Kansas, 1993), 99–100, 167–70, 177–79; *Congressional Quarterly Almanac* 36 (1980): 179.

3. F. Ross Holland to author, 5 July 1996.

4. Harry Pfanz, Acting Chief, Cultural Resources Management Division, to Acting Assistant Director, Planning and Development, 24 March 1977 (drafted by Barry Mackintosh); Philip O. Stewart, Acting Deputy Director, to Regional Director, Rocky Mountain Region, 9 May 1977, Park History Files, National Register, History, and Education, WASO.

5. Rodd L. Wheaton, Historical Architect, RMR, to Associate Regional Director, Professional Support, RMR, 18 July 1975, H2215 (FOUS), THRO; *General Management Plan, Fort Union Trading Post NHS*, August 1978, FOUS.

6. F. Ross Holland Jr. to Assistant Director, Planning and Development, 11 November 1977, Park History Files, WASO.

7. The management objective read in full: "To restore and perpetuate the historic fort scene within practical limits to the period of the mid-1800's in accordance with Management Policies for Historic Preservation." *General Management Plan*, SFM-7,

GDP-2-3; Paul Hedren, "The Reconstruction of Fort Union Trading Post: A Cause, A Controversy, and a Success," *Journal of Interpretation* 13 (1989): 11.

8. Rodd Wheaton to author, 16 September 1997; John Lancaster, National Park Service Open Meeting, Williston ND, 12 April 1978, audiotape, Ben Innis Papers, FOUS; *General Management Plan*, VUP-1, GDP-2-3.

9. Rodd Wheaton to author, 3 September 1997.

10. *General Management Plan*, VUP-3; Dwight F. Rettie, *Our National Park System: Caring for America's Greatest Natural and Historic Treasures* (Urbana: University of Illinois Press, 1995), 108.

11. John Lancaster and William Wellman, National Park Service Open Meeting, Williston ND, 12 April 1978.

12. P.L. 95–625, sec. 309, 10 November 1978; Mark Andrews to author, 7 November 1997.

13. Wildred Husted even made sketches showing how a visitor center and employee work space might fit in the interior of the reconstructed fort. Husted to Chief, Midwest Archeological Center, 5 November 1970, L58 (FOUS), THRO.

14. Wheaton to Associate Regional Director, Professional Support, RMR, 12 August 1975, H2215 (FOUS), THRO. The team's full-time members were Mary Shivers Culpin, architectural historian; Richard Borjes and Willard B. Robinson, historical architects; and project draftsman Robert K. White, an engineering student at Stanford University. Rocky Mountain Region Historic Preservation Team, "Fort Union Reconstruction Analysis" (1979), FOUS.

15. Associate Regional Director, Planning and Resource Preservation, RMR, to Superintendent, THRO, 5 June 1979, Park History Files, WASO; Rodd L. Wheaton, "To Reconstruct or Not to Reconstruct: Decision within Documentation," paper presented at the annual meeting of the Association for Preservation Technology, September 1985, Research Files (0002), FOUS; Wheaton to author, 3 September and 13 November 1997; Mary Shivers Culpin, "Archival Collections—Why They Are Important," *CRM* 14, no. 4 (1991): 13–15.

16. "Fort Union Reconstruction Analysis" (1979), FOUS; Associate Regional Director, Planning and Resource Preservation, RMR, to Superintendent, THRO, 5 June 1979, Park History Files, WASO; Wheaton to author, 7 January 1998. The Historic Preservation Team recommended full reconstruction of the palisades, bastions, Bourgeois House, trade house, powder magazine, bell tower, and flagpole and partial reconstruction of the dwelling range and store range.

17. Holland to Chief, Office of Legislation, 12 October 1979 [memo prepared by Pfanz]; Holland to Jim Tobin, 16 October 1979; Holland to Peter Gove, 21 November 1979, Park History Files, WASO.

18. Bob Herbst, Assistant Secretary for Fish and Wildlife and Parks, to Thomas P. O'Neill Jr., Speaker of the House of Representatives, 23 November 1979, Innis

Papers, FOUS; Holland to Peter Gove, 21 November 1979, Park History Files, WASO; Mark Andrews to Innis, 6 December 1979, Innis Papers, FOUS.

19. Richard Sellars and Dwight Pitcaithley, "Reconstructions—Expensive, Life-Size Toys?" CRM *Bulletin* 2, no. 4 (1979): 6–8; Paul L. Hedren, "Field Notes: Why We Reconstructed Fort Union," *Western Historical Quarterly* 32 (August 1992): 351.

20. Rettie, *Our National Park System*, 129, 183, 209–10; Michael Schaller, *Reckoning with Reagan: America and Its President in the 1980s* (New York: Oxford University Press, 1992), 41–47, 100–102; John Jacobs, *A Rage for Justice: The Passion and Politics of Phillip Burton* (Berkeley: University of California Press, 1995), 417–18. Rettie, no friend of the Reagan administration, determined that the Park Service budget probably grew "at a rate high enough to accommodate the effects of both inflation and the addition of new areas" (183).

21. Schaller, *Reckoning with Reagan*, 100–102; *New York Times*, 6 February 1983, sec. 1, 22.

22. The General Accounting Office reported that Watt had misused nearly nine thousand dollars in order to hold the parties. Watt reimbursed the government, and the Republican party reimbursed Watt. *Washington Post*, 1 January 1982, B1; 25 February 1982, A1; 28 February 1982, B1; Hal K. Rothman, *The Greening of a Nation? Environmentalism in the United States since 1945* (Fort Worth: Harcourt Brace College Publishers, 1998), 169–71. Watt proved an uncommonly clumsy politician and made important enemies within the administration, including Nancy Reagan. Impolitic humor was a special weakness. He was forced to resign in September 1983 after telling an offensive joke at a U.S. Chamber of Commerce meeting. Watt was replaced by William Clark of California, a friend of the president, chosen in part for "his ability to keep out of the limelight" (Rothman, *Greening of a Nation*, 188).

23. Richard F. Fenno Jr., *When Incumbency Fails: The Senate Career of Mark Andrews* (Washington: Congressional Quarterly Press, 1992), 67–68.

24. Interview of William Wellman, 16 July 1996; Andrews to author, 30 August 1997; interview of Andrea Winkjer Collin, 31 July 1996. Andrea Collin said she never heard Fort Union mentioned in Andrews's office during the two years she worked there. For the ubiquity of add-ons in park financing, see Rettie, *Our National Park System*, 182–83.

Wellman believed that there was no malice involved in the incident, just misunderstanding. He guessed that someone in the legislative office had called the planning office and asked, "How much more money do you need for the reconstruction analysis?" The answer was "none" because the reconstruction analysis had already been completed.

25. *Sidney Herald*, 5 October 1977, 4 February 1981, 22 December 1982; *Williston Herald*, 24 December 1979; on the Snowden Bridge, see appendix B. The two Montana counties had a difficult time finding an underwriter for the insurance. Two large bridge insurance firms finally wrote a policy in 1982 but then canceled after

three months when they discovered that vehicles shared the roadbed with trains—something the county commissioners had told them at the start of negotiations but which the insurance companies seem to have had difficulty believing.

26. *Williston Herald*, 24 December 1979; *Sidney Herald*, 24 March 1980.

27. William L. Bowen, Chief, Division of National Park and Recreation Area Planning, to Howard W. Baker, Regional Director, Midwest Region, 18 February 1963; R. J. Elliott, Director, State Parks, to Baker, 21 February 1963; Baker to Director, National Park Service, 1 March 1963, H1415 (FOUS), THRO; Ben Innis, "C of C Bridge Hearing," KEYZ Radio News story, 12 March 1979, courtesy of Rick Collin; interview of Orville Loomer, 2 July 1996; "Transcript of Public Hearing [Regarding the Location of the New Bridge] at Trenton High School, Trenton, ND, and Fairview High School, Fairview, MT, August 6, 1981," Innis Papers (26–061), FOUS.

28. *Williston Herald*, 3 December 1981, 12 April 1984.

29. Wellman to Charles A. Gullicks, Programming and Surveys Engineer, North Dakota State Highway Department, 6 June 1980, Innis Papers; *Williston Herald*, 7 December 1981; interview of Tom Rolfstad, 16 July 1996.

30. Harvey D. Wickware, Superintendent, THRO, to Regional Director, RMR, 21 May 1982; interview of William Wellman, 22 July 1996; "WE, THE PEOPLE" to Andrews, 19 May 1982, D30 (attic), FOUS. Wellman received a supportive call from Secretary Watt's office, and although he soon transferred to another park, he did not believe his transfer had anything to do with the petition.

31. Innis to Greg W. Hennessy, 31 August 1982, Innis Papers; Wellman interview; James E. Sperry, Superintendent, SHSND, to Innis, 22 July 1982; Innis memorandum of a telephone interview with Vern Neff, 26 July 1982; Fort Union–Fort Buford Council Meeting minutes, 4 August 1982, Innis Papers.

32. Innis to Connolly, 16 August 1976; Greg W. Hennessy to David McAdoo, 17 September 1982; Hennessy to Charles A. Gullicks, Program and Project Development Engineer, North Dakota State Highway Department, 28 September 1982; Innis to Duane Liffrig, undated [August or September 1982], Innis Papers. Innis's letter begins, "Yesterday you called me a liar." It should be noted that Ben Innis was no purist regarding the integrity of Fort Union's historic scene. In a discussion probably recorded in 1978 Innis told Wellman that Fort Union, like Mount Rushmore, would eventually have to have a place where visitors could "buy a hamburger or . . . a bottle of pop. . . . You'll have to set up a little concession for selling a lot of this tourist trap stuff. . . . It would be best located at the [Bodmer] Overlook if traffic can be managed up there." Audiotape labeled "Judge Burdick" in Innis Papers.

33. Gardner to Innis, 2 October 1982; Innis to Fort Union-Fort Buford Council "Members and Supporters," 8 October 1982; Frank A. Wenstrom to Innis, 13 October 1982, Innis Papers.

34. Duane R. Liffrig to Frank Wenstrom, 23 July 1982, Innis Papers. The so-called

MonDak Bridge was completed in the summer of 1985, in time for the sugar beet harvest.

35. Hedren, "Field Notes," 351; Rolfstad interview; *Williston Herald*, 12 April 1984; *Sidney Herald*, 4 September 1985.

36. Rettie, *Our National Park System*, 137; *Sidney Herald*, 24 March 1982; interview of Earle Kittleman, 7 August 1996.

37. Kittleman interview; Loomer interview; *The Prism: Williston's Monthly Magazine* (July 1983): 4.

38. Interview of Richard and Andrea Winkjer Collin, 31 July 1996; *Williston Herald*, 21 October 1983; GNDA *Action Alert* 59 (November 1983); *Fort Buford Post*, November–December 1983 [newsletter of the Fort Buford Sixth Infantry Association], 5.

39. Collin interview; Richard Collin diary, 7 November 1983, courtesy of Collin. Collin to Andrews, 7 November 1983, Innis Papers. Andrea Collin recalled that she was "probably the only person in all of Williston who said, 'You know [the proposed $10 million to reconstruct Fort Union] doesn't sound like a lot of money'—having just come from Washington, where these millions are bandied about."

40. Collin interview; Collin diary, 8 December 1983; *Williston Herald*, 19 February 1984.

41. Collin interview; interview of Greg Hennessy, 9 July 1996; Innis to Roy McCluskey, 30 April 1984, Innis Papers.

10. Winning the Appropriation

1. "Oil Boom Goes Bust for Town," *Chicago Tribune*, 17 October 1982, VI, 3; Glenn Wollan, North Dakota Industrial Commission, to author, 25 June 1998; "Behind the Oil Glut: Meaning for Americans," *U.S. News & World Report*, 15 March 1982, 47, 50; *Oil & Gas Journal* 80 (8 March 1982): 99, and (8 November 1982): 105; interview of Rick and Andrea Winkjer Collin, 31 July 1996; interview of Thomas C. Rolfstad, 16 July 1996; David B. Danbom, "Postscript," in Elwyn B. Robinson, *History of North Dakota* (Lincoln: University of Nebraska Press, 1966 [1995 reprint]), 604, 606; interview of Marvin Kaiser, 16 July 1996.

2. Harvey D. Wickware to Regional Director, RMR, 3 January 1980, A2615, THRO.

3. Telephone conversation with Rick Collin, 2 August 1996; Blake A. Krabseth, "Williston Can Become a Destination," *Williston Herald*, 26 May 1985, 9A. The "American Legacy Tour" was a loop between Bismarck and Williston that included Fort Abraham Lincoln, Fort Mandan, Knife River Indian Village NHS, Garrison Dam, Fort Union, Fort Buford, and the North and South units of Theodore Roosevelt National Park.

4. Interview of Paul Hedren, 6 August 1996; Kaiser interview; *Williston Herald*, 13 May 1984.

5. Hedren interviews, 18 June and 6 August 1996; Rolfstad interview; Kaiser interview; *Contemporary Authors, New Revision*, 37:236. Hedren served at Fort Laramie NHS, Wyoming, 1971–76; Big Hole National Battlefield, Montana, 1976–78; and Golden Spike NHS, Utah, 1978–84.

6. Greg Hennessy, Williston lawyer and chairman of the Friends of Fort Union, quoted in *Minot Daily News*, 24 December 1996, A6; Rolfstad interview; *Bismarck Tribune*, 4 January 1997; Hedren to author, 23 November 1997; Bearss to Associate Director, Cultural Resources, 31 July 1991, Park History Files, National Register, History, and Education, WASO; *Williston Herald*, 2 August 1992, 1A.

7. Collin interview; Hedren interview, 6 August 1996; *Bismarck Tribune*, 4 January 1997. In Winkjer's article Hedren argued that it was "time for a change"—by upgrading the museum displays. *Williston Prism*, July 1984, 4; telephone conversation with Michael Jones, 29 January 1998.

8. Hedren, "Field Notes: Why We Reconstructed Fort Union," *Western Historical Quarterly* 23 (August 1992): 351; Hedren interview, 6 August 1996.

9. Dwight F. Rettie, *Our National Park System: Caring for America's Greatest Natural and Historic Treasures* (Urbana: University of Illinois Press, 1995), 133–38; Richard W. Sellars and Melody Webb, *An Interview with Robert M. Utley on the History of Historic Preservation in the National Park Service, 1947–1980* (Santa Fe: Southwest Cultural Resources Center, 1988), 50; Carla Kelly, "Robert Utley: Carrying History to the People," M.A. thesis, Northeast Louisiana University, 1992, 86–87. It should be noted again that the "partial reconstruction" of Fort Union endorsed by the *Reconstruction Analysis* has not been completed and that reconstruction of the store range and the dwelling range awaits only an appropriate political or economic moment.

10. Rolfstad interview; *Sidney Herald*, 8 August 1984, 1; *Williston Herald*, 12 July 1984.

11. Brickshawana's model was highly accurate except for its shape: it was constructed conventionally as a rectangle rather than a parallelogram. About a yard square, the bulky model became a standard prop at promotional activities. Rolfstad recalled a trip to the Sidney Chamber of Commerce in which the model in its glass case was "loaded in the back of a National Park Service station wagon. It looked like a hearse [with] this box in the back; and here we go all dressed up in suits . . . driving this vehicle across the Snowden Bridge." Rolfstad interview. Like the Fort Union model, which is still on display at the park, a model of Louisbourg, built before the partial reconstruction of that site, "survived the test of more than three decades of intensive research" and continues to fascinate visitors. Terry Maclean, *Louisbourg Heritage: From Ruins to Reconstruction* (Sydney, Nova Scotia: University College of Cape Breton Press, 1995), 17–18.

12. "We paid like $1,300 to have those two models built, including all the materials, glass cases, and stands, the whole works. It was the bargain of the century. To be honest [if the models had cost $2,500], I don't know if I could have gotten the re-

sources to make it happen." Rolfstad interview. Rolfstad to Garvin Stevens, 15 September 1989, courtesy of Rolfstad.

13. Rolfstad interview; Hedren interview, 18 June 1996; Kaiser interview; Jones conversation; interview of Greg Hennessy, 9 July 1996.

14. Rolfstad interview; Hedren interview, 18 June 1996; Kaiser interview; Hennessy interview.

15. Jones conversation; Hedren interview, 18 June 1996; Jones to author, 3 February 1998.

16. Collin interview; Rolfstad interview; Hedren interview, 18 June 1996; *Minot Daily News*, 26 September 1993, 100–101.

17. Collin interview; Rolfstad interview; Hedren interview, 18 June 1996; Kaiser interview. Planners of the "Evening at the Confluence" were unaware that the movement to preserve Fort Union National Monument in New Mexico had been stimulated by a similar barbecue held thirty-three years earlier almost to the day. Liping Zhu, *Fort Union National Monument: An Administrative History* (Santa Fe: Southwest Cultural Resources Center, 1992), 22.

18. *Williston Herald*, 14 September 1984, 1; "Frontier State," *American Heritage* 44 (May–June 1993): 30. Schafer brought along a reproduction of a Remington bronco sculpture to be auctioned as a benefit to the Fort Union project. Schafer's Medora is a unique blend of private, state, and federal historic and entertainment attractions that include what *American Heritage* called a "wonderfully hokey variety show."

19. Hennessy interview; Hedren interviews.

20. Kaiser interview; Hedren interviews; *Williston Herald*, 17 May 1987, 1. Kaiser was a former partner in a law firm that included the fathers of Andrea Winkjer and Tom Rolfstad. Kaiser enjoyed making the grand gesture. After learning that the best buckskin clothing was brain-tanned by Larry Belitz of Hot Springs SD, he had his chartered plane diverted there after a business trip to Pierre.

21. Rick Collin to Senator Quentin Burdick, 18 January 1985, courtesy of Collin; Hedren interview, 18 June 1996; Kaiser interview. Eight board members were elected at the first official meeting of the Friends of Fort Union on 3 October 1984: Mike Jones, chairman; Rick Collin, vice-chairman; Dale Sailer, treasurer; Andrea Winkjer, secretary. Additional board members were Tom Rolfstad, Vernon Johnson, Charles Evanson, and Sylvia Harmon. A meeting on 20 November approved formation of five committees with chairmen Marvin Kaiser (Finance), Rick Collin (Legislative), Blake Krabseth (Promotional), Tom Rolfstad (Development), and Charlie Evanson (Historical). Of the nine officers and committee chairmen, seven were from Williston, two (Sailer and Evanson) from Montana.

22. J. M. Shontz to Thomas Rolfstad, 1 March 1985, Mon-Dak Heritage Center, Sidney MT; *Sidney Herald*, 10 April 1985, 3, and 21 April 1985, 5; *Confluence News* (summer 1985), 2; Collin diary, 12 March 1985, courtesy of Rick Collin.

23. Collin interview; Superintendent's Annual Report, 1985, FOUS; *Confluence News* (summer 1985), 2; Rick and Andrea Collin to author, 23 January 1998.

24. Rolfstad to Stevens, 15 September 1989; Hedren interviews.

25. *Sidney Herald*, 23 June 1985. The six senators were Mark Andrews (R-ND), Quentin Burdick (D-ND), Max Baucus (D-MT), John Melcher (D-MT), James McClure (R-ID), and Robert Byrd (D-WV).

26. Russell E. Dickenson to Dennis E. Butler, 28 December 1984, courtesy of Rick Collin.

27. "A Man to Match the Mountains," *National Parks* 67 (January–February 1993): 18–19; Cary Silver, "William Penn Mott: A Mountain of Strength in the Public Parks," *The Rotarian* 149 (December 1986): 18–21; Hedren interview, 18 June 1996. On the solicitation of corporate philanthropy to benefit the parks during the Reagan years, see Rettie, *Our National Park System*, 188.

28. On the Saturday before the Washington trip, the Friends' delegation met at the chamber of commerce to practice its presentation. Civic leaders played U.S. senators, and Harvey Wickware, superintendent of Theodore Roosevelt, took the role of the Park Service's Washington representative. Paul Hedren to author, 20 January 1998.

29. Collin interview; Andrews interview; Rolfstad interview; Collin diary, 18 June 1985. Rolfstad recalled that Senator Byrd said something like, "This Fort Union reconstruction project is a great one, and it has to be done. And to make sure it is, I give you my vote, my proxy, my body—whatever it takes to get this thing done!" "But," he concluded, glancing at his watch, "I've got another meeting. Good day, gentlemen." Rolfstad to Stevens, 15 September 1989.

30. Andrews interview. Andrews also mentioned the *Cardinal* in his flagpole dedication speech on 6 July.

31. The Fort Union Muzzle Loaders had been rescued from inactivity in 1982 by Dave Finders, a fur trade-era reenactor, or "buckskinnner," who had recently moved to Williston from Iowa. Although there was considerable overlap between membership of the Fort Buford Sixth Infantry Association and the Muzzle Loaders, the latter tended to be more family oriented because wives and children could also participate by dressing in period costume. Jones conversation.

32. Superintendent's Annual Report, 1985, FOUS; conversation with Girard Nehring, 30 July 1996; Jones conversation; *Minot Daily News*, 10 May 1985, 2. Among those who discussed the project were Dennis Borud, Dave Dorman, Dave Finders, Jim Gunderson, Jim Hoeflein, Orville Loomer, Girard Nehring, and Michael O'Boyle. The Muzzle Loaders also believed that if the National Park Service developed Fort Union, it might be easier to extract money from the State Historical Society to improve Fort Buford.

33. "Muzzle Loaders to Rebuild Fort Union Flagpole," press release, 19 March 1985, FOUS; Douglas D. Scott, *"This Flag-Staff Is the Glory of the Fort": Archeological Investi-*

gations of the Fort Union Flagpole Remains (Lincoln NE: Midwest Archeological Center, 1986), 1–2; Cronenberger to author, 26 January 1998. Cronenberger also designed, and the Muzzle Loaders rebuilt, the picket fence that had once enclosed the small garden around the flagpole.

34. Press release, 19 March 1985, FOUS; Grayce Ray, "Bauer Is Civilized Buckskinner," *Dakota View*, 21 March 1985, 2, 7; Loomer interview; Jones conversation; Cronenberger to author, 26 January 1998. The completed pole, which weighed about five tons, was eighteen inches wide at the base, ten inches at the crow's nest (a six-foot-by-one-and-a-half-foot platform, fifty-five feet high), and four inches at the top. Michael O'Boyle crafted the copper weathervane (and in the modern version, lightning rod) in the shape of a fish that topped the structure.

35. Douglas Scott, the NPS archaeologist who supervised the flagpole survey, made some unguarded comments to a reporter, who then characterized Scott's archaeological philosophy as the use of "the biggest possible tool for the job . . . to save time and money." A consequent exchange of letters in the *Minot Daily News* between Scott and another archaeologist prefigured the disagreements about Fort Union excavations that were to dog the project during the next few years; see Jane F. Kostenko, letter to the editor, *Minot Daily News*, 1 June 1985, and Scott's reply, 22 June 1985.

36. *Minot Daily News*, 10 May 1985, 2; *Confluence News* (summer 1985): 1; *Williston Herald*, 21 May 1985, 1; interview of Rick Cronenberger, 16 July 1998. Former club president Mike Jones, whose position as a cable television manager provided frequent contacts with other utility companies, arranged to have a local power company drill the hole and set the flagpole.

37. *Richland Free Press* (Sidney MT), 10 July 1985; dedication program, in Mon–Dak Heritage Center, Sidney MT.

38. Transcript of Andrews's speech, 6 July 1985, courtesy of Rick Collin; Hedren interviews. Senator Burdick also promised Hedren that money for the project would be found.

39. Hedren interview, 18 June 1996; Rolfstad interview; *Confluence News* (fall 1985): 4; Hedren, "Reconstruction," 13.

40. Collin diary, 18 and 19 September 1985; taped interview of Mark Andrews, 20 December 1985, courtesy of Collin; *Plains Reporter*, 1 January 1986. The first appropriation for reconstruction was a "redirected appropriation," which meant that Congress told the Park Service how it had to spend money already appropriated. This sort of meddling was, of course, resented at Park Service headquarters. Subsequent appropriations consisted of "new money." Hedren interview, 18 June 1996.

11. Groundwork for the Reconstruction

1. *Williston Herald*, 27 February 1989, 1A; interview of Paul Hedren, 18 June 1996; interview of Marvin Kaiser, 16 July 1996.

2. Paul Hedren, "Field Notes: Why We Reconstructed Fort Union," *Western Histori-

cal Quarterly 23 (August 1992): 352; Marvin Kaiser to Mark Andrews, 26 July 1985, Research Files 506, FOUS; Hedren interview, 18 June 1996; Jerry Rogers, Associate Director for Cultural Resources, to Ed Bearss, Chief Historian, 3 June 1985, Park History Files, National Register, History, and Education, WASO.

3. Interview of Paul Hedren, 6 August 1996; interview of Bill Hunt, 10 July 1996; conversation with Thomas Thiessen, 9 June 1998; Hunt, "The Fort Union Trading Post Reconstruction Project: Archeology Costs and Results" (1988), FOUS; Neckels to Director, 25 September 1985, Park History Files, WASO. Old Fort William, which opened in 1973, is the largest reconstructed fur trading post in North America, but it was rebuilt more than eight miles upriver from its original site. Parks Canada later reconstructed a blockhouse at Coteau-du-Lac NHS, Quebec, immediately adjacent to its archaeological remains.

4. Kaiser to Andrews, 22 November 1985; Andrews to Kaiser, 9 December 1985; Andrews to Neckels, 20 December 1985, Research File 405, FOUS. Transcript of radio interview between Rick Collins and Andrews, 20 December 1985, Research File 506, FOUS. On 11 March 1986 Andrews had Director Mott declare his support for on-site reconstruction during a meeting of the Interior appropriations subcommittee (transcript, D18, FOUS).

5. P.L. 89-665; William J. Murtagh, *Keeping Time: The History and Theory of Preservation in America* (New York: Sterling Publishing Co., 1988), 70; Brit Allan Storey, "The Advisory Council on Historic Preservation: Its Role in the Developing American Preservation Program," in Ronald W. Johnson and Michael G. Schene, *Cultural Resources Management* (Malabar FL: Robert E. Krieger Publishing Co., 1987), 21-48; Thomas F. King, *Federal Planning and Historic Places: The Section 106 Process* (Walnut Creek CA: Alta Mira Press, 2000), 15-22.

6. Neckels to James E. Sperry, SHPO for North Dakota, 7 October 1985; Sperry to Neckels, 16 October 1985; Marcella Sherfy, SHPO for Montana, to Lorraine Mintzmyer, Regional Director, RMR, 17 October 1985, Research Files 506, FOUS; Thomas F. King, Director, Office of Cultural Resource Preservation, to Mintzmyer, 1 April 1986, H30 (attic), FOUS. Cynthia Grassby Baker, Advisory Council on Historic Preservation Chairman, to William Penn Mott, NPS Director, 14 May 1986, Park History Files, WASO.

7. Baker to Mott, 14 May 1986; Mott to Baker, 23 May 1986; Rogers to Mott [handwritten memo], 23 May 1986, Park History Files, WASO; King's comment in *Preservation News* 26 (July 1986): 8.

8. Rogers to Mott, 23 May 1986; Dwight F. Rettie, *Our National Park System: Caring for America's Greatest Natural and Historic Treasures* (Urbana: University of Illinois Press, 1995), 10. Outside the preservationist community, opposition to the Fort Union reconstruction in North Dakota and Montana seems to have been insignificant. Park files include two letters to the editor from fiscal conservatives, one published in the *Sidney Herald* (6 October 1985) and the other in the *Minot Daily News* (15 October

1985), which criticize the proposed reconstruction as an example of irresponsible government spending. But even the North Dakota Republican convention in April 1986 adopted, without debate (although with a few audible "nays"), a resolution supporting the project. *Williston Herald*, 14 April 1986, 2A.

9. Hedren, "Field Notes," 352; Rettie, *Our National Park System*, 188–91; *Sidney Herald*, 16 March 1986, 1; *Minot Daily News*, 16 March 1986. In March 1986 a Friends' delegation again met in Washington with the NPS director in an attempt to order the details of the dual fundraising effort.

10. Interview of Rick and Andrea Winkjer Collin, 31 July 1996; see also comments of Tom Rolfstad in Linda Hunt, "Happy Anniversary, Fort Union!" *North Dakota Horizons* (summer 1996): 15.

11. Hedren interview, 18 June 1996; Kaiser interview; interview of Greg Hennessy, 9 July 1996; interview of Orville Loomer, 2 July 1996.

12. *Williston Herald*, 5, 12, and 21 December 1986, 25 February 1987, 21 and 29 April 1987, 24 May 1987; Greg Hennessy, "Fort Union Reconstruction Will Help the Entire Region," *Williston Herald*, 15 February 1987; Kaiser interview, 16 July 1996; *Confluence News* (fall 1987): 3. Montana fundraising was much slower; by May 1987 Montana had raised only $3,500 toward a $50,000 goal. *Sidney Herald*, 6 May 1987, 6. The Friends of Fort Union concluded its fund drive in September 1987 after raising $136,545. Of that amount, only $4,607 was raised from the heavily promoted coupon drive. *Confluence News* (fall 1987): 4. The most significant in-kind donation was the survey and earthmoving phase of a new access road and parking area. Doug O'Neil, a Williston oil-field engineer, managed the project and raised in-kind contributions of machinery, fuel, and tools from perhaps fifty local businesses—even from the hard-hit oil-field contractors. *Sidney Herald*, 10 June 1987, 1; *Confluence News* (fall 1987): 1.

13. Mott's general plan to raise private funds for the National Park Service anticipated employing a fundraising organization under contract to the National Park Foundation that would raise perhaps $2 billion nationally. Ironically, Mott argued that fundraising was a "sophisticated business and generally . . . not carried out successfully by amateurs." Mott to Regional Director, 27 October 1986, box 5, William Penn Mott Papers, Special Collections, Clemson University Libraries, Clemson SC.

14. Hedren interview, 18 June 1996; Kaiser interview; Priscilla R. Baker to John Jacob Astor VIII, 7 May 1987, Research File 405, FOUS.

15. Priscilla R. Baker to author, 9 July 1996.

16. Baker to Astor, 24 April 1986, Research File 405, FOUS; Baker to author, 9 July 1996; *Minot Daily News*, 8 August 1986, A1.

17. Baker to author, 9 July 1996; Hedren interview, 18 June 1996; *Minot Daily News*, 7 August, 13 and 21 September 1987; Mott to Edward Dzierzawski, 30 September 1987, box 8, Mott Papers, Clemson University; *Confluence News* (fall 1987): 2.

18. Baker to author, 9 July 1996; *Williston Herald,* 13 August 1989, 1A. Both Baker and Marcy Culpin, the project historian, provided photographs of the landscape and drawings of the historic fort from which Back (1922–) recreated the fort on canvas. The painting is carefully composed and well conveys the excitement of the historic scene, although like all reconstructions, it has its idiosyncrasies. In the painting the palisade is not whitewashed because Back had a hard time believing that the "Wild West [would] have bothered to tart the fort up to such a pristine standard." Also, although the scene represents the arrival of the *Yellow Stone,* "c. 1835," the Bourgeois House pictured is the two-story structure of twenty years later. *Williston Herald,* 9 August 1989, 1A; Back to Marcy Culpin, 13 June 1988.

19. Baker to author, 9 July 1996; telephone conversation with John Bennison, 12 August 1998.

20. Hedren interview, 18 June 1996; *Minot Daily News,* 19 September 1987; *Plains Reporter* (Williston ND), 30 September 1987; *Confluence News* (fall 1989): 1; Hedren to author, 18 June 1998. Waiting for the appropriations added "some stress" to the reconstruction project because no one could be completely certain that Congress would vote the money. Rick Cronenberger to author, 8 September 1998.

Although the reasons for Andrews's defeat are beyond the scope of this work, political scientist Richard F. Fenno found them striking enough to write *When Incumbency Fails: The Senate Career of Mark Andrews* (Washington DC: CQ Press, 1992). In short, Fenno's thesis is that politicians do not live by the pork barrel alone. Andrews's support for the Fort Union project was so insignificant in comparison to the millions he directed to other North Dakota projects that Fenno does not even mention the historic site in his monograph.

21. Douglas D. Scott, Thomas D. Thiessen, and William J. Hunt Jr., "Scope of Work for 1986 Archeological Investigations at the Fort Union Trading Post National Historic Site in Preparation for Partial Reconstruction," 19 December 1985 (MWAC), H3015, FOUS; Hunt to Chief, MWAC, 23 June 1982, curatorial file 24–130, FOUS.

22. Interview of William J. Hunt Jr., 9 July 1996; Thomas Thiessen to author, 5 June 1998; *Dakota View* (Williston ND), 5 June 1986, 2; *Minot Daily News,* 15 June 1986, D3; William J. Hunt, "The Fort Union Reconstruction Archeology Project," CRM 12, no. 1 (1989): 2–5; Barry Mackintosh to author, 7 August 1998.

23. A mechanized shaker was used by amateur archaeologist Montague Tallant in west–central Florida as early as the 1930s (South Florida Museum, Bradenton FL). Even grain cleaners had been used before by Gayle F. Carlson at a Fort Atkinson excavation in 1985. Nevertheless, mechanized shakers are used rarely at archaeological sites because they make a significant contribution only to large projects and only where there is a ready source of electricity. Hunt interview; William J. Hunt Jr. and Joseph Brandon, "Using Agricultural Grain Cleaners to Mechanically Screen Earth," *Journal of Field Archaeology* 17 (1990): 116–21; "V[olunteers] I[n] P[arks] Archaeology Orientation," videotape, FOUS Library; *Dakota View,* 5 June 1986, 3.

24. Hunt interview; Hunt, "Fort Union Reconstruction Archeology Project," 3; Bill R. Chada, "AutoCAD and Fort Union Trading Post: The Field Application of a Computer Aided Drafting Program," CRM 12, no. 1 (1989): 5–6. The most serious problem with the CAD experiment at Fort Union was that a single computer operator could not keep pace with forty excavators.

25. Hunt, "Fort Union Reconstruction Archeology Project," 3; "V[olunteers] I[n] P[arks] Archaeology Orientation," videotape, FOUS Library; Hunt interview; *Williston Herald*, 14 March, 8 and 28 July 1986; *The Forum of Fargo-Moorhead*, 23, 25, and 29 June 1986; *Williston Herald*, 25 July 1988, 1A.

26. *Williston Herald*, 28 July 1986, 1; Hunt interview.

27. The three major structures were a large building between the store range and the east palisades, perhaps a warehouse; the fort's first blacksmith shop; and above the latter, another building that may have contained a gun shop. Secondary structures included remains of the palisade bracing, a dairy, the north gate, army-era storerooms and privies, a charcoal house for later blacksmith shops, horse stables, a possible corral, and a late-1850s sawmill.

28. Hunt, "Fort Union Reconstruction Archeology Project," 4; Hunt interview; William J. Hunt Jr., "'At the Yellowstone . . . to Build a Fort': Fort Union Trading Post, 1828–1833," in *Fort Union Fur Trade Symposium Proceedings, September 13–15, 1990* (Williston ND: Friends of Fort Union Trading Post, 1994). Early in the first season both Thiessen and Hunt were bearded by an inebriated Indian who denounced archaeology as ghoulish, predicted the archaeologists would uncover a human burial, and declared that in consequence Hunt would be cursed. To the delight of the media and the dismay of the archaeologists, the excavators discovered a female skeleton in the fort's well. Almost predictably, a tribal chairman complained through his Washington lawyer that the tribes had not been "notified in advance that Indian burial sites were likely to be disturbed." *Billings Gazette*, 8 September 1986, 1; Thiessen to author, 5 June 1998; Steven Leroy DeVore and William J. Hunt Jr., "Fort Union Trading Post National Historic Site (32WI17): Material Cultural Reports, Part X: Native American Burials and Artifacts" (Lincoln NE: Midwest Archeological Center, National Park Service, 1994), 8–13, 19; William Penn Mott to Reid Peyton Chambers, 4 November 1986, Park History Files, WASO.

29. Kaiser to Andrews, 13 June 1986, Research File 405; Kaiser to Neckels, 1 October 1986, H3015 (attic), FOUS. In an effort to be aboveboard in his criticism, Kaiser showed the letter to Thiessen and Hunt. Since Kaiser had been cordial, Thiessen compared reading the letter to "being punched in the gut." Thiessen to author, 5 June 1998.

30. Kevin L. Jones, *Archaeological Site Stabilisation and Reconstruction in the United States* (Wellington, New Zealand: Department of Conservation, 1994), 32–33; Paul Hedren to Kevin Jones, 21 July 1993, H18, FOUS; Hunt interview; Hedren to author, 19 September 1996; Hunt, "Firearms and the Upper Missouri Fur Trade Frontier:

Weapons and Related Materials from Fort Union Trading Post National Historic Site (23WI17), North Dakota," Ph.D. dissertation, University of Pennsylvania, 1989, 109–10.

31. *Confluence News* (winter 1987): 2; Thiessen to author, 5 June 1998.

32. Hedren to author, 19 September 1996; Chief Anthropologist, Chief Historian to Associate Director, Cultural Resources, 19 May 1988, Park History Files, WASO; Kaiser interview. Friends' treasurer Greg Hennessy called the archaeology "a great thing [but] ungodly pricey." Hennessy interview.

33. J. Signe Snortland–Coles to F. A. Calabrese, 17 June 1987, H3015, FOUS; Hedren interview, 18 June 1996; Hedren to Kevin Jones, 26 August 1994, H1417, FOUS: "Certainly we can do much to promote the research that we find so important. . . . But I cannot support the notion that the NPS should . . . take on this research as a self-imposed obligation, which is precisely what the archaeological community has created for itself. It would be like imposing on historians the obligation to write every story possible or desirable from resources in a park library."

34. Hunt interview; Loomer interview; interview of Dennis Borud, 28 June 1996.

35. Hunt interview; Thiessen to author, 5 June 1998.

36. Kaiser interview; Hedren interview, 18 June 1996; Priscilla Baker to author, 9 July 1996. Baker recalled that when archaeologists spoke at WASO managers' meetings, Mott "would tighten up all over and his face would turn red."

37. Based on anecdotal evidence from his peers, Hunt believed that the seventy-seven-year-old Mott might have been suffering some mental confusion at the time of the confrontation. Although Mott's letters and speeches seem lucid enough, it is perhaps noteworthy (or perhaps not) that when Mott appeared at the Waldorf Astoria with Lord Astor later that year, he forgot where he was staying in New York. Because he had left his travel instructions with his luggage and the room key did not include the establishment's name, Mott had to hire a security firm to find his hotel. Hunt interview; Mott to Edward Dzierzawski, 30 September 1987, box 8, Mott Papers, Clemson University.

38. Hunt interview; Hedren interview, 18 June 1996; Rodd Wheaton to author, 29 May 1998; Kaiser interview; Chief Anthropologist [Douglas H. Scovill], Chief Historian [Edwin C. Bearss] to Associate Director, Cultural Resources, 19 May 1988, Park History Files, WASO.

39. Hunt interview; Hedren interview.

40. On several occasions Hunt and MWAC attempted to explain the cost, pace, and value of the excavation to the RMRO and the North Dakota supervisors—with limited success. For instance, THRO superintendent C. Mack Shaver took a dim view of Hunt's claim that the NPS had saved money after archaeologists discovered that ten-inch, rather than twelve-inch, square timbers had been used in the original fort. Shaver asserted that the discovery, although valuable in terms of historical accuracy,

raised the project's cost because smaller timbers increased handling, shipping, and construction expenses. The archaeologists probably had the better of the argument, though. Each twelve-by-twelve-inch timber would have increased the amount of wood in the palisade by twenty square inches. Since the cost of shipping timber was based on weight, transportation costs would also have risen. The larger trees needed to make twelve-by-twelve-inch timbers would have made the wood more expensive, and the smaller timbers actually used were easier to work with. Hunt, "The Fort Union Trading Post Reconstruction Project: Archeology Costs and Results," (1988), FOUS; Shaver to Regional Director, 3 February 1988, H2215, FOUS; Shaver to Hedren, 21 January 1988, H30, FOUS; interview of Rick Cronenberger, 16 July 1998.

12. Reconstructing Fort Union

1. Dwight F. Rettie, *Our National Park System: Caring for America's Greatest Natural and Historic Treasures* (Urbana: University of Illinois Press, 1995), 107–8; interview of Paul Hedren, 6 August 1996; interview of Richard Cronenberger, 16 July 1998. The Denver Service Center received brief media attention during the fall of 1997 when it was discovered that DSC had built a two-hole, earthquake-proof outhouse at Delaware Water Gap National Recreation Area for $333,000. (One visitor mistook the toilet for a visitor center. "It's beautiful," she said, "but I'm glad I always travel with Handi Wipes.") *Greenville News*, 11 October 1997, 1F; *Forbes* 161 (9 January 1998): 90. Since the DSC supported itself on a percentage of building costs, there was a disincentive to design cheaply.

2. Cronenberger interview; interview of Rodd Wheaton, 14 July 1998; Jack Neckels, Acting Regional Director, to Director, 25 September 1985, Park History Files, WASO; Rick Cronenberger to author, 29 October 1997, 26 January 1998. Cronenberger considered participation in the reconstruction a high point of his career: "What an opportunity! . . . How could I pass it up?" Similarly, Rodd Wheaton remembered the excitement of applying his research to actual construction as opposed to preservation projects, which were "much more mundane. . . . It was fun selecting the trim moldings and finding sources; it was fun selecting finials for the newel posts from early-nineteenth-century pattern books. It was a very heady experience for all of us initially involved." Wheaton to author, 21 January 1998.

3. Cronenberger interview; Wheaton interview.

4. Cronenberger to author, 28 January 1998; telephone conversation with Cronenberger, 30 July 1996; Cronenberger interview; interview of William Hunt, 9 July 1996; Wheaton interview; Mary Shivers Culpin, "Archival Collections—Why They Are Important," *CRM* 14, no. 4 (1991): 14.

5. For instance, the Fort Union photographs proved that the earlier, first-floor windows had seven-by-nine-inch panes of glass, indicating French influence and manufacture in New Orleans, whereas the 1850s windows had eight-by-ten-inch panes, suggesting that they had originated in Kansas City. Wheaton interview.

6. Cronenberger enjoyed incorporating pieces of the historic fabric into the reconstructed buildings, including original hearth stones in the trade house, the southeast cornerstone of the palisade, foundation stones at the south (river) entrance, and cobbles outside the north entrance. Cronenberger to author, 8 September 1998.

7. Cronenberger interview; Wheaton interview; *Minot Daily News*, 10 June 1987, D1; *Sidney Herald*, 8 February 1987, 1; Terry Maclean, *Louisbourg Heritage: From Ruins to Reconstruction* (Sydney, Nova Scotia: University College of Cape Breton Press, 1995), 107. A portrait of Martin Van Buren on the Bourgeois House pediment was reproduced by an artist who, ironically, had to hurry off to complete contracts for the Disney Studios. *Williston Herald*, 13 May 1987, 1A.

8. "Composition of Cost for Completion Report, Narrative Statement: The Bourgeois House Construction," FOUS.

9. *Williston Herald*, 14 October 1990; Wheaton interview; Cronenberger interview; Keith Warner, Contracting Officer, RMRO, to Yeater, Hennings, Ruff Architects, Ltd., 18 December 1986, H3015 (attic), FOUS. Rather than redesign the interior to include the heavy masonry necessary to support authentic chimneys, Cronenberger had false chimneys constructed from stucco and plaster.

10. Cronenberger interview; Cronenberger, "Fort Union Recollections," 26 January 1998, in possession of author; Wheaton interview.

11. Cronenberger interview.

12. Cronenberger interview.

13. Cronenberger interview; Cronenberger to author, 8 September 1998.

14. Cronenberger, "Fort Union Recollections"; *The Forum*, 29 June 1986.

15. Cronenberger interview; Cronenberger, "Fort Union Recollections"; *Sidney Herald*, 12 June 1988, 1. The air-drying yard at the Fort Union site was one the largest custom operations in the country. Douglas fir was brought from Washington to a nearby siding, and the heavy logs were stacked to take advantage of prevailing winds. Although the winds tended to blow from the opposite direction during the summer of 1988, the weather was extremely hot, with several days above one hundred degrees. Thirty percent of the timber's weight was lost in the drying process, and the wood dried so quickly that it sometimes exploded with a noise like a gunshot.

16. *Sidney Herald*, 12 June 1988, 1; Cronenberger to author, 25 February 1997; telephone conversation with Cronenberger, 30 July 1996; *Sidney Herald-Leader*, 23 July 1989, 1; interview of Orville Loomer, 2 July 1996; interview of Dennis Borud, 28 June 1996; *Williston Herald*, 26 February 1989, 1A (quotation from stonemason Bill Born); *Williston Herald*, 27 March 1987, 1A (quotation from woodworker Larry Mockel).

17. *Williston Herald*, 30 January 1986, 1A; Wheaton interview; Cronenberger interview. Wheaton spent a lot of emotional energy proving, at least to his own satisfaction, that because the columns on the upper porch were six feet eight inches, the height of the main deck of a riverboat, they had originated as steamboat salvage.

18. Cronenberger to author, 21 and 26 January 1998; Cronenberger interview.

19. Technically, the stonework was a veneer because it was not designed as a structural element. Nevertheless, it was, in Cronenberger's words, a "very substantial veneer.... You could probably fly a 747 into it and not knock it down." Cronenberger interview.

20. "Timber Contract to Be Awarded for Fort Union Trading Post National Historic Site," press release, 21 January 1988, K3415, FOUS; *Williston Herald,* 18 August 1988, 1A; Orville C. Loomer, "Reconstruction of Fort Union: Daily Diary," Research File 497, FOUS; *Williston Herald,* 26 February 1989, 7A; Paul Hedren, "Fort Union Trading Post: Restoring the Grandeur," rev. 26 June 1995 (slide script), 14, FOUS; conversation with Hunt, 1 June 1998; Hedren to author, 18 June 1998.

21. The rear of the Bourgeois House was also designed with boarded-up windows to suggest that although there was no pictorial evidence, one could guess where the windows were. "We thought we did a good job with those boarded-up windows until we read a quote in a local newspaper at the dedication [that said] we had reconstructed it so accurately that we boarded up the windows like they were originally. And that's when we realized ... who we had to design this thing for." Cronenberger interview.

22. *Minot Daily News,* 14 December 1990; *Williston Herald,* 20 July 1993, 1A; Cronenberger interview. In the *Reconstruction Analysis* the Indian trade house is called the "Indian-Artisan House." Since the artisans (blacksmith, tinner, and gunsmith) were displaced by 1851, the target date of the reconstruction, the official name has not been used here.

23. Kevin L. Jones, *Archaeological Site Stabilisation and Reconstruction in the United States* (Wellington, New Zealand: Department of Conservation, 1994), 32; Paul L. Hedren, "Field Notes: Why We Reconstructed Fort Union," *Western Historical Quarterly* 32 (August 1992): 352.

24. Hedren, "Fort Union Trading Post: Restoring the Grandeur," 14; *Williston Herald,* 2 June 1987, 1A; Cronenberger to author, 8 September 1998.

25. "Fort Union Grand Dedication, August 12 and 13, 1989," program booklet, FOUS; *Williston Herald,* 13 and 16 August 1989, 1A; Gavin Scott, "Exploring the Real West," *Time,* 7 August 1989, 65. The Friends of Fort Union raised the major share of the more than $25,000 necessary to pay for the weekend's events.

26. Ben Innis was mentioned in passing during the introduction of his wife, Jane, who had donated his library and papers to the park.

13. The Business of a Park

1. Hank Schoch to author, 26 July 1996; J. B. Lyon Jr., "Ft. Union Restoration Progress Slow," *Williston Herald,* undated clipping [winter 1971], FOUS.

2. Interview of Sylvester Putnam, 23 July 1996; interview of William Wellman, 22

July 1996. Wellman recalled that the cold sometimes froze the trailer doors shut; conversely, "depending on how the building was creaking and moaning," one of the doors wouldn't close at all and had to be wired shut. "But when it iced up real good, it sealed all the cracks in the trailers, and it was actually warmer. It was real common to have a good coat of ice and frost on the inside of the walls."

3. Putnam interview; Wellman interview. Putnam retreated to St. Louis or the South Unit of Theodore Roosevelt in the winter; Wellman maintained an office in Williston during his first two winters.

4. Wellman interview; Lynn Thompson to Paul Hedren, 10 April 1989, research files, FOUS.

5. Putnam interview; Wellman interview; interview of Dennis Borud, 28 June 1996; "Fort Union Trading Post" [brochure], GPO:1972—483-431/8.

6. Putnam interview; Wellman interview; *Williston Herald*, 23 July 1978; interview with Orville Loomer, 2 July 1996; "Monthly Report," 4 September 1975, 3 July 1976, December 1975, A2615, THRO; *Williston Plains Reporter*, 18 May 1974.

7. Wellman interview; Loomer interview; "Monthly Report," 1 July 1974, 2 August 1974, 7 July 1975, 4 February 1976, A2615, THRO.

8. Frazier interviewed by Tim Fought in *Grand Forks Herald*, 15 October 1989, CI.

9. Carroll Van West, "Reconsidering Western Historic Sites," *North Dakota History* 62 (winter 1995): 2–12.

10. Hedren to Interagency Resources Division, 23 September 1993, H32 (413), FOUS.

11. Rendezvous was first scheduled during the first week of July. "Annual Statement for Interpretation and Visitor Services, Fort Union Trading Post National Historic Site, FY 1994," FOUS; "Fort Union Rendezvous, June 13–16 [1996], Costs," FOUS; Loomer interview.

12. Paul Hedren to author, 15 September 1998; Randy Kane to author, 16 August 1998.

13. "Annual Statement for Interpretation and Visitor Services, Fort Union Trading Post National Historic Site, FY 1994," FOUS.

14. Scott Eckberg, "Fort Union Administrative History: I & RM Program Summary for 1991–1995" [hereafter "Summary"], manuscript, FOUS; *Confluence News* (fall 1994): 2.

15. Eckberg, "Summary"; Eckberg to Superintendent, THRO, 21 November 1991, THRO, P4219; *Williston Herald*, 16 August 1992, IA; interview of Paul Hedren, 6 August 1996. In the late 1990s Intertribal Day became "Indian Arts Showcase," which focused more on traditional crafts than did the earlier "pow-wow drum and dance program." Randy Kane to author, 16 August 1998.

16. Rodd Wheaton to Interpretive Planner, Harpers Ferry Center, 24 September

1986, D18, FOUS. By 1998 two barrels marked "Rye" and "High Wine" were displayed in the trade house. Ironically, tobacco was sold without controversy in the Indian trade house while in the same period the tobacco shop at Colonial Williamsburg was converted into a tobacco-free apothecary. "Rewriting Tobacco History," *North Carolina Farm Bureau News* (September 1995): 3.

17. Loomer interview; telephone conversation with Loomer, 12 August 1998. Loomer believed that park interpreters would be able to explain to visitors that the "ratty" whitewash and bone-strewn yard were typical of the fur traders' lifestyle.

18. Hedren interview, 6 August 1996; Hedren to Staff, 8 July 1996, A3415, FOUS; Daniel J. Boorstin, "An American Style in Historical Monuments," in *Hidden History: Exploring Our Secret Past* (New York: Harper & Row, 1987), 157–58.

19. Boorstin, "American Style," 158.

20. Interview of Audrey L. Barnhart, 26 July 1996; Eckberg to Hedren, 22 December 1991, H20, FOUS.

21. Barnhart interview; Hedren to Neckels, 28 November 1989, H3015, FOUS; Hedren to Kevin Jones, 26 August 1994, H1417, FOUS; conversation with Tom Thiessen, 9 June 1998; interview of William Hunt, 10 July 1996; Hedren to author, 24 June 1998.

22. Barnhart interview; Barnhart to author, 10 August 1998; Paul Hedren, "Annual Report," 1994, FOUS. The more fragile and significant items were held in the smaller vault of the Bourgeois House basement.

23. Much larger estimates for the number of Fort Union artifacts were current during the late 1980s and early 1990s. Estimates ranged from 1.5 to 3.1 million items, the larger number being posted at the park's website in 1998. Archaeologist Bill Hunt innocently instigated this artifact inflation with a widely publicized guess of 1.5 million items. No one was in a hurry to make an accurate count. Barnhart noted that the MWAC analysis was very expensive and that "the 1.5 figure didn't hurt us when it came to getting the green stuff." Barnhart to author, 10 August 1998.

24. Barnhart to author, 10 August 1998; Steven Leroy DeVore, *Beads of the Bison Robe Trade: The Fort Union Collection* (Williston ND: Friends of Fort Union Trading Post, 1992); *Confluence News* (spring 1993): 3.

25. P.L. 101–601. A good summary of the background and complications of NAGPRA is Andrew Gulliford, "Bones of Contention: The Repatriation of Native American Human Remains," *Public Historian* 18 (fall 1996): 119–43.

26. *Federal Register* 61 (4 October 1996): 52058–59.

27. Barnhart interview; Hedren interview; Barnhart to author, 26 October 1998.

28. Loomer interview; Borud interview; *Williston Herald*, 20 January 1987, 1A. Borud met Ben Innis when a teenager, considered him a mentor, and joined the Fort Buford Sixth Infantry in 1963.

29. Hedren to Kristin R. Freita, National Biological Service, 2 June 1995, N16; Eckberg, "Summary"; Loomer interview; Borud interview.

30. U.S. General Accounting Office questionnaire, 2 October 1992, N2623, FOUS.

31. Michael D. Snyder, Associate Regional Director, Planning and Assistance, to Daniel E. Cimarosti, U.S. Army Corps of Engineers, 22 March 1993, L7619 (RMR-PP); Eckberg to Hedren, 26 March 1993, L7621; Annual Report, 1993, FOUS.

32. David Harmon, *At the Open Margin: The NPS's Administration of Theodore Roosevelt National Park* (Medora ND: Theodore Roosevelt Nature and History Association, 1986), 70, 79–86. Within the oil industry, "slant drilling" is called "directional drilling."

33. Hedren to Regional Director, 23 August 1985, L2427; Chief, Mineral Resources Branch, to Regional Director, RMR, 28 March 1986, L24, FOUS; interview of Greg Hennessy, 9 July 1996. Oil pumping machinery remained visible at Fort Buford State Historic Site through the 1990s.

34. Appleman to Chief, Division of History and Archeology, 27 September 1962, L58, FOUS.

35. "Land Protection Plan, Fort Union Trading Post National Historic Site," 1985, FOUS.

36. Hedren to Regional Director, 18 October 1985, L1425, FOUS; Young memorandum, 3 October 1985, L1425 (RMR-ML), FOUS.

37. Borud interview; Hedren to Elmer R. Herdt, 2 June 1987, L76, FOUS; Annual Report, 1987; Hedren to author, 15 September 1998.

38. Case incident report, 13 December 1992; Richard Young to Hedren, 15 May 1992, L1425 (RMR-PA); Annual Report, 1992, FOUS; Hennessy interview; Borud interview; Hedren interview, 28 May 1996; Randy Kane to author, 2 October 1998.

39. Merrill J. Mattes, "On the Trail of Lewis and Clark with Thomas Hart Benton," *Montana: The Magazine of Western History*: 16 (summer 1966): 6–22; Acting Chief, Office of Resource Planning, to Assistant Director, Cooperative Activities, 4 April 1967, D18 (attic), FOUS; Loomer interview. Bodmer was a careful artist, but the drawing of Fort Union and the painting derived from it are not absolutely representational. Bodmer telescoped intervening ground to make the fort appear larger than it would with the naked eye.

40. Borud interview; Loomer interview.

41. The actual names of the friends groups vary and include Patriots of Fort McHenry, Washington Association of New Jersey, Los Amigos del Mal Pais, Lassen Volcanic National Park Foundation, and the Denali Citizens Council. Gary E. Machlis and Nancy C. Medlin, *Friends of the National Parks: A Report on Friends Groups throughout the National Park System* (Washington DC: National Park Foundation, 1993), 1, 9; *Williston Herald*, 4 November 1994, 14A.

42. Red River carts were sturdy all-wooden, two-wheeled vehicles first built by Métis in what today is northeastern North Dakota.

43. *Confluence News* (summer 1991): 3; *Sidney Herald*, 23 September 1990; Minutes, Friends of Fort Union, 19 June 1990; *Confluence News* (spring 1993): 2; Randy Kane to author, 16 August 1998; *Fort Union Fur Trade Symposium Proceedings, September 13–15, 1990* (Williston ND: Friends of Fort Union Trading Post, 1994); *Confluence News* (fall 1993): 2.

44. Candi Helseth, "Paddlefishing for $$$," *N.D. REC/RTC Magazine* (April 1996): 39–42; *Federal Register* 55 (25 April 1990): 17473–75; Hennessy interview; Hennessy, "Beaver, Buffalo, and Caviar at Fort Union," *Gavel* (December 1999–January 2000): 8–9; "Memorandum of Understanding between ND Game and Fish Department and Gold Star Caviar," February 1993, A2215, FOUS; *Fargo Forum*, 17 July 1994; *Confluence News* (July 1998): 3; Anita Sharpe, "The 80s Are Gone, but Caviar Is Back," *Wall Street Journal*, 6 September 1996, B1. In order to avoid confusion with a Brooklyn-based fish company, Gold Star Caviar became North Star Caviar in January 2000. *Williston Daily Herald*, 22 January 2000. Because they feed on plankton and will not take a hook, paddlefish are caught by dragging palm-sized treble hooks and chunks of lead across the river bottom. Since seventy-pound paddlefish are not uncommon, heavy salt-water rods and large-spooled reels are used to wrestle in the catch.

45. "Park Service Selects Southwest Parks and Monuments Association as Cooperating Association at Little Bighorn, Bighorn Canyon," NPS press release, 30 September 1993, K3415, FOUS; Dwight F. Rettie, *Our National Park System: Caring for America's Greatest Natural and Historic Treasures* (Urbana: University of Illinois Press, 1995), 94. Concessionaires are private, for-profit businesses franchised by the Park Service to provide services deemed necessary by the NPS, such as food, lodging, and horseback riding. Although NPS employees are allowed to assist cooperative associations, they are prohibited from operating concessions.

46. Eckberg, "Summary"; Minutes, Friends of Fort Union Trading Post, 18 September 1990, 23 July 1991, A2215, FOUS. Hedren's *Great Sioux War, 1876–77* contained material relevant to the history of Fort Union, notably its chapter on steamboating the Yellowstone.

47. Eckberg, "Summary"; interview of Marvin Kaiser, 16 July 1996; "Park Service Cuts Ties with Custer Group," *Billings Gazette*, 28 August 1993, 1A.

48. Eckberg, "Summary"; Kaiser interview; Hart to Homer F. Rouse, Associate Regional Director, Park Operations, 24 January 1992, K18, FOUS.

49. Kaiser to Baker, 8 May 1992, K18 (RMR-MI), FOUS; Eckberg, "Summary"; Kaiser interview; Hennessy interview; Hedren to author, 15 September 1998.

50. Eckberg, "Summary"; Minutes, Friends of Fort Union, 20 September 1994; *Confluence News* (spring 1993): 1. The *Confluence News* shaded the truth a bit, however,

when it announced that the FUA had been founded "through encouragement of the Regional Director" and "support from TRNHA."

51. The bookstore operation owed a good deal of its success to the high quality of the books sold there. Hedren and the chief rangers even encouraged the printing of new material—occasionally by the Fort Union Association itself—as well as reprints of classic out-of-print books and pamphlets. Eckberg, "Summary"; Randy Kane to author, 16 August 1998.

52. Kaiser interview; Eckberg, "Summary"; Kaiser to author, 6 August 1998; Hedren to author, 15 September 1998.

53. Kaiser interview; Eckberg, "Summary"; Kaiser to author, 6 August 1998; Hedren to author, 15 September 1998; *Williston Herald*, 8 September 1994, 1A. Other factors besides the FUA played a role in Eckberg's departure, notably what Hedren called the "horribly substandard quarters" forced on the chief ranger because of his responsibility to live at the site. Replacement of the rodent-infested, prefabricated staff quarters was hampered by an earlier overbuilding of housing at Theodore Roosevelt National Park and by the politics of park housing generally. After Fort Union Trading Post was reassigned to the NPS Midwest Region in 1996, the Omaha office built two new houses in Garden Coulee. Kane also had an advantage over Eckberg in that Kane had lower expectations and was unmarried. Eckberg, "Summary"; Hedren to author, 15 September 1998; Kane to author, 16 August 1998.

54. Eckberg, "Summary"; Hedren to Associate Regional Director, Administration, Midwest Region, 5 January 1995, S74 (MWR-A), FOUS; Kane to author, 16 August 1998.

55. *Confluence News* (July 1998): 4; Kaiser interview.

56. Hedren to author, 21 September 1998. The park was transferred back to the Midwest Region in 1996, and its superintendency became a formal training position.

Conclusion

1. At the same time, the smallpox epidemic that ravaged the Indians of the Great Plains in 1837 did not become so closely identified with Fort Union that the place acquired a "mark of shame"—which might have resulted in denying "the memory of the event by effacing all evidence and obliterating the site." See Kenneth E. Foote, *Shadowed Ground: America's Landscapes of Violence and Tragedy* (Austin: University of Texas Press, 1997), 174–75.

2. Barry Mackintosh to author, 28 August 1996.

3. Transcript of Andrews's speech, 6 July 1985, courtesy of Rick Collin. A similar attempt to justify partial reconstruction of Louisbourg urged Canadians to view the fort not "only in terms of the glories of monarchical France or the triumph of British arms" but in terms "of the two great cultures whose interplay made our nation possible." Terry Maclean, *Louisbourg Heritage: From Ruins to Reconstruction* (Sydney, Nova Scotia: University College of Cape Breton Press, 1995), 76–77.

4. Paul Hedren to author, 23 November 1997; interview of Paul Hedren, 18 June 1996; see also Dwight Rettie, *Our National Park System: Caring for America's Greatest Natural and Historic Treasures* (Urbana: University of Illinois Press, 1995), 137.

5. Rettie, *Our National Park System*, 137. Rettie, of course, intended his observation to be taken as negative criticism. But the "uncommon leeway" allowed by the Park Service also permits able NPS managers to respond creatively to local needs while remaining true to the agency's mission.

6. Michael James Kelleher, "Making History: Reconstructing Historic Structures in the National Park System," M.S. thesis, University of Pennsylvania, 1998, 60–68; Richard W. Sellars and Melody Webb, *An Interview with Robert M. Utley on the History of Historic Preservation in the National Park Service, 1947–1980* (Santa Fe: Southwest Cultural Resources Center, 1988), 34.

7. See Ivor Noël Hume, "Pragmatism and Professionalism: A Cellarman's View of the Ivory Tower," in *Forgotten Places and Things: Archaeological Perspectives on American History*, ed. Albert E. Ward (Albuquerque: Center for Anthropological Studies, 1983), 1–9.

8. One irony of Franklin Court is that although preservationists take pride in the "ghost house," nearby in the interpretive center the Park Service installed a "mirrored wall with flashing neon lights . . . a bank of telephones with recorded messages relaying famous people's opinions of Franklin," and a sound and light show displayed on a miniaturized theater in the round. Constance M. Greiff, *Independence: The Creation of a National Park* (Philadelphia: University of Pennsylvania Press, 1987), 224–26.

9. *Minot Daily News*, 27 August 1989; Bearss to Associate Director, Cultural Resources, 31 July 1991, National Register, History, and Education, WASO; Robert M. Utley to author, 14 July 1996 and 10 August 1997.

Appendix A

1. Lorett Treese, *Valley Forge: Making and Remaking a National Symbol* (University Park: Pennsylvania State University Press, 1995), 13–14.

2. W. A. Shoup to Charles Kessler, 16 January 1917, 11 August 1918, Charles Kessler Papers, William Andrews Clark Memorial Library, UCLA.

3. Charles Kessler to Stella Drumm, 14 June 1919; Joseph Culbertson to Charles Kessler, 12 July 1919, Missouri Historical Society, St. Louis. The map (which shows Fort Union with four bastions rather than two) is labeled "approximate plan of tunnel from Ft. Union to Mo. R. by Joe Culbertson" and is filed with the Kessler-Shoup correspondence at UCLA.

4. Charles Kessler to Ralph Budd, 29 June 1925, Kessler Papers; Frank B. Harper, "Fort Union and Its Neighbors on the Upper Missouri," pamphlet published by the Great Northern Railway, 1925, copy in FOUS Library.

5. Bill Hunt to author, 13 February 1997; Rick Cronenberger to author, 19 February 1997; Paul Hedren to author, 19 September 1996, H1417, FOUS.

Appendix B

1. The bridge originally connected the Great Northern main line with the line connecting Fairview (MT) to Watford City (ND). Snowden was a depot two miles north of the bridge and Nohly a small town to the immediate south. Both hamlets are now only geographic expressions and archaeological remains. Richard E. Johnson, "The Montana Eastern Railway, 1912 to 1935: Great Northern's Envisioned Second Main Line," *Hoofprints for the Yellowstone Corral of the Westerners* (1994): 3–15; Fred Schneider and Wayne Roberson, "Cultural Resource Inventory of the Mondak Bridge Project," State Highway Department of North Dakota and the University of North Dakota, 1981, FOUS Library.

2. James K. Finch, "John Alexander Low Waddell," *Dictionary of American Biography*, Supplement 2, 685–86; Frederic L. Quivik, *Historic Bridges in Montana* (Washington DC: National Park Service, 1982), 38, 71. The substructure for the bridge was built by the Union Bridge and Construction Company of Kansas City; steel for the superstructures was fabricated by the Gary, Indiana, works of the American Bridge Company; and the superstructure was assembled on site by Gerrick and Gerrick of Seattle.

3. Quivik, *Historic Bridges*, 38; Jim Miculka, "Snowden Bridge," leaflet published by the Theodore Roosevelt Nature and History Association (1980), FOUS.

4. Miculka, "Snowden Bridge"; John O. Lancaster to Alice Fryslie, 10 February 1977, H2215 (FOUS), THRO. Motorists stopped at the approach and cranked a box telephone to call a watchman in the lift house. If the bridge was clear of traffic, the watchman would raise an electronically controlled gate and collect the toll when the vehicle passed the center of the bridge. Later a toll booth was constructed on the north approach.

5. "Bridge Replacement—Mondak Bridge . . . Environmental Impact Statement," 1 June 1981, in Ben Innis Papers (26–060), FOUS. The bridge itself was only about a quarter of a mile long (1,159 feet); but before 1939, when the approach trestles were considerably shortened, they more than doubled its length to 3,257 feet. Miculka, "Snowden Bridge."

6. "Bridge Replacement."

7. "Bridge Replacement"; *Sidney Herald*, 5 October 1977, 4 September 1985. Although, practically speaking, the MonDak Bridge connects Montana and North Dakota, the new bridge is located entirely in North Dakota.

8. Barry Mackintosh to author, 7 January 1998.

SELECTED BIBLIOGRAPHY

Manuscript Materials and Government Documents
Interviews
Periodicals
Selected Books, Articles, and Dissertations

Manuscript Materials and Government Documents

By far the most important sources for the history of Fort Union Trading Post NHS (FOUS) are the files, library, and archives of the historic site itself, which include the Ben Innis Papers and the Fort Union–Fort Buford Council Papers. Also significant, especially for the internal NPS debate over reconstruction, are the Park History Files at the Washington DC office of the National Park Service (WASO). Because the superintendent of Theodore Roosevelt National Park (THRO) maintained a supervisory role over other North Dakota parks during this period, helpful material about the early years of the national historic site may be found in THRO files at Medora. For the site's years as a stepchild of the North Dakota state park system, the park files for Fort Buford at the State Historical Society of North Dakota (SHSND) in Bismarck provide assistance. Of nongovernment sources, the most significant are the records of the Great Northern Railway Company, Minnesota Historical Society, St. Paul. The following collections and institutions provided additional information:

> Cary, Charles H. Papers. Oregon Historical Society, Portland.
> Fogarty, Kate Hammon. Papers. Montana Historical Society, Helena.
> Hartzog, George B. Papers. Clemson University, Clemson, South Carolina.
> Kessler, Charles. Papers. William Andrews Clark Memorial Library, UCLA.
> Midwest Archeological Center, Lincoln, Nebraska.

214 SELECTED BIBLIOGRAPHY

Mon-Dak Heritage Center, Sidney, Montana.

Mott, William Penn. Papers. Clemson University, Clemson, South Carolina.

National Park Service, Harpers Ferry Center Library, West Virginia.

Neff, LaVern C. Papers. State Historical Society of North Dakota, Bismarck.

Interviews

The use of the word *interview* in the notes signifies the existence of both a tape recording and a complete catalog—although not a word-for-word transcription—of an oral interview. *Discussion* or *conversation* indicates more informal note taking. Tapes, catalogs, notes, and correspondence cited in the chapter notes have been deposited at Fort Union Trading Post National Historic Site. Interviews were conducted with the following individuals:

>Mark Andrews (10 July 1996)
>Audrey Barnhart (26 July 1996)
>Dennis Borud (28 June 1996)
>Ralph Chase (25 June 1996)
>Richard Collin and Andrea Winkjer Collin (31 July 1996)
>Richard Cronenberger (16 July 1998)
>Paul Hedren (28 May, 18 June, 6 August 1996)
>Greg Hennessy (9 July 1996)
>William Hunt (9 July 1996)
>Wilfred Husted (26 July 1996)
>Jane Innis (26 June 1996)
>Michael Jones (29 January 1998)
>Marvin Kaiser (16 July 1996)
>Earle Kittleman (7 August 1996)
>Orville Loomer (2 July 1996)
>Barry Mackintosh (20 May 1996)
>Sylvester Putnam (23 July 1996)
>Thomas Rolfstad (16 July 1996)
>William Wellman (22 July 1996)
>Rodd Wheaton (14 July 1998)

Periodicals

The chief newspaper source is the *Williston (ND) Daily Herald*, supplemented by the *Sidney (MT) Herald*, the *Minot (ND) Daily News*, the *Bismarck Tribune*, and weekly newspapers in the towns surrounding the confluence. The fourteen-year run of

Mondak's *Yellowstone News* (1906–20) is available on microfilm and as hard copy, largely complete, at the Mon-Dak Heritage Center, Sidney MT. *Confluence News*, the newsletter of the Friends of Fort Union, is helpful for the reconstruction and postreconstruction periods.

Selected Books, Articles, and Dissertations

Barbour, Barton H. *Fort Union and the Upper Missouri Fur Trade*. Norman: University of Oklahoma Press, 2001.

Bennett, Gordon. "Evoking the Past or Provoking the Gods? Some Observations on Period Reconstructions." CRM 15, no. 5 (1992): 21–24.

Boorstin, Daniel J. "An American Style in Historical Monuments." In *Hidden History: Exploring Our Secret Past*. New York: Harper & Row, 1987.

Chittenden, Hiram Martin. *The American Fur Trade of the Far West*. 2 vols. New York: Barnes & Noble, 1935.

Courage Enough: Mon-Dak Family Histories. Sidney MT: Mondak Historical and Arts Society, 1975.

DeVore, Steven Leroy. *Beads of the Bison Robe Trade: The Fort Union Trading Collection*. Williston ND: Friends of Fort Union Trading Post, 1992.

DeVore, Steven Leroy, and William J. Hunt Jr. *Fort Union Trading Post National Historic Site (32WI17): Material Cultural Reports, Part X: Native American Burials and Artifacts*. Lincoln NE: Midwest Archeological Center, National Park Service, 1994.

Fenno, Richard F., Jr. *When Incumbency Fails: The Senate Career of Mark Andrews*. Washington DC: Congressional Quarterly Press, 1992.

Fox, Gregory L. *A Late Nineteenth Century Village of a Band of Dissident Hidatsa: The Garden Coulee Site (32WI18)*. Lincoln NE: J & R Reprint Co., 1988.

Frazier, Ian. *Great Plains*. New York: Farrar, Straus, Giroux, 1989.

Glass, James A. *The Beginnings of a New National Historic Preservation Program, 1957 to 1969*. Nashville: American Association for State and Local History, 1990.

Harmon, David. *At the Open Margin: The NPS's Administration of Theodore Roosevelt National Park*. Medora ND: Theodore Roosevelt Nature and History Association, 1986.

Hedren, Paul L. "Field Notes: Why We Reconstructed Fort Union." *Western Historical Quarterly* 32 (August 1992): 349–54.

———. "The Reconstruction of Fort Union Trading Post: A Cause, A Controversy, and a Success." *Journal of Interpretation* 13 (1989): 10–15.

Historical Research Associates. "Testing and Evaluation of Cultural Resource Site 24RV102, The Mondak Townsite, Roosevelt County, Montana." 1982. [Fort Union Trading Post NHS Library].

Hosmer, Charles B., Jr. *Presence of the Past: A History of the Preservation Movement in the United States before Williamsburg*. New York: G. P. Putnam's Sons, 1965.

———. *Preservation Comes of Age: From Williamsburg to the National Trust, 1926–1949*. 2 vols. Charlottesville: University Press of Virginia, 1981.

Hunt, William J., Jr. "'At the Yellowstone . . . to Build a Fort': Fort Union Trading Post, 1828–1833." In *Fort Union Fur Trade Symposium Proceedings, September 13–15, 1990*. Williston ND: Friends of Fort Union Trading Post, 1994.

———. "Firearms and the Upper Missouri Fur Trade Frontier: Weapons and Related Materials from Fort Union Trading Post National Historic Site (23WI17), North Dakota." Ph.D. diss., University of Pennsylvania, 1989.

———. "The Fort Union Reconstruction Archeology Project." CRM 12, no. 1 (1989): 2–5.

———. *Fort Union Trading Post National Historic Site (32WI17) Material Culture Reports, Part I: A Critical Review of the Archeological Investigations*. Lincoln NE: Midwest Archeological Center, 1986.

Innis, Ben. *Sagas of the Smoky-Water: True Stories Reflecting Historical Aspects of the Missouri-Yellowstone Confluence Region, 1805–1910*. Williston ND: Centennial Press, 1985.

Kelleher, Michael James. "Making History: Reconstructing Historic Structures in the National Park System." M.S. thesis, University of Pennsylvania, 1998.

Kelly, Carla. "Robert Utley: Carrying History to the People." M.A. thesis, Northeast Louisiana University, 1992.

Kurz, Rudolph Friderich. *Journal of Rudolph Friderich Kurz*. Smithsonian Institution, Bureau of American Ethnology, Bulletin 115. Washington DC: Government Printing Office, 1937.

Larpenteur, Charles. *Forty Years a Fur Trader on the Upper Missouri*. Lincoln: University of Nebraska Press, 1989.

Lowenthal, David. *The Past Is a Foreign Country*. Cambridge: Cambridge University Press, 1985.

———. *Possessed by the Past: The Heritage Crusade and the Spirit of History*. New York: Free Press, 1996.

Mackintosh, Barry. "The Case against Reconstruction." CRM 15, no. 1 (1992): 17–18.

———. *The Historic Sites Survey and National Historic Landmarks Program: A History*. Washington DC: National Park Service, 1985.

———. *The National Parks: Shaping the System*. Washington DC: National Park Service, 1991.

———. "Reconstruction: Controversy on Both Sides of the Border." CRM 15, no. 5 (1992): 13.

———. "To Reconstruct or Not to Reconstruct: An Overview of NPS Policy and Practice." CRM 13, no. 1 (1990): 5.

Martin, Albro. "Ralph Budd." In *Railroads in the Age of Regulation, 1900–1980*, ed. Keith L. Bryant Jr. New York: Facts on File, 1988.

Mattes, Merrill J. "From Ruin to Reconstruction, 1920–1976." [Bent's Old Fort]. *Colorado Magazine* 54 (1977): 57–101.

Mattison, Ray H. "The State Historical Society of North Dakota: A Brief History." *North Dakota History* 34 (fall 1967): 295–319.

Merritt, Jane T. *The Administrative History of Fort Vancouver National Historic Site*. Seattle: National Park Service, Pacific Northwest Region, 1993.

Murtagh, William J. *Keeping Time: The History and Theory of Preservation in America*. New York: Sterling Publishing Co., 1988.

Noël Hume, Ivor. "Pragmatism and Professionalism: A Cellarman's View of the Ivory Tower." In *Forgotten Places and Things: Archaeological Perspectives on American History*, ed. Albert E. Ward. Albuquerque: Center for Anthropological Studies, 1983.

Pitcaithley, Dwight T. "Re-Creating the Past." CRM 17, no. 5 (1994): 28–29.

Reid, Russell. "The North Dakota State Park System." *North Dakota Historical Quarterly* 8 (October 1940): 63–78.

Rettie, Dwight F. *Our National Park System: Caring for America's Greatest Natural and Historic Treasures*. Urbana: University of Illinois Press, 1995.

Ricketts, Shannon, "Raising the Dead—Reconstruction within the Canadian Parks Service." CRM 15, no. 5 (1992): 13–20.

Robinson, Elwyn B. *History of North Dakota*. Lincoln: University of Nebraska Press, 1966.

Sellars, Richard, and Dwight Pitcaithley. "Reconstructions: Expensive, Life-Size Toys?" CRM 2, no. 4 (1979): 6–8.

Sellars, Richard W., and Melody Webb. *An Interview with Robert M. Utley on the History of Historic Preservation in the National Park Service, 1947–1980*. Santa Fe: Southwest Cultural Resources Center, 1988.

Sunder, John E. *The Fur Trade on the Upper Missouri, 1840–1860*. Norman: University of Oklahoma Press, 1965.

Sweetman, Alice M. "Mondak: Planned City of Hope Astride Montana-Dakota Border." *Montana* 15 (autumn 1965): 12–27.

Thompson, Erwin N. *Fort Union Trading Post: Fur Trade Empire on the Upper Missouri*. Williston ND: Fort Union Association, 1994.

Treese, Lorett. *Valley Forge: Making and Remaking a National Symbol*. University Park: Pennsylvania State University Press, 1995.

Utley, Robert M. "The Military Frontier on the Northern Plains, 1850–1900." In *Fort Buford and the Military Frontier on the Northern Plains, 1850–1900*, ed. Larry Remele. Bismarck: State Historical Society of North Dakota, 1987.

Van West, Carroll. "Reconsidering Western Historic Sites." *North Dakota History* 62 (winter 1995): 2–12.

Wallace, Michael. "Reflections on the History of Historic Preservation." In *Presenting the Past: Essays on History and the Public*, ed. Susan Porter Benson, Stephen Brier, and Roy Rosenzweig. Philadelphia: Temple University Press, 1986.

Weeks, Kay. "Are We Losing Authenticity to Recover Appearances?" CRM 17, no. 5 (1994): 26.

Wheaton, Rodd L. "Considering Reconstruction as an Educational Tool." CRM 15, no. 1 (1992): 16, 18.

———. "Reconstruction through Documentation." *Park Arts* 3 (summer-fall 1987): 7–9.
White, W. Thomas. "John M. Budd." In *Railroads in the Age of Regulation, 1900–1980*, ed. Keith L. Bryant Jr. New York: Facts on File, 1988.
Williams County Historical Society. *The Wonder of Williams County, North Dakota*. N.p.: Williams County Historical Society, 1975.
Wishart, David J. *The Fur Trade of the American West, 1807–1840: A Geographical Synthesis*. Lincoln: University of Nebraska Press, 1979.
Zhu, Liping. *Fort Union National Monument: An Administrative History*. Santa Fe: Southwest Cultural Resources Center, 1992.

INDEX

Fort Union is abbreviated as FU in the index. Page references in italics indicate illustrations.

Abbot, Lawrence, 38
Abraham Lincoln Birthplace NHS, 157 n.3
"add-ons," 115; defined, 88
Advisory Council on Historic Preservation (ACHP), 107–8
Agate Fossil Beds (NM, NE), 134
Ainslie, George, 122
Albright, Horace, 47, 175 n.18
alcohol: use of at FU, 14, 15–16, 21, 128, 133, 207 n.16; use of at Mondak, 29–30
Allott, Gordon, 4
American Bridge Company (Gary IN), 212 n.2
American Fur Company, 10, 11, 12, 15, 132
American Legacy Tour, 95, 193 n.3
American Society of Travel Agents, 111
Anderson, Adrienne B., 69–70, 106, *126*
Anderson, Clinton, 64
Andrews, Mark, 77, 86, 93, 114, 187 n.16, 191 n.24; and appropriations for FU reconstruction, 104, 127; argument of for FU reconstruction, 104, 147; and authorization for FU reconstruction (1978), 80, 81, 188 n.29; and DOI recommendation about FU reconstruction (1978), 85, 189 n.31; election of as senator (1980), 87; and Friends' lobbying trip to Washington (1985), 101–2; and FU flagpole dedication (1985), 104, 196 n.30; at GNDA meeting (1983), 92–94; and interest in history, 77, 104, 147; and loss of Senate race (1986), 112, 200 n.20; and misunderstanding with NPS (1979), 87– 88, 181 n.31, 191 n.24; and MonDak Bridge, 88, 90; political effectiveness of, 77, 187 n.16; and support for FU reconstruction, 77–80, 104, 112, 149, 200 n.20; and support for on-site reconstruction (1985), 106–7, 198 n.4
"anvil post" at FU, 52, 176 n.24
Appleman, Roy, 5, 61, 67; and land on south bank of Missouri, 80, 137; and FU reconstruction by, 64, 66
Appleton, William Sumner, 36–37
Appomattox Court House National Historical Park (VA), 3

archaeology at FOUS: (1968–72) 67–71, 149, 153, 184 n.21 n.27, 185 n.32, 201 n.27; (1976–77) 70, 112; around flagpole (1985), 103, 197 n.35; (1986–88) 109, 112–17, 152, 201 n.27; artifacts recovered in, 67, 69, 113, 114, 135, 207 n.23; and exhumation of human remains, 69, 71, 135, 201 n.28; Friends irritated by pace of, 115–16, 117, 149, 202 n.32; Mott irritated with, 117; personnel problems of, 116–17; use of computers in, 113–14, 201 n.24; use of grain cleaners in, 113, 200 n.23; use of water screening during, 113, 184 n.16; use of volunteers in, 112, 114
Arickaras, 14, 136
Arlington House (Custis-Lee Mansion), 37, 87
Aspinall, Wayne, 63
Assiniboines, 12, 13, 14, 18, 19, 24, 103, 109, 132, 136
Astor, John Jacob (I), 10, 109
Astor, John Jacob, VIII, third Baron Astor of Hever, 109–11, *110*, *111*
Audubon, John James, 16, 18

Back, Robert, 110–11, 200 n.18
Baker, Priscilla R., 109–11
Baker, Robert M., 142
Barnhart, Audrey L., 134–35
baseball, 39, 40, 43
bastions at FU, 107, 113, 123; reconstructed, 122–24, *124*, 205 n.19; southwest, partially destroyed by gravel extraction, 49–50, *50*
Battin, James F., 64
beads, trade, at FU, 135
Bearss, Edwin C., 96, 150
beaver, 13
Belitz, Larry, 195 n.20
bell tower at FU, 85, 107
Bennett, Charles E., 4, 159 n.14
Bennison, John, 111

Benton, Thomas Hart (1782–1858), 10
Benton, Thomas Hart (1889–1975), 138
Bent's Old Fort NHS (CO), 4–5, 68, 85, 100, 142; maintenance problems with, 5, 86, 119, 122, 146
Bernard Pratte and Company (St. Louis MO), 10
Bible, Alan, 63, 64
bison, 13, 16, 18, 24, 162 n.15
Bjella, Jestrab and Neff, 59
Blackfeet, 12
Bodmer, Karl, 16, 17, 39, 136, 138; sketch of FU by, *17*, 138, 208 n.39
Bodmer Overlook, 99, 117, 138–39
Boller, Henry, 19
Boorstin, Daniel J., 8, 133–34, 161 n.33
Borjes, Richard, 190 n.14
Borud, Dennis, 136, 196 n.32, 207 n.28
Bourgeois House, 12, 18, *20*, 66, 107, 204 n.17; archaeological investigation of (1986), 112–13; dedication of (1987), 11, 117, 119, 137; original hearth stones incorporated in reconstruction of, 119, 204 n.6; reconstruction of (1986–87), 119, 122, 203 n.5 n.17, 205 n.21; and use as visitors' center, 66, 119, 130
Brickshawana, Auggaphol "Duke," 97–98
bridge over Missouri near FU. *See* Mon-Dak Bridge *and* Snowden Bridge
Brotherton, David Hammett, 179 n.8
Buckskinners. *See* Fort Union Muzzle Loaders Association
Buck, Solon J., 170 n.25
Budd, John, 62, 181 n.36
Budd, Ralph, 33–45, *44*, 48, 51, 52, 53, 103, 104, 120, 127, 146, 172–73 n.46; and attempts to interest federal government in FU site, 36–37, 170 n.21; and attempts to purchase FU site, 35–36; character and intellectual interests of, 33–35; and Columbia River Historical Expedition, 43; and FU "tunnel," 45,

151; and planking of Snowden Bridge, 41, 88; and Upper Missouri Historical Expedition, 39–43
buffalo, 13, 16, 18, 24, 162 n.15
Buford ND, 27
Buford-Trenton irrigation project, 54, 58, 179 n.18
Burdick, Quentin, 61, 77, 101, 111, 112, 149, 179 n.23, 187 n.15, 188 n.23, 189 n.31, 197 n.38; and interest in history, 77; and legislation authorizing FOUS development, 79–80; and legislation authorizing FU as NPS unit, 62–63, 77
Burdick, Usher, 77
Bureau of Reclamation, 58, 179 n.18
burials, Indian, at FU, 56, 69, 71, 135, 201 n.28
Burlington Northern Railroad, 88, 99, 153–54. *See also* Great Northern Railroad
Burnison, William, 185 n.33
Burton, Phillip, 3–4, 80, 87, 188–89 n.29
Butler, Pierce, 38
Byrd, Harry, 3
Byrd, Robert, 102, 196 n.29

Cain, Stanley, 64
Calabrese, Francis A. ("Cal"), 117
Cammerer, Arno, 51
Cardinal (Amtrak train), 102, 196 n.30
Carlson, Gayle F., 200 n.23
Carter, Jimmy, 80, 82, 102
cart, Red River, 139, 209 n.42
Carver, John A., 64
Cascade Tunnel (WA), 45
Cass, Lewis, 10, 15, 163 n.26
Cassidy, Hopalong, 46, 173 n.3
Catlin, George, 12, 16, 23
caviar, 139–41
CCC (Civilian Conservation Corps), 47–48, 174 n.6
Chase, Ralph, 32

Chateau de Mores (Medora ND), 48
Chatelain, Verne, 175 n.18
chautauqua, 8
Children's Fairyland (Oakland CA), 102
Chittenden, Hiram Martin, 35, 51
Choteau, Charles, 20–21
Choteau, Pierre, Jr., 10, 11, 12, 15; as patron of scientific expeditions, 16
Civilian Conservation Corps (CCC), 47–48, 174 n.6
Clark, George Rogers, monument to, 45
Clark, William (1770–1838), 18
Clark, William P., 191 n.22
Clary, David, 186 n.8
clinker (scoria), 175 n.13
cocaine, 29
Collin, Andrea Winkjer, 92–94, 96, 191 n.24, 193 n.39, 195 n.21
Collin, Richard, 92–94, 93, 99, 101, 104, 195 n.21
Colonial National Historical Park, Jamestown Island in, 63
Colonial Williamsburg, Inc. (VA), 2, 36, 100, 119, 158 n.7
Columbia River Historical Expedition, 43, 44
computers, used in FOUS archaeology, 113–14, 201 n.24
Confluence Commission. *See* Yellowstone–Missouri–Fort Union Commission
Confluence News, 100, 209–10 n.50
Connally, Ernest, 5
Connolly, James B., 58–59, 60, 61, 63, 67, 76, 78; and view of NPS, 64, 72
Conrad, Kent, 112
Coolidge, Calvin, 37
cooperating association, defined, 141, 209 n.45
Corps of Engineers, U.S., 136, 138
Coteau-du-Lac NHS (Quebec), 198 n.3
county-splitting movement in MT, 32, 168 n.50

222 INDEX

Cramton, Louis C., 37, 38
Crees, 14
CRM. *See* Cultural Resource Management Division of NPS
Cronenberger, Richard, 103, 119–23, *126*, 203 n.2, 204 n.6
Crows, 12, 14
Crow Flies High (Hidatsa chief), 24, 26, 165–66 n.12, 166 n.20; and encampment of his band in Garden Coulee, 24–26, 112, 135, 165 n.9
Culbertson, Alexander, 14
Culbertson, Joseph, 151–52, 211 n.3
Culpin, Mary Shivers ("Marcy"), 119, *126*, 190 n.14
Cultural Resource Management (CRM) Division of NPS, and opposition to FU reconstruction, 82–84, 86
Custer Battlefield Historical and Museum Association, 141

dairy at FU, 123
Dawes, Charles, 172 n.39
Delaware Water Gap National Recreation Area (PA), 203 n.1
Denig, Edwin Thompson, 14, 16, 17, 47, 103
Denver Service Center (DSC) of the NPS, 118, 121, 122, 203 n.1
Depression of the 1930s, 45, 46
Deschamps family, 13, 162 n.17
DeVore, Steven L., 135
Dickenson, Russell, 102
diorama of FU in Interior Department Museum, 50, 175 n.17
Disneyland, 7, 8, 102, 122
Dole, Elizabeth, 92, 93
Dole, Robert, 187 n.16
Dorgan, Byron, 101, 112
Dorman, Dave, 196 n.32
drains at FU, 121, 152
Drury, Newton, 3
dry farming, 34, 169 n.5

earthlodge, 48; as built for Upper Missouri Historical Expedition, 41, 50
Eastern National Park and Monument Association, 141
Eckberg, Scott, 132, 143, 210 n.53
Edsall Construction Company, 121
Evans, Bob, *101*
Evanson, Charles, 195 n.21
"Evening at the Confluence," (Friends' promotional dinner, 1984), 99–100, 195 n.17
Everhardt, Gary, 78, 79, 188 n.27
Ewers, John C., 180 n.28, 185 n.32

Fairview MT, 32, 212 n.1
Fairview Bridge, 153
Farm Security Administration, 53
Federal Highway Administration, 88
Fenno, Richard F., 200 n.20
Finders, Dave, 196 n.31 n.32
flagpole at FU, 40, 41, 183 n.6; reconstruction of (1985), 101, 103–4, 106, 119, 197 n.33 n.34
flag-raising ceremonies at FU: (1925) 40–41; (1972) 71–72, 74; (1985) 103–4
flagstones, original, exposed at FU dairy, 123
Fogarty, Kate Hammond, 30–31
Ford, Gerald, 76
Ford's Theatre NHS, 76
Fort Abraham Lincoln (ND), 48
Fort Atkinson SHP (NE), 200 n.23
Fort Benton (MT), 19
Fort Berthold Indian Reservation (ND), 24, 25, 26
Fort Bowie NHS (AZ), 7, 160 n.29
Fort Buford (ND), 20, 21, 22–23, 24, 25, 27, 165 n.9; 179 n.18
Fort Buford Sixth Infantry Regiment Association, 73–74, 92, 98, 196 n.31
Fort Buford State Historic Site (ND), 91, 100, 138, 176 n.21, 179 n.18, 196 n.32; administratively joined to FU by

SHSND, 55; Appleman and Hartzog oppose incorporation of in FOUS (1965), 64; becomes state park (1924), 177 n.2; Brickshawana model of, 98; and contributions by Friends of Fort Union, 139, 141; and Innis's attempts to have transferred to NPS, 75–76; irrigation canal cut across, 179 n.18; and local interest, 58–59, 60; Masonic sign at, 180 n.28; and NPS report (1962), 62; oil and gas drilling near, 137, 208 n.33; and powder magazine constructed of FU stone, 22

Fort Caroline National Memorial (FL), 4

Fort Clark (ND), 15

Fort Laramie NHS (WY), 96

Fort Larned NHS (KS), 103

Fort Necessity National Battlefield (PA), 68

Fort Peck Indian Reservation (MT), 109, 132, 136

Fortress of Louisbourg NHS (Nova Scotia), 2, 119, 145, 169 n.10, 194 n.11, 210 n.3

Fort Scott NHS (KS), 3–4

Fort Smith NHS (AR), 78, 148

Fort Stanwix (NM, NY), 3, 158 n.11

Fort Totten (ND), 77

Fort Ticonderoga (NY), 1

Fort Union: climate of, 18–19, 132, 164 n.36, 182 n.4, 206 n.2; flooding at, 17–18; water quality of, 16–17. *See also* Fort Union, as archaeological/historical site (1867–1966); Fort Union, artists' reconstructions of; Fort Union, as historic trading post (1828–1867); Fort Union, park management of; Fort Union, reconstruction of; Fort Union Trading Post NHS

Fort Union, as archaeological/historical site (1867–1966), 49, 50; administered by SHSND, 52–57, 60; Columbia River Historical Expedition at, 43, 44; Crow-Flies-High band at, 24–26, 165 n.9; as dumping ground, 31, 56; exhumation of Indian burials at, 31, 56; gravel extraction at, 49, 50, 52, 56; Knights of Columbus marker at, 60; location debated, 51–52, 176 n.21; "pothunting," souvenir collecting, and vandalism at, 31, 52, 55, 56, 181 n.41; purchased for SHSND (1938), 53, 177 n.27; reconstruction suggested for, 35–36, 53–54, 60; as travelers' landmark, 23–24, 165 n.8; Upper Missouri Historical Expedition at, 39–43

Fort Union, artists' reconstructions of: Back painting of (1988), 110–11, 200 n.18; Bodmer drawing of (1833), 17, 138, 208 n.39; Brickshawana model of (1984), 97–98, 101, 194 n.11 n.12; Interior Department Museum diorama of (1936), 50, 175 n.17; Mulford model of (1931), 46–47, 173 n.4; North Dakota Heritage Center model of (1934), 47; Sidney Junior High School model of (1972), 72, 185 n.33

Fort Union, as historic trading post (1828–1867): and alcohol, 14, 15, 21, 207 n.16; cemetery at, 22; construction of, 11, 18, 114; decline of, 19–21; destruction of, 21, 22; dimensions and building arrangements of, 11–12, 17, 114, 162 n.8; employees of, 14; Indian assaults on, 13, 19; name, origin of, 11; odor of, 13, 133–34; relationship between Indians and traders at, 12–13; and small pox epidemic of 1837, 13, 14–15, 133, 163 n.23, 178 n.14, 210 n.1; timber resources of, 18; treatment of in twentieth-century ND histories, 57, 178 n.14

Fort Union, park management of: and Bodmer Overlook, 99, 138–39; and book store, 142, 210 n.51; and brochures, park, 129; and curation,

Fort Union, park management (*cont.*) 134–66, 207 n.22 n.23; and attempts to preserve historic scene, 128, 136–38, 176 n.23; and interpretation, 129–34, 138, 139, 142–43, 207 n.16, 207 n.17; and "Intertribal Day," 132, 206 n.15; and "living history," 132; and maintenance, 136, 138; and museum, 130, 133; and attempts to restore prairie grasses, 136; and "Rendezvous," 92, 131, 141; and staff housing, 128–29, 206 n.2, 210 n.53; and teepee village, 129; and visitation, 114, 131, 132; and visitors' centers, 66, 91, 119, 128–29, 130, 206 n.2; and wayside exhibits, 129

Fort Union, reconstruction of: economic motives for, 63–64, 72, 75, 95, 99–100, 108, 147; original materials included in, 126, 204 n.6; reasons for success of, 145–50; support for and opposition to, 63–64, 66, 74–75, 78–80, 82–83, 85, 86–87, 102, 106, 146, 198 n.8

Fort Union Association (FUA), 142–43, 209–10 n.50

Fort Union Fellowship, 139

Fort Union Formation, 16, 164 n.31

Fort Union-Fort Buford Council, 74, 76, 77, 90, 98, 109

Fort Union Fur Trade Symposium (1990), 139

Fort Union Muzzle Loaders Association, 98, 99, 101, 103, 131, 196 n.30 n.31

Fort Union National Monument (NM), 7, 62, 160 n.28, 175 n.18, 195 n.17

Fort Union Reconstruction Analysis (1979), 85–87, 97, 118, 119, 194 n.9

Fort Union Trading Post NHS (FOUS), 147; origin of name, 62
—chronology: feasibility study for park authorized (1962), 61–62; NPS report declares FU "of national significance" (1962); congressional hearings held (1963), 62–63; becomes NPS unit (1966), 63–64; master plan approved (1967), 65–66, 182 n.4; state lands transferred to NPS (1967), 66–67; exploratory archaeology (1968–72), 67–71, 184 n.21 n.27, 185 n.32; first staff assigned, 70–71 (1971–72); flag-raising ceremony (1972), 71–72, 74; minor archaeological work done (1976–77), 70, 112; Congress authorizes development (1978), 80–81, 137; General Management Plan approved (1978), 82, 83–85, 189 n.7; *Reconstruction Analysis* written (1979), 85–87, 97, 118, 190 n.16, 194 n.9; first (1985) and subsequent reconstruction appropriations approved, 104, 112, 197 n.40, 200 n.20; road to paved (1986); reconstruction opposed by ACH (1986), 107; intensive archaeology by MWAC (1986–88), 109, 112–17, 152, 201 n.27; partial reconstruction (1986–91), 119–25, 194 n.9 (*see also* bastions at FU; bell tower at FU; Bourgeois House; dairy at FU; drains at FU; flagpole at FU; Indian trade house at FOUS; kitchen at FU; palisades at FU); dedication (1989), 125–27

Fort Vancouver NHS (WA), 3, 122

Fort William Historical Park, Old (Ontario), 106, 198 n.3

FOUS. *See* Fort Union Trading Post NHS

Franklin house, Independence National Historical Park (PA), 7, 150, 211 n.8

Frazier, Ian, 16, 130, 150

"friends groups," 139, 208 n.41

Friends of Fort Union Trading Post, 98, 100–101, 105–6, 108, 128, 137, 139; attempts to keep reconstruction nonpolitical by, 98; and conflict with MWAC archaeologists, 115–17, 149; cooperating association organized by

(1993), 141; fund raising for reconstruction by, 100, 108–9, 146, 199 n.12; influence of on reconstruction and park affairs, 139–41, 149; and land purchases on south bank of Missouri, 138; and lobbying trips to Washington, 101–2, 108, 196 n.28, 199 n.9; organization of (1984), 94, 195 n.21; and promotion of economic benefits of reconstruction, 108, 147; and publicizing of FU archaeology, 114; recognition of by National Park Foundation (1994), 139; and recruitment of educated professionals, 98–99; as sponsor of "Evening at the Confluence," 99–100
FUA (Fort Union Association), 142–43, 209–10 n.50

Garden Coulee, 24–25, 165 n.9, 210 n.53
Gardner, Fred, 89–90
The Gauche, (Assiniboine chief), 14, 163 n.22
General Accounting Office, 136
George Rogers Clark National Historical Park (IN), 45
George Washington Birthplace National Mounument (VA), 2, 6
Gettysburg National Military Park (PA), 7, 47
"ghost reconstruction," 106; at FOUS, 120, 123, 124
Gillio, David A., 69, 71
Glacier National Park (MT), 34–35, 39, 96
Glass, Carter, 3
Godfrey, Edward Settle, 23
Golden Spike NHS (UT), 96
Gold Star Caviar Inc., 140–41, 143, 209 n.44
Good, Albert H., 6
Graff House, Independence National Historical Park (PA), 158 n.10
grain cleaners, motorized, 113, 200 n.23

gravel and gravel extraction at FU site, 11, 48–49, 52, 56, 67, 175 n.14
Great Depression, 45, 46
Greater North Dakota Association (GNDA), 59, 64, 92
Great Northern Railroad, 23, 26, 27, 29, 32, 34, 37, 42, 53, 151, 153; as arbiter of place names, 38–39, 169 n.7, 171 n.28, 172 n.46. *See also* Burlington Northern Railroad; Upper Missouri Historical Expedition
Gunderson, Jim, *101*, 196 n.32

Hagan, Edward J. ("Bud"), 99, 100, 109, *111*
Hagedorn, Hermann, 2
Hale, Mary, 143
Hancock, John, house of, 1, 157 n.2
Hansen, Julia Butler, 3
Harmon, Sylvia, 195 n.21
Harper, Frank, 151
Harpers Ferry Center (NPS), 130
Hart, Pete, 142
Hartzog, George B., 64
Hawley, Alpheus F., 21
Hayden, Ferdinand Vandeveer, 16, 72
Hedren, Paul L., 96–98, 101, 102, 103, 104, 105–6, 109, 111, 112, 116, 117, 135, 141, 143–44, 146, 148, 152, 194 n.7; character and abilities of, 96–97; and friendship with Rolfstad, 97–98; and *Great Sioux War, 1876–77*, 141, 209 n.46; importance of to FOUS reconstruction, 96, 148; and interpretation of FOUS, 131, 132–33; reaction of to non-historic intrusions at FOUS, 136–38; and views on archaeological analysis, 116, 134, 202 n.33
Hennessy, Greg W., 90, 100, 109, 138, 142, 202 n.32
Hidatsas, 24–25, 136
Hill, James J., 26, 33–34
Hill, Louis, 34–35, 37

historical archaeology, defined, 68
historical reconstruction. *See* reconstruction, historical: arguments for and against
historic preservation. *See* preservation, historic
Historic Preservation Act of 1966, 2, 103, 106, 179 n.18
Historic Sites and Buildings Act of 1935, 2, 50
Historic Sites Survey, 60–61
Hoeflein, Jim, 196 n.32
Hoffine, Lyla, 180 n.24
Holland, F. Ross, 82, 83; and reconstruction of FU, 86, 87
Hopalong Cassidy, 46, 173 n.3
Hosmer, Charles B., Jr., 1
House of David, 43
Hubbell, James, 21
Hummel, Edward A., 50, 51–53, 175 n.15
Hunt, William J., Jr., 70, 110, 112–17, 121, 202 n.37, 202 n.40
Husted, Wilfred M., 69, 71, 190 n.13
Hydle, Nellie Johnson, 52, 56, 176 n.26

Independence Hall Association, 158 n.10
Independence National Historical Park (PA): Graff House, 158 n.10; Franklin house, 7, 150, 211 n.8
Indian-Artisan House. *See* Indian trade house at FOUS
Indians, 12–16, 27, 41–43, 125, 172 n.44; and "adoption" of whites into tribes, 42, 172 n.39; and alcohol, 15–16; and exhumation of FU burials, 56, 69, 71, 135, 201 n.28; interpretation of at FOUS, 130, 132–33. *See also* Arickaras; Assiniboines; Blackfeet; Crees; Crows; Hidatsas; Mandans; Sioux; Three Affiliated Tribes
Indian trade house at FOUS, 113, 205 n.22; curatorial vault beneath, 123, 134; costumed interpretation in, 132;
trade goods store in, 132, 141–43; reconstructed, 123, *124, 125*, 139
Innis, Ben, Jr., 74, 81, 92, 97, 99, 100, 120, 127, 146, 178 n.13, 180 n.24, 186 n.9 n.12, 188 n.23 n.25, 192 n.32, 205 n.26; attempts to have Fort Buford transferred to NPS by, 75–76; and authorization for FU reconstruction, 75–79; character and abilities of, 73, 76, 186 n.9; as coached by Andrews, 77; death of, 94; and MonDak Bridge controversy, 90; and organization of Fort Union–Fort Buford Council, 74, 76; and publication of *Sagas of the Smoky-Water*, 98
Innis, Jane, 205 n.26
Interior Department Museum, diorama of FU in, 50, 175 n.17
Interstate Commerce Commission, 45
Intertribal Day, 132, 206 n.15

James, D. Willis, 26, 166 n.24
Jamestown Festival Park (Jamestown Settlement; VA), 6, 63, 181 n.39
Java MT, 28
Javits, Jacob, 158 n.11
Jefferson National Expansion Memorial (MO), 129
Jevnager, Anton, 28
Johnson, Lyndon B., 64
Johnson, Vernon, 195 n.21
Jones, Michael, 99, 196 n.21, 197 n.36
Judd, Henry, 84

Kaiser, Marvin L., 100, 102, 109, 111, 142, 149, 187 n.15, 195 n.20; as chairman of FUA, 142–43; and complaints about pace of FOUS archaeology, 114, 115, 201 n.29
Kane, Randy, 143, 210 n.53
Kelly, Luther S. ("Yellowstone"), 23, 24
Kessler, Charles, 151
King, Thomas, 107

Kipp, James, 14
kitchen at FU, partial reconstruction of, 107, 120, 123
Kittleman, Earle B., 91–92, 94
Kleppe, Thomas S., 76, 186 n.10
Knickerbocker Boys' Band of Ray ND, 38
Knife River Indian Villages NHS, 97
Knights of Columbus, marker of at FU, 60, 180 n.28
Krabseth, Blake, *101*, 195 n.21
Kurz, Rudolph Friederich, 13, 14, 16, 18, 103, 132; and discovery of drawing by, 85

Lancaster, John O., 76, 78, 84, 88
L'Anse aux Meadows NHS (Newfoundland), 6
Larpenteur, Charles, 13, 21
Laut, Agnes, 43
Lee, Robert E., 37, 87
Lee, Ronald F., 3, 52, 65
Libby, Orin G., 36, 39, 43, 171 n.28
Like-a-Fishhook Village (ND), 24
Lincoln, Abraham, birthplace of, 157 n.3
Little Bighorn Battlefield National Monument (MT), 141
"living history" at FOUS, 132
Loomer, Orville, 101, 131, 133, 136, 196 n.32, 207 n.17
Louisbourg, Fortress of, NHS (Nova Scotia), 2, 119, 145, 169 n.10, 194 n.11, 210 n.3
Lounsberry, Clement A., 27
lyceum movement, 8
Lyon, J. B., 48, 53

Mackintosh, Barry, 82, 83, 147
Mandans, 136
Mansfield, Mike, 36
Marsh, Grant, 162 n.6
Mattison, Ray H., 54, 61
Maximilian of Wied, Prince, 16
McClellan, John, 78, 148

McClure, James A., 104
McKenzie, Kenneth, 10–12, 14, 140; and operation of still at FU, 15
McLean House, Appomattox Court House National Historical Park (VA), 3
Medora ND, 100, 195 n.18
Mercer, John and Sarah, 58
Metcalf, Perry, 121
Midwest Archeological Center (MWAC), 69, 112, 113, 114, 117, 134–35, 184 n.19, 202 n.40
Miner (steamboat), 21
Minninick, 44
Mintzmyer, Lorraine, 119, 142
Mission 66 (NPS), 60
Missouri River, flooding of, at FU, 17, 49
Missouri River Basin Survey, 68, 181 n.31, 184 n.18
models of FU: Brickshawana (1984), 97–98, 100, 101, 194 n.11 n.12; by Clarence Mulford (1931), 46–47, 173 n.4; at North Dakota Heritage Center (1934), 47; proposed by RMR planning team (1977–78), 83–84, 86; by Sidney Junior High School students (1972), 72, 185 n.33
MonDak Bridge, 154, 212 n.7; debate over location of, 62, 88–91
Mon-Dak Heritage Center, 185 n.33
Mondak MT, 27–32, *28*, 42, 167 n.32, 167 n.36, 168 n.52; and NPS report (1962), 62; reasons for decline of, 28, 31–32; renamed Fort Union, 33, 38, 171 n.28
Moore, Jackson W. ("Smoky"), 4, 68–69
Morison, Samuel Eliot, 173 n.46
mosquitoes, at FU, 18
Mott, William Penn, 102, 105, 106, 108, 110, *111*, *116*, 146, 198 n.4, 202 n.36 n.37; background and interests of, 102; fund raising for FU reconstruction by, 109, 199 n.13; outburst at FOUS by (1987), 117

Mount Rushmore National Memorial (SD), 51
Mount Vernon Ladies' Association, 2
Mulford, Clarence E., 46–47, 51, 173 n.3 n.4
MWAC. *See* Midwest Archeological Center

NAGPRA (Native American Graves Protection and Repatriation Act), 135–36
National Audubon Society, 60, 76
National Environmental Policy Act (1969), 75
National Farm Loan Association, 53
National Historic Preservation Act (1966), 107
National Park Foundation, 109, 139
National Park Service (NPS), 37, 47, 60–61, 75; and congressional budget cuts (1978), 80, 82; and cooperating associations, 141–42; coordination between SHSND and, 53–55; development of history section by (1960s), 65; and historical reconstructions, 2–6, 75, 86–87, 96, 107–8, 119, 148; and historic preservation, 2–3, 7, 54, 65, 78; internal disunity of, 148; *Management Policies* (1975) of, 5–6, 148; and *Mission 66,* 60; and Organic Act of 1916, 6; under Reagan administration, 87; and the "stall," 97, 148
National Park Service, and FU: fundraising failure of, 109, 199 n.13; opposes reconstruction of, 63–64, 74, 75, 78–81, 82–84, 86–87, 102, 106, 146; and interest in site, 51–53, 61–62, 102; and inability to present anti-reconstruction position effectively, 148; underestimation of archaeological resources by, 68–70
National Register of Historic Places, 65, 154
National Survey of Historic Sites and Buildings. *See* Historic Sites Survey

Native Americans. *See* Indians
Native American Graves Protection and Repatriation Act (NAGPRA), 135–36
Neckels, Jack, 105–6, 107, 114; and new cooperating association (FUA), 142; and off-site reconstruction of FU, 106
Neff, LaVern C., 60, 64, 90
Nehring, Girard, 196 n.32
Neihardt, John, 30
New Salem SHS (IL), 157 n.3
New York World's Fair (1964), 73–74
Noël Hume, Ivor, 160 n.27, 184 n.16
Nordell, Ben G., 62, 67
Norris, Philetus W., 23
North Dakota: political culture of, 76; tourism in, 59, 95–96, 100
North Dakota Automobile Association, 58
North Dakota Federation of Women's Clubs, 52
North Dakota Game and Fish Department, 140
North Star Caviar, 209 n.44
North Western Fur Company, 21
NPS. *See* National Park Service
Nutt, R. S., 48, 60, 88, 174 n.10

Oakes, John B., 179 n.20
O'Boyle, Michael, 196 n.32, 197 n.34
Ocmulgee (NM, GA), 47
off-site historical reconstruction, 5–6, 106, 115, 198 n.3; pros and cons of at FOUS, 106
oil and gas exploration and drilling, 57–58, 95, 136–37, 208 n.32
Old Fort William Historical Park (Ontario), 106, 198 n.3
Olmstead, Frederick Law, Jr., 6
O'Neil, Doug, 199 n.12
Organic Act of 1916, 6
Overson, Willard B., 36, 39, 43, 48, 53, 56

paddlefish, 139–41, 209 n.44
palisades at FU, 113; air drying of wood for, 204 n.15; reconstruction of, 122–23, *124*, 205 n.19; and size of original timbers discovered, 202 n.40
"park barrel," origin of term, 80
Parkhurst, Charles, 166 n.24
parking lots at FOUS, 124–25, 130, 199 n.12
petroleum exploration and drilling, 57–58, 95, 136–37, 208 n.32
Pfaller, Louis, 180 n.24 n.28
Pfanz, Harry, 82, 86
Pioneer Daughters of North Dakota, 52
Pirnie, Alexander, 158 n.11
Plimoth Plantation Inc. (MA), 6
Poplar MT, 32
Popular Science Monthly, 46–47
"pothunting," souvenir collecting, and vandalism, at FU site, 31, 52, 55, 56, 63, 71, 181 n.41, 185 n.31
prairie grasses, attempts to restore at FOUS, 136; recommended by 1967 Master Plan, 66
Pratte, Bernard, and Company (St. Louis MO), 10
preservation, historic, 36, 37, 59, 160 n.26; difficulties of, 160 n.27 n.28 n.29 n.30; NPS *Management Policies* (1975) concerning, 5–6, 148
Pullman strike of 1894, 23
Putnam, Sylvester, 71, 129, 185 n.31, 206 n.3

Reagan, Ronald, 87, 102, 104, 106
reconstruction, historical, arguments for and against, 6–9, 75, 82, 106, 107, 133–34; "ghost," 106, 123, *124*; lessons of FOUS for supporters and opponents of, 146–47, 205 n.21; "off-site," 5–6, 106, 115
Reconstruction Analysis, of Fort Union (1979), 85–87, 97, 118, 119, 194 n.9

reconstruction of FU, economic motives for, 72, 75, 95, 99–100, 108, 147; original materials included in, *126*, 204 n.6; reasons for success, 145–50; supported and opposed, 66, 74–75, 78–80, 82–83, 85, 86–87, 102, 106, 107–8, 146, 198 n.8
Redlin, Rolland, 63–64
Red River cart, 139, 209 n.42
Reid, Russell, 47–48, 56, 59, 61, 72, 146, 179 n.18; and saving of FU site, 52–53
Rendezvous, 92, 131, 141
Rettie, Dwight, 84, 148, 191 n.20, 211 n.5
Reynolds, Charles ("Lonesome Charley"), 23
Riddle, Simon, 30
River Basin Surveys of the Smithsonian Institution, 68
Robinson, Willard B., 190 n.14
Rockefeller, John D., Jr., 2, 36
Rocky Mountain Regional Office (RMRO) of the NPS (Denver), 70, 91, 137, 141, 142; and FU reconstruction, 79, 83, 104, 105, 118–19, 120
Rogers, Jerry, 107–8
Rolfstad, Thomas C., 97–100, 194 n.11 n.12, 195 n.21
Rome NY, 3, 158 n.11
Roosevelt, Franklin, 47
Roosevelt, Theodore, 1–2, 34
Roosevelt County MT, creation of, 32
Roosevelt Memorial Association, 2
Rose, Vivien, 161 n.30
Ross, Lester, 135
Rotary Club of Williston ND, 48, 58
Russell, Charles ("Charley"), 39

Sailer, Dale, 195 n.21
Schafer, Harold, 100, 195 n.18
Scopes Trial (1925), 43, 172 n.43
scoria (clinker), 175 n.13
Scott, Douglas, 197 n.35
Scott, Hugh Lenox, 38, 41, 43, 44, 165 n.8

Seel, Jacob, 27
Shaver, C. Mack, 202 n.40
Shiloh National Military Park (TN), 47
Shoup, W. A., 151
SHSND. *See* State Historical Society of North Dakota
Sidney MT, 72, 89, 194 n.11
Singing Paddles (1935), 3
Sinner, George, 101
Sioux, 19, 20, 24
Sitting Bull, 22, 23, 179 n.18
Skubitz, Joe, 3–4
Slemp, C. Bascom, 37
smallpox epidemic of 1837, 13, 14–15, 133, 163 n.23, 178 n.14, 210 n.1
Smithsonian Institution, River Basin Surveys of, 68
Snowden Bridge, 28, 41, 88, 89, 91, 153–54, 191–92 n.25, 212 n.4 n.5
Sousa, John Philip, 32
South Halsted Street Bridge (Chicago), 153
souvenir collecting, "pothunting," and vandalism at FU site, 31, 52, 55, 56, 63, 71, 181 n.41, 185 n.31
State Historical Society of North Dakota (SHSND), 45, 61, 90; administration of FU site by, 55–56; and donation of FU site to NPS, 66–67; and MonDak Bridge controversy, 90; purchases FU by, 52–53; and relationship with NPS during Depression, 53–55
State Historic Preservation Officers (SHPOS), 107
Stevens, George, 27
Stevens, John F., 33, 39, 171 n.30
St. Paul, Minneapolis, and Manitoba Railway, 23
Stuart, James, 23
sugar beet farming, 89–90
Sullivan, Arthur, 186 n.9
Sully, Alfred, 19

Sutter's Fort SHP (CA), 1
Sweetman, Luke, 27

Tallant, Montague, 200 n.23
Theodore Roosevelt Association, 157 n.3
Theodore Roosevelt Birthplace NHS, 1
Theodore Roosevelt National [Memorial] Park, 59, 100, 105, 137, 142, 179 n.23, 210 n.53
Theodore Roosevelt Nature and History Association (TRNHA), 141–42
Thiessen, Thomas D., 112, 114, 115, 117, 201 n.29
Thompson, David, monument to, 39, 171 n.29
Thompson, Erwin ("T"), 66, 85, 183 n.7
Three Affiliated Tribes, 135–36
Ticonderoga, Fort, 1
tourism, increase in, during the 1950s, 59
trade beads at FU, 135
trade house at FOUS. *See* Indian trade house at FOUS
Trenton ND, 60, 168 n.52
TRNHA (Theodore Roosevelt Nature and History Association), 141–42
tunnel at FU, legend of, 45, 151–52, 211 n.3

Union Bridge and Construction Company (Kansas City KS), 212 n.2
Upper Missouri Historical Expedition, 37–43, 50, 103, 146, 153; and FU flagpole, 40, 41, 183 n.6; "Indian congress" during, 41–43, 172 n.44; invitation to, 39, 40
Upper Missouri Outfit (UMO), 11
Utley, Robert, 5, 54, 75, 97, 150, 186 n.8; and proposed reconstruction of Fort Smith, 148; and delayed reconstruction of FU, 78; and departure from NPS, 79

Valley Forge National Historical Park (PA), 151
vandalism, souvenir collecting, and "pothunting" at FU site, 31, 52, 55, 56, 63, 71, 181 n.41, 185 n.31
Van Orsdel, William Wesley ("Brother Van"), 30
Van West, Carroll, 130
Verendrye ND, 38–39
Villa Militaire (Mercer home at Fort Buford), 58
Virginia City MT, 19
volunteers, importance of in FU archaeology and reconstruction, 102, 104, 108, 112, 114

Waddell, John Alexander Low, 89, 153
Waldorf Astoria, 110, 111
War, Department of, 37, 53, 153
Washington birthplace (Westmoreland County VA), 2, 6
water quality at FU, 17
water screening, used in FOUS archaeology, 113
Watford City ND, 212 n.1
Watt, James, 87, 191 n.22
Weinrich, Frank A., 35–36, 39, 43, 48–49, 52–53
Wellman, William, 71, 76, 84, 88, 185 n.31, 186 n.12, 191 n.24, 206 n.3; and FOUS interpretation, 129; and Mon-Dak Bridge controversy, 88, 89–90, 91, 192 n.30
Wenstrom, Frank, 59–60, 90
Wheaton, Rodd L., 85, 119, 120, 122, 123, 126, 133, 203 n.2, 204 n.17
White, Robert K., 190 n.14
Whitehill, Walter Muir, 6
Wickware, Harvey, 104, 196 n.28
William Crooks (locomotive), 37

Williamsburg, Colonial, Inc. (VA), 2, 36, 100, 119, 158 n.7
Williston Basin, 57, 95
Williston (ND) Chamber of Commerce, 100, 102, 140
Williston Jobs and Industries, 98, 99
Williston ND, 26, 41, 42, 73, 75, 84, 89, 92, 98, 149, 166 n.24; and CCC, 53–54; interest of in FU, 53, 56, 59, 75–77, 79, 98, 99–100, 108, 146; and oil booms, 57–58, 95; and tourism, 95–96, 99–100, 108, 114
Wilson, Milburn Lincoln, 35–36, 169 n.12; and photographs of FU site, 49, 175 n.15
Winkjer, Andrea. *See* Collin, Andrea Winkjer
Wirth, Conrad L., 61, 62–63
Wolf Point MT, 32
Women's Clubs, North Dakota Federation of, 52
Women's Rights National Historical Park (NY), 7, 161 n.30
Women's Roosevelt Memorial Association, 1
Works Progress Administration (WPA), 53–54
Wright, Dana, 55, 56

Yeater Hennings Ruff, 119–20
Yellow Stone (steamboat), 12
Yellowstone–Missouri–Fort Union Commission (Confluence Commission), 59–60, 61, 88, 183 n.8
Yellowstone National Park, 96; and centennial commemoration at FOUS (1972), 71–72
Yellowstone News, 27, 30, 31
Young, Milton R., 76, 78, 187 n.14